low-fat no-fat
mediterranean

low-fat no-fat
mediterranean

**With 200 inspiring and
delicious recipes from
a region famous for long
life and active health**

Consultant editor: Anne Sheasby

LORENZ BOOKS

This edition is published by Lorenz Books

Lorenz Books is an imprint of Anness Publishing Ltd
Hermes House, 88–89 Blackfriars Road, London SE1 8HA
tel. 020 7401 2077; fax 020 7633 9499
www.lorenzbooks.com; info@anness.com

© Anness Publishing Ltd 2005

UK agent: The Manning Partnership Ltd
tel. 01225 478 444; fax 01225 478 440
sales@manning-partnership.co.uk

UK distributor: Grantham Book Services Ltd
tel. 01476 541080; fax 01476 541061
orders@gbs.tbs-ltd.co.uk

North American agent/distributor: National Book Network
tel. 301 459 3366; fax 301 429 5746; www.nbnbooks.com

Australian agent/distributor: Pan Macmillan Australia
tel. 1300 135 113; fax 1300 135 103
customer.service@macmillan.com.au

New Zealand agent/distributor: David Bateman Ltd
30 Tarndale Grove, Off Bush Road, Albany, Auckland
tel. (09) 415 7664; fax (09) 415 8892

Publisher: Joanna Lorenz
Editorial Director: Helen Sudell
Editor: Simona Hill
Designer: Ian Sandom
Editorial Reader: Rosanna Fairhead
Production Controller: Wendy Lawson

10 9 8 7 6 5 4 3 2 1

NOTES

Bracketed terms are intended for American readers.

For all recipes, quantities are given in both metric and
imperial measures and, where appropriate, in standard cups
and spoons. Follow one set, but not a mixture, because they
are not interchangeable.

Standard spoon and cup measures are level. 1 tsp = 5ml,
1 tbsp = 15ml, 1 cup = 250ml/8fl oz.

Australian standard tablespoons are 20ml. Australian readers
should use 3 tsp in place of 1 tbsp for measuring small
quantities of gelatine, flour, salt, etc.

The nutritional analysis given for each recipe is calculated per
portion (i.e. serving or item), unless otherwise stated. If the
recipe gives a range, such as Serves 4–6, then the nutritional
analysis will be for the smaller portion size, i.e. 6 servings.
Measurements for sodium do not include salt added to taste.

Each recipe title in this book is followed by a symbol that
indicates the following:
★ = 5g of fat or fewer per serving
★★ = 10g of fat or fewer per serving
★★★ = 15g of fat or fewer per serving
Medium (US large) eggs are used unless otherwise stated

CONTENTS

INTRODUCTION

For many of us the Mediterranean conjures up idyllic images of sun-soaked beaches, pretty provincial villages tucked away up in the mountains and on the coast, sun-drenched olive groves. With it goes the colourful chaos of a bustling food market full of an array of fresh fruit, vegetables, herbs and spices, eating *al fresco* and enjoying the delicious food and drink from the many different regions. This all contributes to an appealing and relaxed vision of life, far away from the hassles of our normal routines.

Throughout the Mediterranean there is a passion for food and cooking, and eating plays an important part in everyday lives. The warm Mediterranean sea borders a large and varied area and encompasses many different countries, including Spain, southern France, Italy, Greece, Turkey and the Middle East, plus North African countries such as Morocco and Tunisia, as well as the islands of Malta and Cyprus. Much of the fresh produce eaten in Mediterranean countries is grown or produced locally, and quality and freshness of foods is of great importance in these regions. Many of the provincial and regional specialities are created from the seasonal food to hand.

A HEALTHY DIET

Generally speaking, people from the Mediterranean countries live longer and have a lower incidence of cancers, heart disease and obesity than people from other countries such as the UK, Canada and the USA – and their diet is probably one of the main reasons why. The types of food traditionally eaten in Mediterranean countries have been proven to offer a variety of health benefits and protection against disease.

The Mediterranean diet generally includes lots of fresh and flavourful sun-ripened fruit and vegetables, fresh herbs, fresh fish, pasta, rice and bread. Although some dishes are high in calories and fat, many traditional dishes from all over the region can still be enjoyed as part of a healthy low-fat eating plan. With a few basic guidelines, therefore, a low-fat Mediterranean diet is simple to achieve.

LOOKING AT FAT

Olive oil is the primary fat used for cooking throughout the Mediterranean. Olive oil is a "healthier" type of fat, which is high in monounsaturated fat and low in saturated fat, and so long as it is used in moderation, it can also be enjoyed as part of a low-fat diet.

Some other ingredients typically used in Mediterranean countries, such as pancetta, Parmesan and mozzarella, are high in fat but are easily substituted with lower-fat foods such as lean bacon and reduced-fat mozzarella. Alternatively, in many recipes the quantity of the high-fat food can simply be reduced to lower the fat content of the dish. For many dishes, you will be surprised at how little an amount of olive oil you will need for cooking some foods such as sautéed vegetables or lean meat. Foods such as pasta and rice are also ideal for a low-fat diet as they are naturally high in carbohydrates and low in fat.

Most of us eat fats in some form or another every day and we all need a small amount of fat in our diet to maintain a healthy,

Left: Minimal and flavourful ingredients are the hallmark of Mediterranean-style dining.

Above: Pasta is a key ingredient in Italian cooking. It is naturally low in fat and the basis of a healthy meal.

balanced eating plan. However, many of us eat far too much fat and we should all be looking to reduce our overall fat intake, especially saturated fats. Regular exercise is also an important factor in a healthy lifestyle.

By cutting down on the amount of fat you eat and making simple changes to your diet, you will soon be reducing your overall fat intake and are likely to feel less bloated and more comfortable in your skin, without really noticing any difference to the food you eat.

This cookbook aims to bring you a wide selection of delicious and nutritious dishes from many regions of the Mediterranean, all of which are low in fat, and are ideal to include as part of a healthy and low-fat eating plan.

It includes lots of useful and informative advice. A short introduction provides information about basic healthy eating guidelines; helpful hints and tips on low-fat and fat-free ingredients and low-fat or fat-free cooking techniques; practical tips on how to reduce fat and saturated fat in your diet; an interesting and useful insight into many of the different

ingredients typically found in the Mediterranean kitchen and used widely in Mediterranean cooking; as well as over 200 delicious and easy-to-follow low-fat Mediterranean recipes for all the family to enjoy. The tempting selection of recipes ranges from appetizers, soups and salads, to vegetarian, fish and meat dishes, and also includes a tasty collection of home-baked bread and delicious desserts.

THE RECIPES IN THIS BOOK

Each recipe includes a nutritional breakdown, providing at-a-glance calorie and fat contents (including saturated fat content) per serving, as well as other key nutrients such as protein, carbohydrate, calcium, cholesterol, fibre and sodium. All the recipes in this cookbook are low in fat – many containing five grams of fat or fewer per serving, and a few containing less than one gram of fat per serving.

In the first four chapters of this book – Appetizers, Soups, Salads and Side Dishes, as well as the final chapter on Breads – each recipe contains five grams of fat or fewer per serving. In the remaining five chapters of the book, representing recipes for the main meal of the day – Vegetarian, Fish and Shellfish,

Above: Herbs and natural sweeteners, such as honey, are a traditional feature of Mediterranean cooking.

Poultry and Game, Lamb, Pork, Beef and Veal, and Desserts – most recipes contain ten grams of fat or fewer per serving. A few recipes in these chapters such as Moussaka and Beef Stew with Red Wine and Peas, contain a slightly higher maximum of 15 grams of fat or fewer per serving, but are included because they are such classic dishes of the region. For ease of reference, throughout the recipe section, all recipes with a single ★ following the recipe name contain five grams of fat or fewer, those with ★★ contain ten grams of fat or fewer and those with ★★★ contain 15 grams of fat or fewer. All the recipes contain less fat than similar traditional recipes and yet they are still packed full of delicious flavour.

This practical cookbook will enable you to enjoy Mediterranean food that is healthy, delicious and nutritious as well as being low in fat.

Left: Olives are an everyday healthy food served throughout the Mediterranean as appetizers or tapas, or cooked in a wide variety of dishes. They contain beneficial fats, but should be eaten in small quantities when following a low-fat diet.

HEALTHY EATING GUIDELINES

A healthy diet is one that provides us with all the nutrients we need. By eating the right types, balance and proportions of foods, we are more likely to feel healthy, have plenty of energy and have a higher resistance to disease. We will be less likely to develop illnesses such as heart disease, cancers, bowel disorders and obesity.

By choosing a variety of foods every day, you will ensure that you are supplying your body with all the essential nutrients, including vitamins and minerals, it needs. To get the balance right, it is important to know just how much of each type of food you should be eating.

Of the five main food groups, it is recommended that we eat plenty of fruits and vegetables (at least five portions a day, not including potatoes) and foods such as cereals, pasta, rice and potatoes; moderate amounts of meat, fish, poultry and dairy products, and only small amounts of foods containing fat or sugar. By choosing a good balance of foods from these groups every day, and by choosing lower-fat, lower-sugar and lower-salt alternatives, we will be supplying our bodies with all the nutrients they need for optimum health.

THE ROLE AND IMPORTANCE OF FAT IN THE DIET

Fats shouldn't be cut out of our diets completely. We need a small amount of fat for general health and well-being; fat is a valuable source of energy, and also helps to make foods more palatable to eat. However, if you lower the fats, especially saturated fats, in your diet, it may help you to lose weight, as well as reducing your risk of developing some diseases, such as heart disease.

Aim to limit your daily intake of fats to no more than 30–35 per cent of the total number of calories. Since each gram of fat provides nine calories, for anyone eating 2,000 calories a day, the total daily intake should be no more than around 70g fat. Your total intake of saturated fats should be no more than approximately ten per cent of the total number of calories.

Types of fat

All fats in our foods are made up of building blocks of fatty acids and glycerol, and their properties vary according to each combination.

There are two main types of fat, which are referred to as saturated and unsaturated. The unsaturated group of fats is divided into two further types – polyunsaturated and monounsaturated fats. There is usually a combination of these types of unsaturated fat in foods that contain fat, but the amount of each type varies from one kind of food to another.

Saturated fats

These fats are usually hard at room temperature. They are not essential in the diet, and should be limited, as they are linked to increasing the level of blood cholesterol, which can increase the likelihood of heart disease.

The main sources of saturated fats are animal products, such as fatty cuts of meat and meat products, spreading fats, such as butter, lard and margarine, that are solid at room temperature, and full-fat dairy products such as cream and cheese. However, there are also saturated fats of vegetable origin, notably coconut and palm oils, and some margarines and oils, which, when processed, change the nature of the fat from unsaturated fatty acids to saturated ones. These fats are labelled "hydrogenated", such as hydrogenated vegetable oil, and should be limited. Saturated fats are also found in many processed foods, such as chips (French fries), savoury snacks and crisps (potato chips), as well as cookies, pastries and cakes.

Left: Monounsaturated fats, which are beneficial for our bodies, are found in foods such as olive oil, oily fish and nuts such as almonds.

Above: Saturated fats are found in foods such as butter, lard and margarine, and full-fat dairy products such as cheese and cream.

Above: Cheese is full of saturated fats and should be eaten in moderation in a healthy diet. For those following a low-fat diet, cheese should be restricted.

Above: Polyunsaturated fats are found in foods such as sunflower oil and oily fish including herring, mackerel and sardines.

Polyunsaturated fats

There are two types of polyunsaturated fats: those of vegetable or plant origin (known as omega 6), such as sunflower oil, soft margarine and seeds, and those from oily fish (known as omega 3), such as salmon, herring, mackerel and sardines. Both fats are usually liquid at room temperature. Small amounts of polyunsaturated fats are essential for good health and are thought to help reduce the blood cholesterol level.

Monounsaturated fats

Foods such as rapeseed oil, olive oil, some nuts, such as almonds and hazelnuts, oily fish and avocados all contain monounsaturated fats. They are also thought to have the beneficial effect of reducing the blood cholesterol level. This could explain why in some Mediterranean countries there is such a low incidence of heart disease.

CUTTING DOWN ON FATS AND SATURATED FATS IN THE DIET

Generally about one-quarter of the fat we eat comes from meat and meat products, one-fifth from dairy products and margarine and the rest from cakes, cookies, pastries and other foods. It is relatively easy to cut down on

obvious sources of fat in the diet, such as butter, oils, margarine, cream, whole milk and full-fat cheese, but we also need to know about, and check our consumption of, "hidden" fats. Hidden fats can be found in foods such as cakes, chips, cookies and nuts.

By educating yourself and being aware of which foods are high in fats, particularly saturated fats, and by making simple changes to your diet, you can reduce the total fat content of your diet quite considerably.

Whenever possible, cut out fattening foods and choose reduced-fat or low-fat alternatives to foods such as milk, cheese and salad dressings, and fill up on very low-fat foods, such as fruits and vegetables, and foods that are high in carbohydrates, such as pasta, rice, bread and potatoes.

Cutting down on fat doesn't mean sacrificing taste. It's easy and enjoyable to follow a sensible healthy-eating plan without having to forgo all your favourite foods.

THE CHOLESTEROL QUESTION

Cholesterol is a fat-like substance that plays a vital role in the body. It's the material from which many essential hormones and vitamin D are made. Too

much saturated fat encourages the body to make more cholesterol than it uses or can rid itself of. Cholesterol is carried around the body, attached to proteins called high density lipoproteins (HDL), low-density lipoproteins (LDL), and very low-density lipoproteins (VLDL or triglycerides).

After eating, the LDLs carry the fat in the blood to the cells where it's required. Any surplus should be excreted from the body, however, if there is too much LDL in the blood, some of the fat will be deposited on the walls of the arteries. This furring up gradually narrows the arteries and is one of the most common causes of heart attacks and strokes. In contrast, HDLs appear to protect against heart disease. Whether high triglyceride levels are risk factors remains unknown.

For some people, an excess of cholesterol is a hereditary trait; in others, it's mainly due to the consumption of too much saturated fat. In both cases it can be reduced by a low-fat diet. Many believe naturally high cholesterol foods such as egg yolks and offal should be avoided, but research has shown that it is more important to reduce total fat intake. A typical low-fat Mediterranean diet is naturally low in cholesterol.

PLANNING A LOW-FAT DIET

Most of us eat about 115g/4oz of fat every day. Yet just 10g/¼oz, about the amount in a single packet of crisps (potato chips) or a thin slice of Cheddar cheese, is all we actually need.

Current nutritional advice isn't quite that strict though and suggests that we should limit our daily intake of fat to no more than 30 per cent of total calories. In real terms, since each gram of fat provides nine calories, this means that for an average intake of 2,000 calories a day, the total daily intake should be around 600 calories or fewer.

CUTTING DOWN ON FAT IN THE DIET

There are lots of simple no-fuss ways of reducing the fat in your diet. Just follow the simple "eat less, try instead" suggestions below to discover how easy it is.
• Eat less butter, margarine, other spreading fats and cooking oils.
• Eat fewer full-fat dairy products such as whole milk, cream, butter, hard margarine, crème fraîche, whole-milk yogurts and hard cheese.
• Try instead semi-skimmed (low-fat) or skimmed milk, low-fat or reduced-fat milk products, low-fat yogurts, low-fat fromage frais and low-fat soft cheeses, reduced-fat hard cheeses such as Cheddar, and reduced-fat crème fraiche.

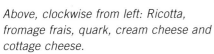

Above, clockwise from left: Ricotta, fromage frais, quark, cream cheese and cottage cheese.

• Try instead reduced-fat spreads, low-fat spreads or fat-free spreads. If you must use butter or hard margarine, make sure they are softened at room temperature and spread them very thinly, or try low-fat cream cheese or low-fat soft cheese for sandwiches and toast.

• Eat fewer fatty cuts of meat and high-fat meat products, such as meat pâtés, burgers, pies and sausages.
• Try instead naturally low-fat meats such as skinless chicken and turkey, and venison. Use only the leanest cuts of meats such as lamb, beef and pork. Always cut away and discard any visible fat and skin from meat before cooking. Choose reduced-fat sausages and meat products, and eat fish more often. Try using low-fat protein products such as peas, beans, lentils or tofu instead of meat in recipes.
• Eat fewer hard cooking fats, such as lard or hard margarine.
• Try instead polyunsaturated or monounsaturated oils, such as sunflower, corn or olive oil for cooking (but don't use too much).
• Eat fewer rich salad dressings, and less full-fat mayonnaise.
• Try instead reduced-fat or fat-free mayonnaise or dressings. Make your own salad dressings at home with low-fat yogurt or fromage frais.
• Eat less fried food.
• Try instead fat-free cooking methods such as grilling (broiling), baking, microwaving or steaming whenever possible. Try cooking in non-stick pans with only a very small amount of oil. Always roast or grill (broil) meat or poultry on a rack.
• Eat fewer deep-fried and sautéed potatoes.
• Try instead low-fat starchy foods such as pasta, couscous and rice. Choose baked or boiled potatoes.
• Eat less added fat in cooking.
• Try instead to cook with little or no fat. Use heavy, good quality non-stick pans so that the food doesn't stick. Try using a small amount of spray oil in cooking to control exactly how much fat you are using. Use fat-free or low-fat ingredients for cooking, such as fruit juice, low-fat or fat-free stock, wine or even beer.
• Eat fewer high-fat snacks, such as chips (French fries), fried snacks and pastries, cakes, doughnuts and cookies.
• Try instead low-fat and fat-free fresh or dried fruits, breadsticks or vegetables. Make your own home-baked low-fat cakes. Buy low-fat and reduced-fat versions of cookies.

Below: Sardines are a good source of unsaturated fat.

Avocados

Below: Choose lean cuts of meat and naturally low-fat meats such as skinless chicken and turkey.

FAT-FREE COOKING METHODS

Once you get into the habit, it's easy to cook without fat. For example, whenever possible grill (broil), bake, microwave and steam foods without the addition of fat, or try stir-frying with little or no fat. Alternatively, try using a low-fat or fat-free stock, wine or fruit juice for cooking, instead of fat.

• By choosing good quality, non-stick cookware, you'll find that the amount of fat needed for cooking foods can be kept to an absolute minimum. When making casseroles or meat sauces such as Bolognese, dry-fry the meat to brown it, and then drain off all the excess fat before adding the other ingredients. If you do need a little fat for cooking, choose an oil that is high in unsaturates, such as olive, sunflower or corn oil, and always use as little as possible, or use an unsaturated spray oil.

• When baking low-fat cakes and cookies, use good quality non-stick bakeware that doesn't need greasing before use, or use baking parchment and only lightly grease before lining.
• Look for non-stick coated fabric sheets. This re-usable non-stick material is amazingly versatile, as it can be cut to size and used to line cake tins (pans), baking sheets or frying pans. Heat-resistant up to 550°F and microwave-safe, it will last for up to five years.

• Sauté vegetables in low-fat or fat-free stock, wine or fruit juice instead of oil.

• When baking foods such as chicken or fish, rather than adding a knob (pat) of butter to the food, try baking it in a loosely sealed package of foil or baking parchment and adding some wine or fruit juice and herbs or spices before sealing the parcel.

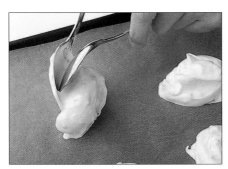

• When grilling (broiling) foods, the addition of fat is often unnecessary. If the food shows signs of drying, lightly brush with a small amount of unsaturated oil, such as olive, sunflower or corn oil.
• Microwaved foods rarely need the addition of fat, so add herbs or spices for extra flavour and colour.

• Steaming and boiling are easy, fat-free ways of cooking many foods. Cook vegetables in a covered pan over a low heat with a little water so they cook in their own juices.

• Try poaching foods such as chicken, fish and fruit in low-fat or fat-free stock or syrup.
• Try braising vegetables in the oven in low-fat or fat-free stock, wine or simply water with the addition of some chopped fresh or dried herbs.

• Marinate foods such as meat, poultry and game in mixtures of alcohol, herbs or spices, and vinegar or fruit juice. This will help to tenderize the meat and add flavour and colour. The leftover marinade can be used to baste the food while it is cooking. Fish can also be marinated before cooking to add flavour.

• When serving vegetables resist the temptation to add a knob (pat) of butter or margarine. Instead, sprinkle with chopped fresh herbs or ground spices.

LOW-FAT SPREADS IN COOKING

There is a huge variety of low-fat and reduced-fat spreads available at our supermarkets, along with some spreads that are very low in fat. Generally speaking, any very low-fat spreads with a fat content of around 20 per cent or less have a high water content. These are unsuitable for cooking and can only be used for spreading.

VEGETABLES

Naturally low in fat and bursting with vitamins and minerals, vegetables are one food group that should ideally make up the bulk of our daily diet. Vegetables have always played an important role in Mediterranean cooking. They are sometimes served as dishes in their own right, and sometimes as accompaniments. Either way, the range of imaginative low-fat recipes from all over the Mediterranean incorporating vegetables is vast, from salads to hearty stews. A whole range of flavourings, such as herbs, will bring out the best flavour in vegetables

Asparagus

Cultivated in the Mediterranean for hundreds of years, asparagus is still highly prized as a luxury vegetable all over Europe. It has a very short growing season, from spring to early summer, and is really only worth eating during this period. Both green and white asparagus are cultivated. The green variety is grown above ground, so that the entire spear is bright green, and is harvested when it is about 15cm (6in) high. The fat white spears with their pale yellow tips are grown under mounds of soil to protect them from the light.

Asparagus spears can be boiled, steamed, grilled (broiled) or roasted in a little olive oil, and served as a first

Below: Aubergines (eggplants) have an oily quality and a meaty texture.

course with a light sprinkling of freshly grated Parmesan cheese, or served with a light vinaigrette. Asparagus spears make an ideal accompaniment to low-fat Mediterranean-style meals and asparagus tips also make a luxury addition to risottos.

Above: Asparagus has been cultivated in the Mediterranean for hundreds of years.

Aubergines (eggplants)

Although aubergines originated in Asia, they feature in dishes from many Mediterranean countries. The plump purple variety is the most common and they are available in a range of sizes. Look for firm, shiny-skinned specimens with green stalks, that are heavy for their size. A light aubergine may have a dry, spongy inside and could contain a lot of seeds. Do not buy those with wrinkled or damaged skins. Aubergines will keep in the refrigerator for up to a week and are a very versatile vegetable. They can be grilled (broiled), baked, stuffed, stewed or lightly sautéed, either on their own or with other vegetables, and since they absorb flavours well, they can be used with most seasonings.

Left: Broad (fava) beans are at their best when they are small and tender.

Above: Fennel bulb, when cooked, has a subtle aniseed flavour.

Broad (fava) beans

These beans are at their best in late spring or early summer when they are small and tender, or cooked and skinned later in the season. When young they can be cooked and eaten, pods and all. Cooked broad beans have a milder flavour than raw. Dried broad beans are popular in the Middle East where they are cooked with spices or added to stews.

Courgettes (zucchini)

These summer squash typically have shiny green skin, a sweet delicate flavour and a crisp texture. They are at their best when they are small. The green variety is most common, but yellow ones are sometimes available. They can be sliced or grated and eaten raw, or they can be cooked, combining well with other Mediterranean vegetables. The larger courgettes become, the less flavour they have. When buying, choose firm, shiny specimens. Do not buy flabby courgettes, or those with blemished skins. In Italy and France the golden courgette flowers are also highly prized for eating. Courgettes are available almost all year round, but are at their best in spring and summer. They are perhaps best known

Above: Garlic has an unmistakable aroma unlike any other herb.

as a key ingredient with tomatoes and onions in the popular Mediterranean dish ratatouille.

Fennel bulb/Florence fennel

So called to distinguish it from the feathery green herb, fennel bulb or Florence fennel resembles a fat white root with overlapping leaves and green, wispy fronds. It has a delicate but distinctive flavour of aniseed and a crisp, refreshing texture. It can be eaten raw, dressed with a low-fat vinaigrette or served in a mixed salad. It can also be lightly sautéed, baked or braised. When cooked, the aniseed flavour becomes more subtle and the texture

Below: Courgettes (zucchini) are a good vegetable to provide bulk for stews.

resembles cooked celery. Choose firm, rounded bulbs, in which the outer layers are crisp and white, and if possible, buy those with the feathery green fronds intact.

Garlic

Sold in strings or as separate bulbs, the main consideration when buying garlic is that the cloves are plump and firm. Garlic is one of the most vital ingredients in Mediterranean cooking and there are few recipes in which its addition would be out of place. Used crushed, sliced or even whole, garlic develops a smooth, gentle flavour with long, slow cooking. Used raw in salads, light sauces and dressings, garlic adds a delicious, strong flavour. Garlic also has a medicinal value, being a decongestant, helping to lower blood pressure and blood cholesterol.

Globe artichokes

Not to be confused with Jerusalem artichokes, globe artichokes are at their best in summer. These tall vegetables grow a round head on a long stem and are visibly striking when cultivated. Look for artichoke heads with tightly-packed leaves, as open leaves indicate that the vegetable is too mature. When an artichoke is old, the tops of the leaves will turn brown. If possible, buy artichokes that are attached to their stems, as they will stay fresh for longer. Artichokes will keep fresh for several days if you place the stalks in water. Otherwise wrap them in clear film (plastic wrap) and keep in the vegetable drawer of the refrigerator for a day or two.

Jerusalem artichoke

The Jerusalem artichoke is an entirely different vegetable from the globe artichoke. It is, in fact, a tuber belonging to the sunflower family. Jerusalem artichokes look rather like knobbly potatoes, and can be treated as such. They have a lovely distinctive flavour and are good in Mediterranean-style soups. They are also delicious baked, braised, lightly sautéed or puréed.

Mushrooms

Button (white), open cup and flat mushrooms are used in Mediterranean cooking all year round. Regional wild species such as ceps, chanterelles and oyster mushrooms are to be found in

Left: Mushrooms of all varieties are used in Mediterranean cooking. They impart a subtle flavour to dishes.

the markets during autumn. Mushrooms can be sliced and eaten raw, dressed with a dash of extra virgin olive oil, or they can be lightly brushed with olive oil and grilled (broiled). Mushrooms also add subtle flavour to many other low-fat dishes such as sauces, stocks, soups and risottos.

To clean mushrooms, cut off the earthy base of the stalk and lightly brush the caps with a soft brush or wipe them clean with a damp cloth.

Peppers

Capsicums, or bell peppers, as they are also known, come in a range of colours including green, red, yellow, orange and even a purplish-black, though they all have the same sweetish flavour and crunchy texture. Peppers are commonly used in Mediterranean dishes. They can be used raw or lightly roasted in salads or as an antipasto, and can be cooked in a variety of ways – roasted and dressed with a light olive oil or vinaigrette dressing, grilled (broiled) or stuffed and baked. To make the most of their flavour, grill (broil) peppers until charred, then rub off and discard the skins. Peppers have a great affinity with other Mediterranean ingredients such as olives, capers, aubergines (eggplants), courgettes (zucchini), tomatoes and anchovies.

Left: The tightly packed heads of the green leafy globe artichoke are not to be confused with the root vegetable Jerusalem artichoke. Very small heads can be grilled and eaten whole.

Left: Jerusalem artichokes have a very distinctive flavour and are delicious baked, braised, lightly sautéed or puréed.

Above: Bell peppers are a very healthy food, being naturally low in fat and rich in vitamin C.

Tomatoes

Sun-ripened and full of flavour, tomatoes form the basis of many traditional Mediterranean recipes and come in many varieties, including beefsteak, plum, cherry and baby pear-shaped ones, as well as vine-ripened varieties. Bright red fruits literally bursting with aroma and flavour, tomatoes are essential ingredients in so many dishes.

They can be eaten raw, sliced and served with a trickle of extra virgin olive oil and some torn fresh basil leaves. Raw ripe tomatoes can be chopped with herbs and garlic to make a fresh-tasting pasta sauce. They can be grilled (broiled), lightly fried, baked, stuffed or stewed and made into tasty low-fat sauces and soups. Tomatoes are at their best when they have ripened naturally in the sun.

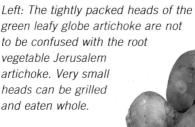

Above: Tomatoes form the basis of many traditional Mediterranean dishes, especially soups and sauces.

Choose your tomatoes according to how you wish to prepare them. Salad tomatoes should be bright red showing they are flavourful and ripe, yet firm and easy to slice. The best tomatoes for cooking are plum tomatoes, which have a superb flavour and hold their shape well. Beefsteak tomatoes are the best for stuffing or for slicing for salads. As well as fresh tomatoes, canned and sun-dried tomatoes are invaluable store cupboard (pantry) items, together with passata (bottled strained tomatoes) and tomato purée (paste). Remember, dry-packed sun-dried tomatoes are lower in fat than the oil-packed ones.

Below: Onions vary in taste and sweetness, as well as size and colouring.

Onions

These strongly flavoured vegetables are an essential component of virtually all savoury low-fat Mediterranean dishes. There are many varieties of onion, differing in colour, size and strength of flavour. Red- or white-skinned varieties have a sweet, mild flavour and are good used raw in salads. Large, Spanish onions are also mild and are a good choice when a large quantity of onion is called for in a recipe. Baby (pearl) onions are perfect for adding whole to stews, or serving as a vegetable dish. Choose firm onions that show no signs of sprouting green leaves. Onions should have thin, almost papery skins that are unblemished.

Okra

This unusual vegetable, sometimes called lady's fingers, is a long, five-sided green pod with a tapering end. It has a subtle flavour and a gelatinous texture, which helps to thicken and enrich dishes. It is used in Middle Eastern and Greek cooking and goes well with garlic, onion and tomatoes. Choose small, firm specimens with no dark patches, and use sliced or whole.

Spinach

This green, leafy vegetable is very popular in the Mediterranean area. Young, tender spinach leaves can be

Below: Okra is a vegetable pod that is added to soups and stews.

Above: Spinach is rich in iron.

eaten raw and need little preparation, but older leaves should be washed well, then picked over and the tough stalks removed. Spinach is used in many recipes including Middle Eastern dishes, Spanish tapas and French recipes. Eggs and fish make very good partners. Spinach wilts dramatically when cooked so allow at least 250g/9oz raw weight per person.

Vine leaves

These pretty leaves have been used in Mediterranean cooking for hundreds of years. They can be stuffed with a variety of low-fat fillings and also make perfect wrappers for lean meat, fish and poultry. Fresh vine leaves should be young and soft. If using brined vine leaves, soak them in hot water for 20–30 minutes before stuffing or wrapping them.

Below: Vine leaves are a key ingredient in Greek cooking.

FRUIT AND NUTS

The Mediterranean region produces a wonderful array of fruits and nuts, which are used extensively in its cuisine. Fruit and nuts are used in both sweet and savoury dishes and complement both flavours well. Raw fruit may also be eaten on its own as a simple dessert. Many fruits enjoyed in the Mediterranean, such as figs, melons, lemons, oranges, peaches and nectarines, are naturally low in calories and fat and provide plenty of vitamin C. Although tasty and nutritious, nuts should be eaten in moderation as they are high in fat.

Dates

When plump and slightly wrinkled fresh dates have a rich honey-like flavour and dense, slightly chewy texture. They are delicious stoned (pitted) and served with Greek (US strained plain) yogurt. Dried dates can be used in the same way, but fewer are needed as the flavour is concentrated.

Figs

Fresh figs are strongly associated with all Mediterranean countries and are delicious served simply on their own. They vary in colour, from dark purple to green to a golden yellow, but all are made up of hundreds of tiny seeds, surrounded by soft pink flesh, which is perfectly edible. Choose firm,

Below: Dates go particularly well with oranges and make a good addition to fruit salads.

PRESERVED LEMONS AND LIMES

These are used in many Mediterranean dishes, and are particularly popular in North African countries. The lemons or limes are preserved in salt and develop a wonderfully mellow flavour.

To preserve lemons or limes, scrub and quarter almost through to the base of the fruits and rub the cut sides with salt. Pack tightly into a large sterilized jar. Half fill the jar with salt, adding bay leaves, peppercorns and cinnamon, if you like. Pour lemon juice over the fruit to cover, then seal and store for two weeks, shaking the jar daily. Add a little olive oil and use within one to six months, washing off the salt before use.

unblemished fruit that just yields to the touch. They are highly perishable so use quickly. Fresh figs can also be served raw as a first course with prosciutto, or with low-fat Greek (US strained plain) yogurt and honey, or stuffed with raspberry coulis and served as a dessert. Poached in a little water or wine flavoured with cinnamon or nutmeg, they make an excellent accompaniment to lean game or lamb dishes.

Below: Lemons have an aromatic flavour, which enhances many Mediterranean dishes.

Grapes

Grown all over the Mediterranean, grapes are good for you. Fresh grapes are naturally low in fat and are rich in potassium and vitamins. Choosing white, black or red grapes is simply a matter of preference. Beneath the skin the flesh is always pale green and juicy. Buy bunches of grapes with fruit which is of equal size and not too densely packed on the stalk.

Lemons

These bright yellow citrus fruits are low in calories and fat and rich in vitamin C. They have an aromatic flavour which enhances almost any dish. Depending on the variety, lemons may have a thick indented skin or be perfectly smooth. Their appearance does not affect the flavour, but they should feel heavy for their size. Buy unwaxed lemons if you intend to use the rind in recipes.

Lemons are grown all over the Mediterranean and are very versatile. The juice can be squeezed to make a drink, or it can be added to tea, low-fat dressings and sauces. It is an antioxidant, and prevents discoloration when brushed over fruits and vegetables that have a tendency to turn brown when cut. The rind also imparts a wonderful flavour to savoury dishes, light salad dressings and low-fat desserts.

Below: Melons come in many different varieties, sizes, shapes and colours. The riper the melon, the sweeter the flavour.

Melons

This fruit comes in many different varieties, sizes, shapes and colours, including cantaloupe, Charentais, Galia, honeydew and Ogen, which are orange- and green-fleshed varieties, and also the wonderful pink-fleshed watermelon. Melons are often served in slices and decorated with other fresh fruits, simply as dessert fruit on their own. Ripe melons should yield to gentle pressure from your thumbs at the stalk end and have a fragrant, slightly sweet scent. If they smell highly perfumed and musky, they will probably be over-ripe. Melons contain mostly water, are naturally low in calories and fat, and provide some vitamin C.

Oranges

Many varieties of the orange are grown all over the Mediterranean, particularly in Spain. Varieties include seedless navel oranges, red-fleshed blood oranges and Seville oranges. Seville oranges, the bitter marmalade variety, have a very short season, just after Christmas. Oranges should have unblemished shiny skins and feel heavy for their size, which indicates that they contain plenty of juice and that the flesh is not dry. Orange varieties vary in levels of sweetness. Choose unwaxed oranges if you intend to use the rind in recipes.

Below: Peaches and nectarines are typically grown in France, Spain and Italy.

Peaches and nectarines

These are among the most delicious summer fruits. They need plenty of sun to ripen them and are grown in France, Spain and Italy. Peaches may be yellow-, pink- or white-fleshed, with a velvety, fuzzy skin. Nectarines are smooth-skinned, with all the luscious flavour of peaches. They also come in yellow and white varieties and, like peaches, the white nectarines have a finer flavour. Look for bruise-free specimens that just give when squeezed gently and choose fruits with an intense, sweet scent. Peaches and nectarines are interchangeable in recipes, whether cooked or raw. They can both be macerated in fortified wine or spirits or poached in white wine and syrup. They also have a special affinity with almonds. Peaches and nectarines are also delicious served with raspberries or made into fruit drinks and smoothies, low-fat ice creams and sorbets.

Pomegranates

These golden, apple-shaped fruits are often associated with Mediterranean cooking. Inside the tough skin are hundreds of seeds, which are covered with a deep pink flesh that has a delicate, slightly tart flavour. They are often sprinkled over meat dishes and sweet dishes such as fruit salads.

Below: Pistachio nuts originated in the Middle East. These small nuts are great to serve as a tapas or appetizer.

Almonds

Cultivated commercially in Spain, Italy and Portugal, the almond is widely used in all the Arab-influenced countries. It is an important ingredient in sweet pastries and is often added to savoury dishes too. Almonds are sold fresh in their green velvety shells in Mediterranean markets. Due to their high-fat content, almonds should be used sparingly in low-fat cooking.

Pine nuts

These little nuts or yellowish kernels have a resinous flavour. They are used in sweet and savoury dishes, and are one of the principal ingredients in pesto, the basil sauce from Italy. They are high in fat, so should be used in small amounts.

Pistachio nuts

These colourful nuts originated in the Middle East. They have flesh which ranges from pale to dark green, and a dry, papery, purple-tinged skin. Pistachio nuts have a subtle flavour and are traditionally used in a wide range of dishes, from pastries to ice creams and nougats. They are also delicious when eaten from the shell. Pistachio nuts are also high in fat, so should be used in moderation. Like all nuts, their texture is dry.

Below: Almonds are cultivated in Spain, Italy and Portugal. Flaked almonds are a good addition to tagines and desserts.

FISH AND SHELLFISH

The waters of the Mediterranean offer an abundant source of food. Fish and shellfish are often cooked simply, drizzled with olive oil and lemon juice and grilled (broiled), or roasted with herbs and garlic. Plainly cooked white fish is a superb low-fat food. Oily fish, such as sardines, contains omega 3 fat, and are good for you.

Clams

These attractive bivalves have a fine, sweet flavour and a firm texture. Like mussels, clams that do not close when tapped sharply should be discarded. Clams can be steamed open and are delicious served in low-fat pasta sauces, stews and soups

Crab

Brown and spider crabs are the most common in the Mediterranean. The meat is divided into brown and white. Crabs are often sold cooked and dressed, ready to eat, since the process of dressing them is quite fiddly. Choose cooked crabs which are heavy for their size and therefore meaty.

Monkfish

Usually only the tail of this very ugly fish is eaten and, as a general rule, the larger the tail, the better the quality. It can be studded with herbs and garlic and roasted whole, or grilled (broiled),

Below: Fresh prawns (shrimp) are low in fat, but high in cholesterol.

Above: Salt cod cooked in the Mediterranean style is delicious.

made into kebabs, lightly pan-fried, poached or braised.

Mussels

These shellfish have their own distinct flavour and are an acquired taste. They can be bought fresh with the shell still in place, or shelled. Any open mussels that do not close when sharply tapped should be discarded as this indicates that they are old. Mussels are easy to steam for just a few minutes in a covered pan. They can then be eaten as they are, stuffed and grilled, or added to sauces, soups and stews.

Prawns (shrimp)

The classic Mediterranean prawn is very large, about 20cm/8in long, reddish brown when raw and pink when cooked. Prawns can be bought fresh or frozen, raw or cooked, peeled or with the shell on.

Red mullet

This pretty fish is usually cooked by grilling over a wood fire, often with the liver still inside to add flavour. It can also be filleted and lightly fried or grilled (broiled), or included in stews and soups.

Salt cod

Most salt cod is prepared in Norway, Iceland and Newfoundland and then exported to Mediterranean countries. It has a pungent smell, but after being soaked for 48 hours and cooked in the Mediterranean style, with olives and tomatoes, it is delicious.

Sardines

These silvery fish are abundant throughout the Mediterranean. They tend to be about 13cm/5in long, and are cooked and eaten whole. They are grilled (broiled), barbecued or pan-fried and are often added to pasta sauces.

Sea bass

The flesh is soft and delicate and needs careful attention when cooking. Cooking methods include baking, grilling, (broiling), poaching and steaming.

Squid

Popular throughout Portugal, Spain and Italy, squid vary in size from the tiny specimens that can be eaten whole, to larger varieties, which are good for stuffing, grilling (broiling) or stewing. The flesh is sweet and tender when cooked for only a short time.

Swordfish

The steaks can be very large. Lightly brush with oil when grilling (broiling).

Tuna

An oily fish belonging to the same family as mackerel. The flesh, which is sold in steaks or large pieces, is dark red and dense. Marinating before cooking helps to keep the flesh moist, as does basting while cooking. It can be baked, fried, grilled (broiled) or stewed.

Below: Red mullet is very popular along the coasts of the Mediterranean.

MEAT AND POULTRY

Meat, poultry and game are enjoyed all around the Mediterranean and play an important role in its cuisine. Slow-cooked stews and casseroles are favoured throughout the whole region. Quickly grilled (broiled) kebabs are popular in Turkey. Poultry and game are often oven-baked or roasted. Meat is also grilled (broiled), particularly in Greece and the Middle East.

Some types of meat are lower in fat than others, for example, poultry and pork contain less fat than beef and lamb. For maximum flavour choose an animal that has been fed a good diet, always choose cuts of meat that are lean, and use healthy cooking methods.

Beef

Cattle are a rare sight and in times past, beef was considered a luxury. Using minced (ground) meat in meatballs, sausages, fillings and pasta sauces is very popular. Meat is often padded out with other ingredients to make a more economical dish. Pulses, rice, bulgur wheat and potatoes are all used to add bulk to traditional dishes to make the meat go further.

Cured meats

Italy is famous for its prosciutto crudo – salted and dried ham that requires no cooking. The most famous of these hams is prosciutto di Parma, or Parma

Below: Beef is higher in fat than white meat, but has a high nutritional value.

Above: Poultry is naturally low in fat, and the basis of many low-fat dishes.

ham, which has a medium fat content, but is served in wafer-thin slices so can be incorporated into low-fat dishes. Pancetta, bresaola, mortadella and salami are also popular Mediterranean cured meats. Meats such as pancetta, mortadella and salami are high in fat and should be used sparingly in low-fat Mediterranean recipes. Bresaola has a similar fat content to prosciutto.

Lamb

In Greece, minced (ground) lamb is layered with aubergines (eggplants), tomato sauce and a white sauce to create a low-fat moussaka, whereas in Turkey minced lamb is used to stuff vegetables such as courgettes (zucchini) and aubergines. Stewed or slow-roasted lamb dishes are also popular.

Below: Lamb is a fatty meat, so choose lean cuts of meat and eat small portions.

Pork

Many rural Mediterranean families traditionally kept a pig, which was slaughtered in the autumn and the meat was preserved to feed them through the chilly winter months. The meat was used to make cured meats and sausages, each with their own unique taste and texture, as well as the variety of cured hams which are still popular around the Mediterranean today.

Poultry and game

These have always played an important role in Mediterranean cooking, largely because of the dry and rugged land. Chickens and ducks have always been particularly popular at the table as peasants were able to raise them on their own land.

Chicken is the most widely used type of poultry in low-fat cooking. It is often cooked with fresh, dried or preserved fruits, nuts and spices. In the Middle East, chickens were kept for their eggs, so only older birds were eaten and slow cooking with highly flavoured sauces and stuffings developed.

Rabbit is widely eaten and game birds such as partridge, quail and pigeon are typical of the region. They are often lightly cooked in sauces or served with polenta (in Italy). Removing and discarding the skin before cooking or eating ensures the meat is very lean.

Below: Traditionally, many rural families in the Mediterranean region kept a pig.

DAIRY PRODUCE

The countries of the Mediterranean produce a diverse range of cheeses and yogurt, made from cow's, goat's, sheep's and, in the case of Italian mozzarella, buffalo's milk. The flavour of the cheese or yogurt depends on the type of milk used and varies from mild and creamy ricotta to sharp and tangy feta, strong and salty halloumi and distinctively flavoured Greek (US strained plain) yogurt. The flavour of the milk depends upon the land that the animal grazes upon.

Low-fat varieties of dairy foods such as yogurt and mozzarella cheese are widely available and ideal for creating delicious low-fat Mediterranean dishes. Full-fat cheeses such as Parmesan can also be used sparingly to add extra flavour, but because of the generally high fat content, they should only be used in small amounts.

CHEESE

The variety of cheeses from Mediterranean countries is huge, ranging from fresh mild cheeses such as mozzarella to soft, blue-veined ones such as Gorgonzola, as well as aged hard types with a strong, mature (sharp)

Below: Choose reduced-fat or low-fat varieties of cheese, such as mozzarella, or use full-fat cheeses such as feta (pictured) in small amounts.

flavour such as Parmesan and Pecorino. Cream cheese is also common to many countries, varying a little according to the milk of the region where the cheese is made, and the method used for preparing it. Choose reduced- or low-fat versions, where possible.

Feta

This crumbly, white Greek cheese is made from sheep's milk. It tends to be rather salty and has a very distinctive, sharp, tangy flavour. It is relatively high in fat, so should be used in small amounts.

Mozzarella

This pure white egg-shaped fresh cheese, whose melting quality makes it perfect for so many dishes, is used widely in Mediterranean dishes, especially in Italy. The best mozzarella is made in the area around Naples in Italy, using water buffalo's milk. Reduced-fat mozzarella is also readily available and is ideal for use in low-fat Mediterranean cooking. It is delicious served with sliced fresh red tomatoes and green basil leaves. When cooked, mozzarella becomes uniquely stringy and is ideal for topping pizzas.

Below: Reduced-fat or low-fat Greek (US strained plain) yogurt is ideal for use in low-fat Mediterranean cooking, for desserts, dips and marinades.

Parmesan

Perhaps the best known cheese used in the Mediterranean region is Italian Parmesan. There are two types of this cheese available, Parmigiano Reggiano and Grana Padano, the former being infinitely superior. A really fine Parmesan may be aged for up to seven years, during which time it matures, becoming pale golden with a slightly granular, flaky texture and a nutty, mildly salty flavour. Always buy Parmesan in the piece and freshly grate it yourself, rather than buying it ready grated. Full-fat cheeses such as Parmesan should be used in moderation – these are flavourful cheeses and a little finely grated fresh Parmesan goes a long way adding delicious flavour to many dishes, from pasta and polenta to risotto and minestrone soup.

Ricotta

This is a fresh, soft Italian cheese made from cow's, ewe's or goat's milk. It is used widely in Italy for both sweet and savoury recipes. Ricotta has a medium fat content so should be used in moderation in low-fat Mediterranean cooking. It has an excellent texture and a mild flavour, so it makes a perfect vehicle for seasonings such as black pepper, nutmeg and chopped fresh herbs. It is also puréed with cooked spinach to make a classic filling for ravioli, cannelloni or lasagne. It is often used in desserts and can be sweetened and then served with fresh fruit, or used as a filling for a tart.

YOGURT

This live produce (pasteurized milk combined with two beneficial bacteria) is perhaps most associated with the Middle Eastern countries, where it is used extensively in cooking. Greek (US strained plain) yogurt is thick and creamy, and French yogurt is traditionally of the set variety. Yogurt is used as a marinade, a dip and to enrich soups and stews. Choose low-fat, reduced-fat or fat-free varieties, to keep the fat content of your Mediterranean dishes down.

PASTA, RICE, GRAINS AND PULSES

Throughout the Mediterranean, these important staple ingredients are used in almost every meal. They may be added to hearty soups or meat and vegetable stews such as tagines, used in salads such as tabbouleh, or served as accompaniments to meat dishes. They are versatile, healthy, nutritious and delicious, as well as naturally low in fat.

Bulgur wheat

Also known as cracked wheat or burghul, this low-fat cereal has been partially processed, so cooks quickly. It is made from cooked wheat berries, which have the bran removed, and are then dried and crushed. This light, nutty grain is soaked in boiling water for 20 minutes, then drained. Bulgur wheat is the main ingredient in the Middle Eastern salad, tabbouleh. It is also used as an accompaniment or as an ingredient in low-fat stuffings.

Couscous

This tiny yellowish grain is a form of pasta made from semolina. The grains are rolled, dampened and cooked with fine wheat flour. Couscous simply needs soaking, although it can also be steamed or baked. It is quick-cooking. Couscous has a light and fluffy texture and a fairly bland flavour, which makes it a good foil for spicy dishes, such as low-fat meat or vegetable stews. It is also ideal for salads and stuffings.

Lentils

These low-fat nutritious pulses come in different sizes and can be yellow, red, brown or green. The tiny green Puy lentils are favoured in France, whereas the brown and red ones are more popular in the Middle East, where they are often cooked with spices. They do not need soaking before cooking.

Pasta

The Latin word for pasta is *paste*, the flour and egg-based dough from which it is made. In Italy there are countless varieties of pasta, from flat sheets of lasagne and ribbon noodles to pressed and moulded shapes such as ravioli and tortelloni. Pasta is naturally low in fat

Above: Polenta is a grainy yellow flour that is a type of cornmeal.

and therefore ideal for creating delicious low-fat dishes. Dried pasta, made from hard durum wheat, is a good store cupboard (pantry) standby. Fresh pasta has a better flavour and texture, but will only keep for a couple of days in the refrigerator, although it can successfully be frozen.

Polenta

This grainy yellow flour is a type of cornmeal made from ground maize, which confusingly is the Italian name for both cornmeal and a dish made with the grain. The cooked dish is a thick, golden porridge, which is often served plain or flavoured with a little butter, olive oil or grated Parmesan cheese, and topped with chopped fresh herbs. Once cooked and cool, it can be cut into pieces and barbecued, grilled (broiled), griddled or lightly fried. Polenta grain is available in grades from fine to coarse to suit different dishes, and it is naturally low in fat.

Rice

For over half the world's population rice is a staple food. In Italy, there are at least four different short-grained types such as Arborio and Carnaroli, used for risotto. In Spain, Valencia rice is the preferred variety for paella. This valuable low-fat food provides a

good source of vitamins and minerals, and creates an ideal basis for a wide variety of nutritious, low-fat Mediterranean dishes.

Chickpeas

This pulse looks like a pale golden hazelnut. Chickpeas are naturally low in fat, have a nutty flavour and firm texture and are used in stews. They can also be served cold as a salad, lightly dressed with lemon juice, fresh herbs and extra virgin olive oil. In the Middle East they are made into flour, and in Greece and Turkey they are puréed to make a dip.

Dried and canned chickpeas are available. Dried chickpeas should be soaked overnight before being used.

Haricot (navy) beans

There are several varieties of these beans, including red- and cream-speckled borlotti, pale green flageolet, small white cannellini and navy, and black-eyed beans (peas). These small plump beans, which are soft when cooked, are added to casseroles and soups. They are also good served as a side dish or added to salads.

Haricot beans are available dried or canned. Dried beans should be soaked overnight before cooking.

Below: Lentils are a nutritious addition to soups and stews and are low in fat.

FLAVOURINGS: HERBS, SPICES AND OLIVE OIL

Around the Mediterranean, many ingredients are added to dishes to give essential extra flavour or to enhance those already present. In Italy, for example, good quality olive oil is drizzled lightly over many dishes, imparting a warm, nutty flavour, while in the eastern Mediterranean rose water is sometimes added to desserts, providing a wonderfully fragrant aroma and taste. Many flavourings such as herbs and spices are also naturally low in fat, so adding lots of flavour and colour, without extra fat, makes them ideal for creating a wide range of delicious and nutritious low-fat Mediterranean dishes.

Basil

One of the herbs most crucial to Mediterranean cooking, particularly in Italian dishes, basil has a wonderful intense aroma, sweet flavour and bright green colour. The sweet, tender leaves have a natural affinity with tomatoes, aubergines (eggplants), (bell) peppers, courgettes (zucchini) and cheese. Basil is perhaps best known as the basis of the Italian sauce pesto, but a handful of torn leaves will also enliven a green salad. Tear the leaves rather than chopping them, as they bruise easily, and add basil to dishes towards the end of the cooking time.

Bay leaves

Taken from the hardy bay shrub or tree, these are widely used to flavour slow-cooked recipes such as low-fat stocks, soups and stews. They are also added to

Above: Bay leaves and seasonings are used to flavour slow-cooked recipes.

marinades, threaded on to kebab skewers, thrown on the barbecue to invigorate the smoky flavour, or used for garnishing.

Coriander (cilantro)

Huge bunches of fresh coriander (cilantro) are a familiar sight in eastern Mediterranean markets, their warm, pungent aroma rising at the merest touch. The leaves impart a distinctive flavour to low-fat soups, stews, sauces and spicy dishes when added towards the end of cooking. Coriander is also used in salads and yogurt dishes.

Mint

In Greece, chopped mint accompanies other herbs to enhance stuffed vegetables and fish dishes, and in Turkey and the Middle East, finely chopped mint adds a cooling tang to yogurt dishes as well as teas and iced drinks.

Oregano

This herb is a wild form of marjoram, and has a slightly stronger flavour. There are several varieties of both oregano and marjoram, which grow wild throughout the Mediterranean region, but are also cultivated. They are very popular herbs, widely used in cooking, particularly in tomato-based sauces and vegetable stews.

Left: Mint is one of the oldest herbs used throughout the Mediterranean.

Parsley

Flat leaf parsley is far more widely used in Mediterranean cooking than the tightly curled variety. It is commonly used to add flavour and colour.

Rosemary

Cut from the pretty flowering shrub, rosemary grows well throughout the Mediterranean and is most widely used in meat cooking. Several sprigs, tucked under a roast chicken or lamb joint with plenty of garlic, impart an inviting warm, sweet flavour.

Thyme

There are many types of thyme, from lemon thyme to plain garden thyme, ranging in colour from yellow to grey-green. A few sprigs will add a warm earthy flavour to slow-cooked meat and poultry dishes, low-fat pâtés, soups, marinades and vegetable dishes.

Chillies

These are the small fiery relatives of the sweet (bell) pepper family and are used extensively in Mediterranean cooking. Chillies, both fresh and dried, may be used in tagines and spicy stews, as well as in many Spanish and Italian dishes.

Cumin seeds

These dark, spindly seeds are frequently married with coriander (cilantro) in spicy dishes that are typical of the eastern Mediterranean. Cumin

Below: Oregano has a distinct aroma.

Above: Chillies add intense heat and a crunchy texture to all dishes.

has a strong, spicy, sweet aroma with a slightly bitter, pungent taste. They are crushed or used whole.

Nutmeg

The sweet, warm aroma of nutmeg makes a good addition to many sweet and savoury dishes, particularly those containing spinach, cheese and eggs. For the best flavour, buy whole nutmegs and grate them freshly as required.

Pepper

This is one of the most versatile of all spices. There are several types of peppercorns, all of which are picked from the pepper vine. Black peppercorns have the strongest flavour, which is rich, earthy and pungent. Green peppercorns are the fresh unripe berries that are bottled while soft.

Below: Olives are high in fat, but the fat they contain is beneficial to our bodies.

Above: Nutmeg makes a good addition to many sweet and savoury dishes.

Honey

An ancient sweetener, honey depends on the flowers on which the bees have fed for its fragrance and flavour. It is used in mainly sweet, but also some savoury, Mediterranean dishes.

Tomato purée (paste)

A thick, concentrated paste made from fresh tomatoes with a very intense flavour. It is perfect for giving a boost to the flavour of bland tomatoes in low-fat soups, stews and sauces. Sun-dried tomato paste has an even richer, riper flavour. Both are available in jars, cans and tubes.

Olives

The fruit of one of the earliest known trees native to the Mediterranean, olives are extremely popular in Mediterranean cooking. There are many varieties, differing in size and taste. Colour depends purely on ripeness – the fruit changes from yellow to green, purple, brown and finally black when fully ripened. Fresh olives are picked at the desired stage, then soaked in water, bruised and immersed in brine to produce the familiar-tasting result. Olives are available loose, bottled or canned and may be whole or pitted. They are sometimes stuffed with pimientos, anchovies or nuts, or bottled with

Right: Olive oil is the traditional fat used for Mediterranean cooking.

flavourings such as garlic and chilli. Olives are quite high in monounsaturated fat and low in saturated fat, but should be used in moderation.

Olive oil

This is indispensable to the Mediterranean cuisine, but should be used in moderation in low-fat cooking because of its high fat content. Unlike other oils, which are extracted from the seeds or dried fruits of plants, olive oil is pressed from the pulp of ripe olives, which gives it an inimitable richness and flavour. Besides being high in monounsaturated fat and low in saturated fat, making it a healthy alternative to many other fats, olive oil is valued for its fine, nutty flavour. Italy, France and Spain produce some of the best, and different regions produce distinctively different oils. The richest and best oil comes from the first cold pressing of the olives, with no further processing, producing a rich green "extra virgin" oil. Virgin olive oil is pressed in the same way, but is usually from a second pressing. Extra virgin olive oil is ideal used "raw" in salad dressings, uncooked sauces and for drizzling lightly over vegetables. Virgin olive oil is used as a condiment or for general cooking and baking.

FAT AND CALORIE CONTENTS OF FOOD

The figures show the weight of fat (g) and the energy content per 100g (3½oz) of each of the following foods used in Mediterranean cooking. Use the table to help work out the fat content of favourite dishes.

	Fat (g)	Energy
MEAT PRODUCTS		
Bacon rasher, streaky (strip, fatty)	39.54	14kcals/1710kJ
Beef mince (ground), raw	16.2	225kcals/934kJ
Chicken fillet, raw	1.1	106kcals/449kJ
Chicken drumstick	5.7	170kcals/720kJ
Chicken, roasted	12.5	218kcals/910kJ
Lamb chops, loin, lean and fat	23.0	277kcals/1126kJ
Lamb, average, lean, raw	8.3	156kcals/651kJ
Liver, lamb, raw	6.2	137kcals/575kJ
Pork chops, loin, lean and fat	21.7	270kcals/1119kJ
Pork, average, lean, raw	4.0	123kcals/519kJ
Prosciutto	12.7	223kcals/892kJ
Rump (round) steak, lean only	4.1	125kcals/526kJ
Salami	45.2	491kcals/2031kJ
Turkey, meat only, raw	1.6	105kcals/443kJ
FISH AND SHELLFISH		
Clams, canned	0.6	77kcals/325kJ
Crab, canned	0.5	77kcals/326kJ
Lemon sole, raw	1.5	83kcals/351kJ
Mackerel, smoked	30.9	354kcals/1465kJ
Monkfish, raw	0.4	66kcals/264kJ
Mussels, raw, weight without shells	1.8	74kcals/312kJ
Mussels, raw, weight with shells	0.6	24kcals/98kJ
Prawns (shrimp)	0.9	99kcals/418kJ
Salmon, poached	11.9	194kcals/812kJ
Sardine fillets, grilled (broiled)	10.4	195kcals/815kJ
Sardines, grilled, weight with bones	6.3	119kcals/497kJ
Sea bass, raw	2.5	100kcals/400kJ
Squid, raw	1.7	81kcals/324kJ
Trout, grilled	5.4	135kcals/565kJ
Tuna, canned in brine	0.6	99kcals/422kJ
Tuna, canned in oil	9.0	189kcals/794kJ

	Fat (g)	Energy
VEGETABLES		
Asparagus	0	15kcals/63kJ
Aubergines (eggplants)	0.4	15kcals/63kJ
Beetroot (beets), cooked	0.1	36kcals/151kJ
(Bell) peppers	0.4	32kcals/128kJ
Broad (fava) beans	0.8	48kcals/204kJ
Broccoli	0.9	33kcals/138kJ
Cabbage	0.4	26kcals/109kJ
Carrots	0.3	35kcals/146kJ
Cauliflower	0.9	34kcals/146kJ
Celery, raw	0.2	33kcals/142kJ
Courgettes (zucchini)	0.4	18kcals/74kJ
Cucumber	0.1	10kcals/40kJ
Fennel	0	14kcals/56kJ
Globe artichoke	0	9kcals/35kJ
Green beans	0	22kcals/92kJ
Jerusalem artichoke	0	41kcals/207kJ
Mushrooms	0.5	13kcals/55kJ
Okra	0	26kcals/110kJ
Onions	0.2	36kcals/151kJ
Peas	1.5	83kcals/344kJ
Potatoes	0.2	75kcals/318kJ
Chips (French fries), home-made	6.7	189kcals/796kJ
Potato crisps (potato chips)	34.2	530kcals/1924kJ
Spinach (fresh, cooked)	0	21kcals/84kJ
Tomatoes	0.3	17kcals/73kJ
FRUITS AND NUTS		
Apples, eating	0.1	47kcals/199kJ
Avocados	19.5	190kcals/784kJ
Bananas	0.3	95kcals/403kJ
Dates	0	226/kcals/970kJ
Dried mixed fruit	0.4	268kcals/1114kJ
Figs	0	43kcals/185kJ

Below: Red meat products, such as sausages and bacon, have a higher quantity of fat per 100g than white meat.

Below: Seafood contains less fat per 100g than meat, but oily fish such as mackerel contains more fat than white fish.

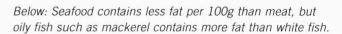

	Fat (g)	Energy
Grapefruit	0.1	30kcals/126kJ
Grapes	0	63kcals/265kJ
Lemons, with peel	0.2	9kcals/38kJ
Melon	0	32kcals/135kJ
Olives (green)	11	112kcals/422kJ
Oranges	0.1	37kcals/158kJ
Peaches/nectarines	0.1	33kcals/142kJ
Pomegranate	0.2	51kcals/218kJ
Almonds	55.8	612kcals/2534kJ
Brazil nuts	68.2	682kcals/2813kJ
Hazelnuts	63.5	650kcals/2685kJ
Pine nuts	68.6	688kcals/2840kJ
Pistachio nuts	58.3	632kcals/2650kJ
Walnuts	68.5	688kcals/2840kJ

BEANS, PULSES AND CEREALS

	Fat (g)	Energy
Brown rice, raw	2.8	357kcals/1518kJ
Bulgur (cracked wheat)	2.5	319kcals/1340kJ
Chickpeas, canned	2.9	115kcals/487kJ
Couscous (cooked)	0	112kcals/470kJ
Pasta, white, raw	1.8	342kcals/1456kJ
Pasta, wholemeal (whole-wheat), uncooked	2.5	324kcals/1379kJ
Polenta	1.6	330kcals/1383kJ
Red kidney beans, canned	0.6	100kcals/424kJ
Red lentils, cooked	0.4	100kcals/424kJ
White rice, raw	3.6	383kcals/1630kJ

BAKING AND SPREADS

	Fat (g)	Energy
Bread, brown	2.0	218kcals/927kJ
Bread, white	1.9	235kcals/1002kJ
Bread, wholemeal (whole-wheat)	2.5	215kcaqls/914kJ
Chocolate, milk	30.7	520kcals/2157kJ
Chocolate, plain (semisweet)	28.0	510kcals/2116kJ
Croissant	20.3	360kcals/1505kJ
Flour, plain (all-purpose) white	1.3	341kcals/1450kJ
Flour, self-raising (self-rising)	1.2	330kcals/1407kJ
Flour, wholemeal (whole-wheat)	2.2	310kcals/1318kJ
Fruit jam	0.26	268kcals/1114kJ

	Fat (g)	Energy
Honey	0	288kcals/1229kJ
Sugar, white	0.3	94kcals/1680kJ

FATS, OILS AND EGGS

	Fat (g)	Energy
Butter	81.7	737kcals/3031kJ
Margarine	81.6	739kcals/3039kJ
Low-fat spread	40.5	390kcals/1605kJ
Very low-fat spread	25.0	273kcals/1128kJ
Cooking oil	99.9	899kcals/3696kJ
Eggs	10.8	147kcals/612kJ
Egg yolk	30.5	399kcals/1402kJ
Egg white	Trace	36kcals/153kJ
French dressing	49.4	462kcals/1902kJ
Fat-free dressing	1.2	67kcals/282kJ
Mayonnaise	75.6	691kcals/kJ

CREAM, MILK AND CHEESE

	Fat (g)	Energy
Cream, double (heavy)	48.0	449kcals/1849kJ
Reduced-fat double (heavy) cream	24.0	243kcals/1002kJ
Cream, single (light)	19.1	198kcals/817kJ
Cream, whipping	39.3	373kcals/1539kJ
Crème fraîche	40.0	379kcals/156kJ
Reduced fat crème fraîche	15.0	165kcals/683kJ
Milk, skimmed	0.1	33kcals/130kJ
Milk, full cream (whole)	3.9	66kcals/275kJ
Cheddar cheese	34.4	412kcals/1708kJ
Cheddar-type, reduced-fat	15.0	261kcals/1091kJ
Cottage cheese	3.9	98kcals/413kJ
Cream cheese	47.4	439kcals/1807kJ
Curd cheese (medium-fat)	11.7	173kcals/723kJ
Feta cheese	20.2	250kcals/1037kJ
Fromage frais, plain	7.1	113kcals/469kJ
Fromage frais, very low-fat	0.2	58kcals/247kJ
Mozzarella cheese	21.0	289kcals/1204kJ
Parmesan cheese	32.7	452kcals/1880kJ
Ricotta cheese	10	150kcals/625kJ
Skimmed-milk soft cheese	trace	74kcals/313kJ
Low-fat yogurt, natural (plain)	0.8	56kcals/236kJ
Greek (US strained plain) yogurt	9.1	115kcals/477kJ

Below: Vegetables are very low in fat. Eat them raw for a filling snack, or steam them to retain maximum nutritional value.

Below: Cheese is very high in fat and should be eaten as an occasional treat when following a low-fat diet.

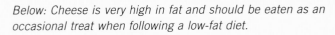

THE RECIPES

This delicious and nutritious collection of
low-fat Mediterranean dishes embraces the
best of traditional and contemporary cooking
from a region of the world famed for its cuisine
and the healthiness of its population.

APPETIZERS

Many Mediterranean countries are well-known
for their appetizers, including Italian antipasti,
Greek meze and Spanish tapas. This chapter
features a tempting selection of low-fat
appetizers from all over the Mediterranean,
including Spiced Dolmades and Tsatziki from
Greece and Bruschetta and Crostini from Italy.

OLIVE AND ANCHOVY BITES ★

THESE LITTLE MELT-IN-THE-MOUTH MORSELS ARE MADE FROM TWO INGREDIENTS THAT ARE FOREVER ASSOCIATED WITH TAPAS — OLIVES AND ANCHOVIES. BOTH INGREDIENTS CONTAIN SALT, WHICH HELPS TO STIMULATE THIRST AND THEREFORE DRINKING.

3 Preheat the oven to 200°C/400°F/Gas 6. Roll out the dough thinly on a lightly floured surface.

4 Cut the dough into 5cm/2in-wide strips, then cut across each strip in alternate directions, to make triangles. Transfer to non-stick baking sheets and bake for 8–10 minutes, until golden. Cool on a wire rack. Sprinkle with sea salt.

VARIATIONS
• To add a little extra spice, dust the olive and anchovy bites lightly with cayenne pepper before baking.
• Crisp little nibbles set off most drinks. Serve these bites alongside little bowls of seeds and nuts such as sunflower seeds and pistachio nuts. Toasted chickpeas are another popular tapas snack.

MAKES ABOUT FORTY-FIVE

INGREDIENTS
   115g/4oz/1 cup plain
     (all-purpose) flour
   115g/4oz/½ cup chilled
     butter, diced
   115g/4oz/1 cup finely grated
     Manchego, mature (sharp) Cheddar
     or Gruyère cheese
   50g/2oz can anchovy fillets
     in oil, drained and roughly
     chopped
   50g/2oz/½ cup pitted black olives,
     roughly chopped
   2.5ml/½ tsp cayenne pepper
   sea salt, to serve

1 Place the flour, butter, cheese, anchovies, olives and cayenne pepper in a food processor and pulse until the mixture forms a firm dough.

2 Wrap the dough loosely in clear film (plastic wrap). Chill for 20 minutes.

Energy per bite 42kcal/173kJ; Protein 1.2g; Carbohydrate 2g, of which sugars 0.1g; Fat 3.2g, of which saturates 1.9g, of which polyunsaturates 0.2g; Cholesterol 9mg; Calcium 27mg; Fibre 0.1g; Sodium 103mg.

BANDERILLAS ★

THESE MINIATURE SKEWERS ARE KNOWN IN SPAIN AS PINCHOS, WHICH LITERALLY MEANS "STUCK ON A THORN". THE CHOICE OF INGREDIENTS MAY INCLUDE COLD OR CURED MEAT, PICKLED TUNA, SALTED FISH OR EVEN HARD-BOILED EGGS AS WELL AS AN ASSORTMENT OF VEGETABLES.

SERVES SIX

INGREDIENTS
    12 small capers
    12 canned anchovy fillets in
      oil, drained
    12 pitted black olives
    12 cornichons or small gherkins
    12 silverskin pickled onions

VARIATION
You can vary the ingredients using cold lean meats, reduced fat cheeses and vegetables. Choose ingredients with different textures, tastes and colours.

1 Using your fingers, place a caper at the thicker end of each anchovy fillet and carefully roll it up, so that the caper is completely enclosed.

2 Thread one caper-filled anchovy, one olive, one cornichon or gherkin and one pickled onion on to each of 12 cocktail sticks (toothpicks). Chill and serve.

Energy 27kcal/110kJ; Protein 1.8g; Carbohydrate 1g, of which sugars 0.7g; Fat 1.7g, of which saturates 0.3g, of which polyunsaturates 0.3g; Cholesterol 4mg; Calcium 29mg; Fibre 0.5g; Sodium 462mg.

GRILLED AUBERGINE IN HONEY AND SPICES ★

HOT, SPICY, SWEET AND FRUITY ARE A CLASSIC COMBINATION IN THIS DELICIOUS MOROCCAN DISH. BABY AUBERGINES ARE VERY EFFECTIVE FOR THIS RECIPE AS YOU CAN SLICE THEM IN HALF LENGTHWAYS AND HOLD THEM BY THEIR STALKS.

SERVES FOUR

INGREDIENTS
  2 baby aubergines (eggplants),
    thickly sliced
  25ml/1½ tbsp olive oil
  2–3 garlic cloves, crushed
  5cm/2in piece fresh root ginger,
    peeled and grated
  5ml/1 tsp ground cumin
  5ml/1 tsp harissa
  75ml/5 tbsp clear honey
  juice of 1 lemon
  salt, to taste

1 Preheat the grill (broiler) or a griddle. Lightly brush each aubergine slice with olive oil and cook under the grill or in a griddle pan. Turn the slices during cooking so that they are lightly browned on both sides.

VARIATION
If you want to make a feature out of this sumptuous dish, serve it with other grilled (broiled) vegetables and fruit, such as (bell) peppers, chillies, tomatoes, oranges, pineapples and mangoes.

2 In a wide non-stick frying pan, fry the garlic in the remaining oil for a few seconds, then stir in the ginger, cumin, harissa, honey and lemon juice. Add enough water to cover the base of the pan and to thin the mixture, then lay the aubergine slices in the pan. Cook the aubergines gently for about 10 minutes, or until they have absorbed all the sauce.

3 Add a little extra water, if necessary, season to taste with salt, and serve at room temperature, with chunks of fresh bread to mop up the juices.

Energy 111kcal/466kJ; Protein 1.4g; Carbohydrate 17.2g, of which sugars 16g; Fat 4.6g, of which saturates 0.7g, of which polyunsaturates 0.5g; Cholesterol 0mg; Calcium 10mg; Fibre 1.8g; Sodium 4mg.

HERBY TORTILLA <u>WITH</u> BEANS ★

THE ADDITION OF CHOPPED HERBS AND A FEW SKINNED BEANS TO THE CLASSIC TORTILLA MAKES THIS A VERY SUMMERY DISH. CUT IT INTO SMALL PIECES AND SERVE AS A TAPAS DISH. TORTILLA IS A TYPICAL MEDITERRANEAN DISH AND A MUST IN TAPAS SELECTIONS.

SERVES TWELVE

INGREDIENTS
  20ml/4 tsp olive oil
  2 Spanish (Bermuda) onions,
   thinly sliced
  300g/11oz waxy potatoes, diced
  250g/9oz/1¾ cups shelled broad
   (fava) beans
  5ml/1 tsp chopped fresh thyme or
   summer savory
  6 eggs
  45ml/3 tbsp mixed chopped fresh
   chives and fresh flat leaf parsley
  salt and ground black pepper

1 Heat half the oil in a deep 23cm/9in non-stick frying pan. Add the onions and potatoes and stir to lightly coat. Cover and cook gently, stirring occasionally, for 20–25 minutes, or until the potatoes are cooked and tender.

2 Meanwhile, cook the beans in a pan of salted boiling water for 5 minutes. Drain well and set aside to cool.

3 When the beans are cool enough to handle, peel off and discard the grey outer skins. Add the beans to the frying pan, together with the thyme or summer savory and season with salt and pepper to taste. Stir well to mix and cook for a further 2–3 minutes.

4 Beat the eggs with a little salt and pepper to taste and add the mixed herbs. Pour the egg mixture over the potatoes and onions and increase the heat slightly. Cook gently for about 5 minutes, or until the egg on the bottom sets and browns. During cooking, gently pull the tortilla away from the sides of the pan and tilt to allow the uncooked egg to run underneath.

5 Cover the frying pan with a large, upside-down plate and invert the tortilla on to it. Add the remaining oil to the pan and heat until hot. Slip the tortilla back into the pan, uncooked side down, and cook for 3–5 minutes, or until the underneath browns.

6 Slide the tortilla out on to a plate. Cut into 12 thin wedges or cubes and serve warm rather than piping hot.

Energy 98kcal/410kJ; Protein 5.8g; Carbohydrate 9.9g, of which sugars 3g; Fat 4.3g, of which saturates 1g, of which polyunsaturates 0.5g; Cholesterol 95mg; Calcium 45mg; Fibre 2.4g; Sodium 42mg.

TOMATO AND GARLIC BREAD ★

A BASKET OF WARM, CRUSTY, GARLIC-FLAVOURED BREAD IS A COMPULSORY ADDITION TO ANY TAPAS TABLE, ESPECIALLY WHEN IT IS LOW IN FAT TOO!

SERVES SIX

INGREDIENTS

4 large ripe tomatoes,
  roughly chopped
2 garlic cloves, roughly chopped
1.5ml/¼ tsp sea salt
grated rind and juice of ½ lemon
5ml/1 tsp soft light brown sugar
1 flat loaf of bread, such as ciabatta
15ml/1 tbsp olive oil
freshly ground black pepper, to taste

3 While the bread is baking, stir the lemon juice and olive oil into the tomato mixture. Cook, uncovered, for a further 8 minutes, or until the mixture is thick and pulpy, stirring occasionally.

4 Spread the tomato mixture on the hot bread pieces, sprinkle with black pepper and serve immediately.

1 Preheat the oven to 200°C/400°F/Gas 6. Place the tomatoes, garlic, salt, lemon rind and brown sugar in a small pan. Cover and cook gently for 5 minutes, or until the tomatoes have released their juices and the mixture is quite watery.

2 Split the loaf in half horizontally, then cut each half widthways into 3 equal pieces. Place on a baking sheet and bake for 5–8 minutes, or until hot, crisp and golden brown.

Energy 145kcal/613kJ; Protein 4.6g; Carbohydrate 24.1g, of which sugars 4.6g; Fat 4g, of which saturates 0.6g, of which polyunsaturates 0.7g; Cholesterol 0mg; Calcium 54mg; Fibre 1.7g; Sodium 222mg.

MARINATED PIMIENTOS ★

PIMIENTOS ARE SIMPLY SKINNED, COOKED PEPPERS. YOU CAN BUY THEM IN CANS OR JARS, BUT THEY ARE MUCH TASTIER WHEN HOME-MADE. THEY CREATE A TASTY LOW-FAT APPETIZER.

SERVES FOUR

INGREDIENTS
  3 red (bell) peppers
  2 small garlic cloves, crushed
  45ml/3 tbsp chopped fresh parsley
  15ml/1 tbsp sherry vinegar
  25ml/1½ tbsp olive oil
  salt, to taste

1 Preheat the grill (broiler) to high. Place the peppers on a baking sheet and grill (broil) for 8–12 minutes, turning occasionally, until the skins have blistered and blackened. Remove the peppers from the heat, cover with a clean dish towel and leave for 5 minutes so that the steam softens the skin.

2 Make a small cut in the bottom of each pepper and squeeze out the juice into a jug. Peel away the skin and cut the peppers in half. Remove and discard the core and seeds.

3 Using a sharp knife, cut each pepper in half lengthways into 1cm/½in-wide strips. Place them in a small bowl.

4 Whisk the garlic, parsley, vinegar and oil into the pepper juices. Add salt to taste. Pour over the pepper strips and toss well. Cover and chill, but, if possible, bring the peppers back to room temperature before serving.

Energy 84kcal/349kJ; Protein 1.7g; Carbohydrate 8.7g, of which sugars 8.3g; Fat 4.9g, of which saturates 0.8g, of which polyunsaturates 0.6g; Cholesterol 0mg; Calcium 33mg; Fibre 2.7g; Sodium 9mg.

OVEN-BAKED PEPPERS AND TOMATOES ★

MAKE SURE THERE IS A BASKET OF WARM, FRESH BREAD ON HAND SO THAT NONE OF THE DELICIOUS JUICES FROM THIS LOW-FAT APPETIZER ARE WASTED.

SERVES EIGHT

INGREDIENTS

   2 red (bell) peppers
   2 yellow (bell) peppers
   1 red onion, sliced
   2 garlic cloves, halved
   6 plum tomatoes, quartered
   50g/2oz/⅓ cup black olives
   5ml/1 tsp soft light brown sugar
   45ml/3 tbsp sherry
   3–4 rosemary sprigs
   20ml/4 tsp olive oil
   salt and ground black pepper

1 Preheat the oven to 200°C/400°F/ Gas 6. Seed the red and yellow peppers, then cut each into 12 even strips.

2 Place the peppers, onion, garlic, tomatoes and olives in a large roasting pan. Sprinkle over the sugar, then pour over the sherry. Season well, cover with foil and bake for 30 minutes.

3 Remove the foil from the tin and stir the vegetables to mixwell. Add the rosemary sprigs.

4 Drizzle over the olive oil. Return the pan to the oven for a further 20–30 minutes, or until the vegetables are tender. Serve hot.

Energy 78kcal/327kJ; Protein 1.7g; Carbohydrate 10g, of which sugars 9.3g; Fat 3.1g, of which saturates 0.5g, of which polyunsaturates 0.6g; Cholesterol 0mg; Calcium 21mg; Fibre 2.6g; Sodium 152mg.

AUBERGINE PURÉE ★

SERVE THIS VELVET-TEXTURED LOW-FAT DIP IN THE SUMMERTIME, WHEN THERE IS A READY SUPPLY OF FIRM, GLOSSY AUBERGINES TO MAKE IT WITH, AND CRISP VEGETABLES TO SERVE IT WITH.

SERVES FOUR

INGREDIENTS
1 large aubergine (eggplant)
25ml/1½ tbsp olive oil
2 garlic cloves, finely chopped
30ml/2 tbsp chopped fresh
  coriander (cilantro)
juice of ½ lemon
cayenne pepper, to taste
salt and ground black pepper
fresh coriander (cilantro) leaves,
  to garnish

1 Preheat the oven to 200°C/400°F/ Gas 6. Place the aubergine on a baking sheet and bake for 30 minutes, or until the skin is blackened and the aubergine is very soft.

2 Remove from the oven and allow the aubergine to cool slightly. Cut it in half and use a spoon to scoop out the flesh into a bowl; discard the skin.

COOK'S TIP
The aubergine can be grilled (broiled) for 20 minutes; keep turning it while cooking.

3 Mash the aubergine flesh using a fork to form a purée.

4 Stir in the olive oil, garlic, chopped coriander and lemon juice, with enough cayenne, salt and pepper to suit your taste. Allow the mixture to cool. Serve garnished with coriander leaves.

Energy 57kcal/236kJ; Protein 1.3g; Carbohydrate 2.9g, of which sugars 1.6g; Fat 4.6g, of which saturates 0.7g, of which polyunsaturates 0.5g; Cholesterol 0mg; Calcium 9mg; Fibre 1.8g; Sodium 2mg.

KING PRAWNS IN SHERRY ★

THESE PRAWNS ARE SIMPLY STIR-FRIED IN A LITTLE OIL AND THEN FLAVOURED WITH SHERRY. THE ADDITION OF TABASCO SAUCE ADDS A FIERY ACCENT TO THE DISH. USE WHICHEVER SHERRY YOU PREFER — FINO, AMONTILLADO AND OLOROSO WORK EQUALLY WELL.

SERVES FOUR

INGREDIENTS
  12 fresh raw king prawns or tiger
    prawns (jumbo shrimp), peeled
  15ml/1 tbsp olive oil
  30ml/2 tbsp sherry
  few drops of Tabasco sauce
  salt and ground black pepper

COOK'S TIP
Cook the prawns just before you eat them, so that they are piping hot and have a melt-in-the-mouth texture.

1 Make a shallow cut down the back of each prawn using a sharp knife, then pull out and discard the dark intestinal tract. Rinse the prawns and pat dry on kitchen paper.

2 Heat the oil in a non-stick frying pan and stir-fry the prawns for 2–3 minutes, or until pink. Pour over the sherry and season with Tabasco sauce, salt and pepper. Tip into a dish; serve immediately.

Energy 72kcal/298kJ; Protein 8.8g; Carbohydrate 0.1g, of which sugars 0.1g; Fat 3.1g, of which saturates 0.5g, of which polyunsaturates 0.3g; Cholesterol 98mg; Calcium 40mg; Fibre 0g; Sodium 96mg.

GUACAMOLE WITH CRUDITÉS ★

*THIS FRESH-TASTING SPICY DIP IS MADE USING PEAS INSTEAD OF THE TRADITIONAL AVOCADOS. THE
PEAS CREATE A DIFFERENT TASTE AND TEXTURE, BUT FOR A LOW-FAT DIP, IT'S WELL WORTH TRYING.
SERVE WITH FRUIT AND SALAD VEGETABLES.*

SERVES SIX

INGREDIENTS
 350g/12oz/3 cups frozen peas,
  thawed
 1 garlic clove, crushed
 2 spring onions (scallions), trimmed
  and chopped
 5ml/1 tsp finely grated lime rind
 juice of 1 lime
 2.5ml/½ tsp ground cumin
 dash of Tabasco sauce
 15ml/1 tbsp reduced-calorie
  mayonnaise
 30ml/2 tbsp chopped fresh
  coriander (cilantro)
 salt and ground black pepper
 pinch of paprika and lime slices,
  to garnish
For the crudités
 6 baby carrots
 2 celery sticks
 1 red-skinned eating apple
 1 pear
 15ml/1 tbsp lemon or lime juice
 6 baby corn

1 Put the peas, garlic clove, spring
onions, lime rind and juice, cumin,
Tabasco sauce, mayonnaise and salt
and ground black pepper in a blender
or food processor and process for a few
minutes, or until smooth.

2 Add the coriander and process for
a few seconds. Spoon the mixture
into a serving bowl, cover with clear
film (plastic wrap) and refrigerate for
30 minutes, to let the flavours develop.

3 For the crudités, trim and peel
the carrots. Halve the celery sticks
lengthways and trim into sticks the
same length as the carrots. Quarter,
core and thickly slice the apple and
pear, then dip into the lemon or lime
juice to prevent discolouration. Arrange
with the baby corn on a serving platter.

4 Sprinkle the paprika over the
guacamole and garnish with lime
slices. Serve.

VARIATION
Use ground coriander in place of ground
cumin, if you like.

Energy 93kcal/386kJ; Protein 5.2g; Carbohydrate 14.7g, of which sugars 9g; Fat 1.9g, of which saturates 0.3g, of which polyunsaturates 0.9g; Cholesterol 1mg; Calcium 41mg; Fibre 5.1g; Sodium 232mg.

HOT SPICY PRAWNS WITH CORIANDER ★

THIS IS A QUICK, EASY AND LOW-FAT WAY OF PREPARING PRAWNS FOR AN APPETIZER. IF YOU INCREASE THE QUANTITIES, IT CAN BE SERVED AS A MAIN COURSE. SCALLOPS AND MUSSELS ARE ALSO DELICIOUS COOKED IN THIS WAY. SERVE THE PRAWNS WITH BREAD TO MOP UP THE TASTY JUICES.

SERVES FOUR

INGREDIENTS

20ml/4 tsp olive oil
2–3 garlic cloves, chopped
25g/1oz fresh root ginger, peeled
  and grated
1 fresh chilli, seeded and chopped
5ml/1 tsp cumin seeds
5ml/1 tsp paprika
450g/1lb fresh raw king prawns
  (jumbo shrimp), shelled
bunch of fresh coriander (cilantro),
  chopped
salt, to taste
1 lemon, cut into wedges, to serve

1 In a large, heavy, non-stick frying pan, heat the oil with the garlic. Stir in the ginger, chilli and cumin seeds.

2 Cook briefly, until the ingredients give off a lovely aroma, then add the paprika and toss in the prawns.

3 Fry the prawns over a fairly high heat, turning them frequently, for 3–5 minutes, or until just cooked. Season to taste with salt and add the coriander.

4 Serve immediately, with lemon wedges for squeezing over the prawns.

Energy 134kcal/560kJ; Protein 21.2g; Carbohydrate 2.4g, of which sugars 0.5g; Fat 4.4g, of which saturates 0.6g, of which polyunsaturates 0.4g; Cholesterol 219mg; Calcium 116mg; Fibre 1.1g; Sodium 219mg.

SPICED DOLMADES ★

THESE TASTY DOLMADES CONTAIN SUMAC, A SPICE WITH A SHARP LEMON FLAVOUR. IT IS AVAILABLE FROM SPECIALIST FOOD SHOPS. SERVE THESE DOLMADES WITH A MIXTURE OF OTHER TRADITIONAL APPETIZERS, SUCH AS OLIVES AND CRUSTY BREAD, FOR A SPECIAL DINNER.

MAKES TWENTY

INGREDIENTS
　20 vacuum-packed vine leaves in brine
　90g/3½oz/½ cup long grain rice
　25ml/1½ tbsp olive oil
　1 small onion, finely chopped
　50g/2oz/½ cup pine nuts
　45ml/3 tbsp raisins
　30ml/2 tbsp chopped fresh mint
　2.5ml/½ tsp ground cinnamon
　2.5ml/½ tsp ground allspice
　10ml/2 tsp ground sumac
　10ml/2 tsp lemon juice
　30ml/2 tbsp tomato purée (paste)
　salt and ground black pepper
　lemon slices and mint sprigs,
　　to garnish

1 Rinse the vine leaves well under cold running water, then drain. Bring a pan of lightly salted water to the boil. Add the rice, lower the heat, cover and simmer for 10–12 minutes, or until almost cooked. Drain.

2 Heat 10ml/2 tsp of the olive oil in a non-stick frying pan, add the onion and cook until soft. Stir in the pine nuts and cook until lightly browned, then add the raisins, chopped mint, cinnamon, allspice and sumac, with salt and pepper to taste. Stir in the rice and mix well. Leave to cool.

COOK'S TIP
Vacuum-packed vine leaves are available from Cypriot and Middle Eastern food shops, as well as some delicatessens.

3 Line a pan with any damaged vine leaves. Trim the stalks from the remaining leaves and lay them flat. Place a little filling on each. Fold the sides over and roll up each leaf neatly. Place the dolmades side by side in the leaf-lined pan, so that they fit tightly.

4 Mix 300ml/½ pint/1¼ cups water with the lemon juice and tomato purée in a bowl. Whisk in the remaining olive oil. Pour the mixture over the dolmades and place a heatproof plate on top to keep them in place.

5 Cover the pan and simmer the dolmades for about 1 hour, or until all the liquid has been absorbed and the leaves are tender. Transfer to a platter, garnish with lemon slices and mint sprigs and serve hot or cold.

VARIATION
Fresh vine leaves may be used but must be blanched in boiling water first to make them pliable.

Energy 52kcal/216kJ; Protein 1g; Carbohydrate 6.1g, of which sugars 2.4g; Fat 2.6g, of which saturates 0.2g, of which polyunsaturates 1.1g; Cholesterol 0mg; Calcium 12mg; Fibre 0.3g; Sodium 6mg.

SIMPLE AUBERGINE, GARLIC AND RED PEPPER PÂTÉ ★

SERVE THIS LOW-FAT, ITALIAN-STYLE CHUNKY, GARLICKY PÂTÉ OF SMOKY BAKED AUBERGINE AND RED PEPPERS, ON A BED OF SALAD, ACCOMPANIED BY CRISP TOASTS.

SERVES FOUR

INGREDIENTS
- 3 aubergines (eggplants)
- 2 (bell) red peppers
- 5 garlic cloves
- 7.5ml/1½ tsp pink peppercorns in brine, drained and crushed
- 30ml/2 tbsp chopped fresh coriander (cilantro)

1 Preheat the oven to 200°C/400°F/ Gas 6. Arrange the whole aubergines, peppers and garlic cloves on a baking sheet. Bake in the oven for 10 minutes, then remove the garlic cloves to a plate. Set aside. Turn over the aubergines and peppers, return to the oven and bake for a further 20 minutes.

2 Meanwhile, peel the garlic cloves and place them in a blender or food processor.

3 Remove the charred peppers from the oven and place in a plastic food bag. Set aside to cool.

4 Return the aubergines to the oven and bake for a further 10 minutes. Split each aubergine in half and scoop out the flesh into a sieve (strainer) placed over a bowl. Discard the skin. Press the flesh with a spoon to remove the bitter juices. Discard the juices.

5 Add the aubergine to the garlic in the blender or food processor and process until smooth. Put the mixture in a bowl.

6 Skin, core and seed the red peppers and finely chop the flesh; stir into the aubergine mixture. Mix in the peppercorns and chopped coriander until thoroughly combined. Spoon into a serving dish and serve immediately.

VARIATION
Use orange or yellow (bell) peppers in place of the red ones.

Energy 69kcal/292kJ; Protein 3.5g; Carbohydrate 11.8g, of which sugars 10g; Fat 1.3g, of which saturates 0.3g, of which polyunsaturates 0.7g; Cholesterol 0mg; Calcium 31mg; Fibre 6.2g; Sodium 8mg.

CANNELLINI BEAN PURÉE <u>WITH</u> GRILLED CHICORY ★

THE SLIGHTLY BITTER FLAVOURS OF THE CHICORY AND RADICCHIO MAKE A WONDERFUL MARRIAGE WITH THE CREAMY BEAN PURÉE TO CREATE THIS LOW-FAT APPETIZER OR SNACK.

SERVES FOUR

INGREDIENTS

400g/14oz can cannellini beans
45ml/3 tbsp low-fat sour cream
finely grated rind and juice of
 1 large orange
15ml/1 tbsp finely chopped
 fresh rosemary
4 heads of chicory (Belgian endive)
2 heads of radicchio
10ml/2 tsp walnut oil
longer shreds of orange rind,
 to garnish (optional)

1 Drain the beans, then rinse and drain them again. Place the beans in a blender or food processor with the sour cream, orange rind and juice and chopped rosemary and process until smooth and well mixed. Set aside.

2 Cut the heads of the chicory in half lengthways.

3 Cut each radicchio head into eight even wedges using a sharp knife. Preheat the grill (broiler) to medium.

4 Lay the chicory and radicchio on a baking sheet and brush lightly with the walnut oil. Grill (broil) for 2–3 minutes. Serve with the bean purée and garnish with orange shreds, if using.

Energy 129kcal/542kJ; Protein 6.8g; Carbohydrate 17.3g, of which sugars 3.3g; Fat 4.9g, of which saturates 1.9g, of which polyunsaturates 1.6g; Cholesterol 7mg; Calcium 48mg; Fibre 5.5g; Sodium 427mg.

TSATZIKI ★

YOU CAN SERVE THIS REDUCED-FAT VERSION OF THE CLASSIC GREEK DIP WITH STRIPS OF PITTA BREAD TOASTED ON THE BARBECUE, OR YOU COULD USE VEGETABLE STRIPS. THE TANGY CUCUMBER MAKES IT A LIGHT, REFRESHING SNACK FOR WARM SUMMER DAYS.

2 Trim the spring onions and garlic, then chop both very finely.

3 Beat the yogurt in a bowl until smooth, if necessary, then gently stir in the chopped cucumber, spring onions, garlic and mint until well combined.

4 Add salt and plenty of ground black pepper to taste, then transfer the mixture to a serving bowl. Chill in the refrigerator until ready to serve, then garnish with a small mint sprig. Serve the dip with slices of pitta bread that have been toasted on the barbecue.

SERVES FOUR

INGREDIENTS
- 1 mini cucumber
- 4 spring onions (scallions)
- 1 garlic clove
- 200ml/7fl oz/scant 1 cup low-fat Greek (US strained plain) yogurt
- 45ml/3 tbsp chopped fresh mint
- salt and ground black pepper
- fresh mint sprig, to garnish (optional)
- toasted pitta bread, to serve

1 Trim the ends from the cucumber, then cut it into 5mm/¼in dice.

Energy 76kcal/316kJ; Protein 3.7g; Carbohydrate 3.7g, of which sugars 2.9g; Fat 5g, of which saturates 3.4g, of which polyunsaturates 0.2g; Cholesterol 8mg; Calcium 95mg; Fibre 0.3g; Sodium 36mg.

BYESAR ★

BYESAR IS SIMILAR TO HUMMUS IN CONSISTENCY, BUT USES BROAD BEANS INSTEAD OF CHICKPEAS. IT IS EATEN BY DIPPING A MEDITERRANEAN-TYPE BREAD INTO GROUND SPICES AND THEN SCOOPING UP THE PURÉE. THIS LOW-FAT VERSION IS HARD TO BEAT FOR A TASTY APPETIZER.

SERVES EIGHT

INGREDIENTS
    115g/4oz dried broad (fava)
      beans, soaked
    2 garlic cloves, peeled
    5ml/1 tsp cumin seeds
    45ml/3 tbsp olive oil
    salt, to taste
    mint sprigs, to garnish
    extra cumin seeds, cayenne pepper
      and fresh bread, to serve

COOK'S TIP
To soak dried beans, rinse them in a sieve (strainer) under the cold tap, then place them in a large bowl. Cover with plenty of cold water and leave to soak.

1 Put the beans in a pan with the whole garlic cloves and cumin seeds and add enough water just to cover. Bring to the boil, then reduce the heat and simmer until the beans are tender. Drain, cool and then slip off and discard the outer skin of each bean.

2 Place the beans in a blender or food processor and process, adding the oil and sufficient water to give a smooth soft dip. Season to taste with salt. Garnish with mint sprigs; serve with extra cumin seeds, cayenne pepper and plenty of fresh bread.

Energy 63kcal/261kJ; Protein 2.5g; Carbohydrate 3.7g, of which sugars 0.4g; Fat 4.3g, of which saturates 0.6g, of which polyunsaturates 0.4g; Cholesterol 0mg; Calcium 19mg; Fibre 2g; Sodium 3mg.

SPICED CLAMS ^{WITH} CHILLI ^{AND} GARLIC ★

Spanish clams, especially in the North, are much larger than clams found elsewhere, and have more succulent bodies. This modern recipe uses Arab spicing to make a hot dip or sauce. Serve with fresh bread to mop up the delicious juices.

SERVES FOUR

INGREDIENTS
1 small onion, finely chopped
1 celery stick, sliced
2 garlic cloves, finely chopped
2.5cm/1in-piece fresh root
  ginger, grated
15ml/1 tbsp olive oil
1.5ml/¼ tsp chilli powder
5ml/1 tsp ground turmeric
30ml/2 tbsp chopped
  fresh parsley
500g/1¼lb small clams, in
  the shell
30ml/2 tbsp dry white wine
salt and ground black pepper
celery leaves, to garnish

COOK'S TIPS
• One of the best clams is known as the *almeja fina* (the carpet shell clam), which is perfect used in this dish. They have grooved brown shells with a yellow lattice pattern.
• Before cooking the clams, check that all the shells are closed. Any clams that do not open after cooking should be discarded.

1 Place the onion, celery, garlic and ginger in a large pan, add the olive oil, spices and chopped parsley and stir-fry for about 5 minutes. Add the clams to the pan and cook for 2 minutes.

2 Add the wine, then cover and cook gently for 2–3 minutes, shaking the pan occasionally. Season. Discard any clams whose shells remain closed, then serve, garnished with the celery leaves.

Energy 78kcal/326kJ; Protein 8.6g; Carbohydrate 2.6g, of which sugars 1.2g; Fat 3.3g, of which saturates 0.5g, of which polyunsaturates 0.3g; Cholesterol 34mg; Calcium 67mg; Fibre 0.9g; Sodium 609mg.

MINI SAFFRON FISH CAKES WITH CHILLED SWEET CUCUMBER AND CINNAMON SALAD ★

THIS SCENTED CUCUMBER SALAD MAKES A SUPERBLY REFRESHING ACCOMPANIMENT FOR THE FISH CAKES. BOTH THE FISH CAKES AND SALAD INCLUDE SWEET AND SPICY FLAVOURS. IF YOU CAN'T GET FRESH FISH, TUNA CANNED IN SPRING WATER OR BRINE (DRAINED) IS A GOOD SUBSTITUTE.

SERVES SIX

INGREDIENTS

    450g/1lb white fish fillets, such as
      sea bass, ling or haddock, skinned
      and cut into chunks
    10ml/2 tsp harissa
    rind of ½ preserved lemon,
      finely chopped
    small bunch of fresh coriander
      (cilantro), finely chopped
    1 egg
    5ml/1 tsp clear honey
    pinch of saffron threads, soaked in
      5ml/1 tsp hot water
    15ml/1 tbsp sunflower oil
    salt and ground black pepper
For the salad
    2 cucumbers, peeled and grated
    juice of 1 orange
    juice of ½ lemon
    15–30ml/1–2 tbsp orange flower
      water
    15–20ml/3–4 tsp caster
      (superfine) sugar
    2.5ml/½ tsp ground cinnamon

1 Make the salad in advance to allow time for chilling before serving. Place the cucumber in a colander over a bowl and sprinkle with some salt. Leave to drain for about 10 minutes.

2 Using your hands, squeeze out the excess liquid and place the cucumber in a bowl.

3 To make the dressing, in a small jug (pitcher) combine the orange and lemon juice, orange flower water and sugar and pour over the cucumber. Toss well to mix, sprinkle with cinnamon and chill for at least 1 hour.

4 To make the fish cakes, put the fish in a food processor. Add the harissa, preserved lemon, chopped coriander, egg, honey, saffron with its soaking water, and seasoning, and whizz until smooth. Divide the mixture into 18 equal portions. Wet your hands under cold water to prevent the mixture from sticking to them, then roll each portion into a ball and flatten in the palm of your hand.

5 Heat the oil in a large non-stick frying pan and fry the fish cakes in batches, until golden brown on each side. Drain on kitchen paper and keep hot until all the fish cakes are cooked. Serve with the chilled cucumber salad.

Energy 115kcal/481kJ; Protein 15.6g; Carbohydrate 5.6g, of which sugars 5.5g; Fat 3.5g, of which saturates 0.6g, of which polyunsaturates 1.5g; Cholesterol 66mg; Calcium 42mg; Fibre 0.8g; Sodium 63mg.

CANNELLINI BEAN AND SUN-DRIED TOMATO BRUSCHETTA ★

THIS TRADITIONAL ITALIAN-STYLE DISH IS A SOPHISTICATED VERSION OF CANNED BEANS ON TOAST. THE BEANS ADD FLAVOUR WHILE MAKING THIS APPETIZER MORE SUBSTANTIAL AND FILLING, BUT THEY ARE STILL LOW IN FAT. EAT IT AT ANY TIME OF DAY.

SERVES SIX

INGREDIENTS
150g/5oz/¾ cup dried
  cannellini beans
5 tomatoes
10ml/2 tsp olive oil
2 sun-dried tomatoes in oil, drained
  and finely chopped
2 garlic cloves
30ml/2 tbsp chopped fresh rosemary
12 slices Italian-style bread, such
  as ciabatta
salt and ground black pepper
a handful of fresh basil leaves,
  to garnish

VARIATION
Make the tomato base as
in steps 2 and 3 and mix with canned,
flaked tuna (in brine), olives or chopped
cooked ham instead of the beans.

1 Soak the beans in water overnight. Drain and rinse, place in a pan and cover with water. Bring to the boil, boil rapidly for 10 minutes. Reduce the heat and simmer for 50–60 minutes. Drain.

2 Meanwhile, place the tomatoes in a bowl, cover with boiling water, leave for 30 seconds, then refresh in cold water. Skin, seed and chop the flesh.

3 Heat the oil in a pan and add the fresh and sun-dried tomatoes. Crush 1 garlic clove and add it to the pan with the rosemary. Cook for 2 minutes.

4 Add the tomato mixture to the cooked cannellini beans, season to taste with salt and ground black pepper, and mix well. Heat through gently.

5 Preheat the grill (broiler) to high. Cut the remaining garlic clove in half and rub the cut sides of the bread slices with it. Toast the bread lightly on both sides. Spoon the cannellini bean mixture on top of the toast. Sprinkle with basil leaves to garnish and serve immediately.

COOK'S TIP
Canned beans can be used instead of dried; use 275g/10oz/2 cups drained, canned beans and add to the tomato mixture in step 4. If the beans are in brine, rinse and drain well before use.

Energy 284kcal/1203kJ; Protein 12.7g; Carbohydrate 49.7g, of which sugars 5.3g; Fat 5g, of which saturates 0.7g, of which polyunsaturates 1.5g; Cholesterol 0mg; Calcium 127mg; Fibre 5.1g; Sodium 376mg.

CROSTINI WITH TOMATO, RED PEPPER AND VEGETABLE TOPPING ★

THIS POPULAR ITALIAN HORS D'OEUVRE WAS ORIGINALLY A WAY OF USING UP LEFTOVERS AND THE OVERABUNDANCE OF TOMATOES FROM THE HARVEST. PLUM TOMATOES ARE TRADITIONALLY USED, BUT CHERRY TOMATOES ARE A DELICIOUS ALTERNATIVE.

MAKES SIXTEEN

INGREDIENTS
1 ciabatta loaf or French baguette
For the tomato, (bell) pepper and anchovy topping
    400g/14oz can or bottle Italian roasted red (bell) peppers and tomatoes, in vinegar or brine
    50g/2oz can anchovy fillets
    15ml/1 tbsp extra virgin olive oil
    15–30ml/1–2 tbsp balsamic vinegar
    1 garlic clove
    25ml/1½ tbsp red pesto
    30ml/2 tbsp chopped fresh chives, oregano or sage, to garnish
    15ml/1 tbsp capers, to garnish
For the mozzarella and tomato topping
    25ml/1½ tbsp green pesto
    120ml/4fl oz/½ cup thick home-made or bottled tomato sauce or pizza topping
    75g/3oz reduced-fat mozzarella cheese, cut into 8 thin slices
    2–3 ripe plum tomatoes, seeded and cut into strips
    fresh basil leaves, to garnish

COOK'S TIP
For an extra healthy version, use wholemeal (whole-wheat) toast instead of a ciabatta loaf or French bread.

1 Preheat the grill (broiler) to high. Cut the ciabatta or French bread into 16 even slices. Toast until crisp and golden on both sides. Cool on a wire rack.

2 For the tomato, pepper and anchovy topping, drain the tomatoes and peppers and wipe dry with kitchen paper. Cut into 1cm/½in strips and place in a shallow dish.

3 Rinse and dry the anchovy fillets and add to the peppers and tomatoes. Drizzle with the olive oil and sprinkle with the balsamic vinegar.

4 Using a sharp knife, peel and halve the garlic clove. Rub 8 toasts with the cut edge of the clove and lightly brush the toasts with a little red pesto. Arrange the tomatoes, peppers and anchovies decoratively on the toasts and sprinkle with chopped herbs and capers.

5 For the mozzarella and tomato topping, lightly brush the remaining toasts with the green pesto and spoon on some tomato sauce. Arrange a slice of mozzarella on each and cover with the tomato strips. Garnish with basil leaves.

Energy 116kcal/488kJ; Protein 4.8g; Carbohydrate 15.9g, of which sugars 3.2g; Fat 4.1g, of which saturates 1g, of which polyunsaturates 1g; Cholesterol 5mg; Calcium 60mg; Fibre 1.3g; Sodium 301mg.

PROSCIUTTO AND PEPPER PIZZAS ★

THE DELICIOUS FLAVOURS OF THESE QUICK AND EASY ITALIAN PIZZAS ARE HARD TO BEAT. SERVE WITH MIXED SALAD GREENS AND SLICED PLUM TOMATOES.

MAKES FOUR

INGREDIENTS

½ ciabatta loaf
1 red (bell) pepper, roasted, peeled and seeded
1 yellow (bell) pepper, roasted, peeled and seeded
4 thin slices prosciutto, cut into thick strips
50g/2oz reduced-fat mozzarella cheese
ground black pepper, to taste
tiny fresh basil leaves, to garnish

1 Preheat the grill (broiler) to high. Cut the ciabatta bread into four thick slices and toast until crisp and golden on both sides.

2 Cut the roasted red and yellow pepper flesh into thick strips and arrange on the toasted bread slices. Top with the strips of prosciutto.

3 Thinly slice the mozzarella and arrange on top, then season with plenty of black pepper. Grill (broil) for 2–3 minutes, or until the cheese is melting.

4 Sprinkle the basil leaves on top to garnish and serve immediately.

Energy 202kcal/854kJ; Protein 9.5g; Carbohydrate 31.7g, of which sugars 7g; Fat 5g, of which saturates 2.2g, of which polyunsaturates 0.7g; Cholesterol 11mg; Calcium 113mg; Fibre 2.6g; Sodium 397mg.

SUN–DRIED TOMATO, BASIL AND OLIVE PIZZA BITES ★

THIS RECIPE USES SCONE PIZZA DOUGH WITH THE ADDITION OF CHOPPED FRESH BASIL TO CREATE THE BASIS FOR THESE TASTY LOW-FAT APPETIZERS.

MAKES TWENTY FOUR

INGREDIENTS
For the scone dough
   115g/4oz/1 cup self-raising
      (self-rising) flour
   115g/4oz/1 cup self-raising
      (self-rising) wholemeal
      (whole-wheat) flour
   pinch of salt
   9–10 fresh basil leaves
   50g/2oz/¼ cup butter, diced
   about 150ml/¼ pint/⅔ cup
      semi-skimmed (low-fat) milk
For the tomato sauce
   10ml/2 tsp olive oil
   1 onion, finely chopped
   1 garlic clove, crushed
   400g/14oz can chopped tomatoes
   15ml/1 tbsp tomato purée (paste)
   15ml/1 tbsp chopped fresh mixed
      herbs, such as parsley, thyme, basil
      and oregano
   pinch of granulated sugar
   salt and ground black pepper
For the topping
   15ml/1 tbsp tomato oil (from the jar
      of sun-dried tomatoes)
   115g/4oz (drained weight) sun-dried
      tomatoes in oil, chopped
   10 pitted black olives, chopped
   9–10 fresh basil leaves, shredded
   50g/2oz reduced-fat mozzarella
      cheese, grated
   30ml/2 tbsp freshly grated
      Parmesan cheese
   extra shredded fresh basil leaves,
      to garnish

1 Preheat the oven to 220°C/425°F/ Gas 7. To make the dough, mix together the flours and salt in a bowl. Tear the basil leaves into small pieces and add to the flour mixture. Rub in the butter until the mixture resembles fine breadcrumbs. Stir in enough milk to form a soft dough.

2 Knead the dough gently on a lightly floured surface. Roll out and use to line a 30 x 18cm/12 x 7in Swiss roll tin (jelly roll pan). Push up the edges of the dough to make a thin rim. Set aside.

3 To make the tomato sauce, heat the oil in a non-stick pan, add the onion and garlic and cook gently for about 5 minutes, until softened. Add the tomatoes, tomato purée, chopped herbs, sugar and seasoning. Simmer uncovered, stirring occasionally, for 15–20 minutes, or until the tomatoes have reduced to a thick pulp. Leave to cool slightly.

4 For the topping, brush the scone base with 7.5ml/1½ tsp of the tomato oil, then spread over the tomato sauce. Scatter over the sun-dried tomatoes, olives and shredded basil leaves.

5 Mix together the mozzarella and Parmesan cheeses and sprinkle over the top. Drizzle over the remaining tomato oil. Bake for about 20 minutes.

6 Cut lengthways and across into 24 bitesize pieces. Garnish with the extra shredded basil leaves and serve immediately.

Energy 73kcal/307kJ; Protein 2.4g; Carbohydrate 8g, of which sugars 1.4g; Fat 3.7g, of which saturates 1.9g, of which polyunsaturates 0.3g; Cholesterol 7mg; Calcium 42mg; Fibre 0.9g; Sodium 69mg.

SOUPS

A steaming bowl of hot soup served with
fresh crusty bread is always appealing, and on a
warm summer's day a refreshing chilled soup is
hard to beat. You will find a tempting collection
of light and tasty recipes from different regions
of the Mediterranean in this chapter; all are full
of flavour but low in fat.

ROASTED PEPPER SOUP ★

GRILLING INTENSIFIES THE FLAVOUR OF SWEET RED AND YELLOW PEPPERS AND HELPS THIS LOW-FAT SOUP TO KEEP ITS STUNNING COLOUR AND DELICIOUS FLAVOUR.

SERVES FOUR

INGREDIENTS
  3 red (bell) peppers
  1 yellow (bell) pepper
  1 onion, chopped
  1 garlic clove, crushed
  750ml/1¼ pints/3 cups vegetable stock
  15ml/1 tbsp plain (all-purpose) flour
  salt and ground black pepper
  red and yellow (bell) peppers, seeded
    and diced, to garnish

1 Preheat the grill (broiler) to high. Halve the peppers lengthways, then remove and discard their stalks, cores and seeds.

2 Line a grill (broiling) pan with foil and arrange the pepper halves skin side up in a single layer. Grill (broil) until the skins have blackened and blistered.

3 Transfer the peppers to a plastic food bag and leave until cool, then peel away and discard their skins. Roughly chop the pepper flesh and set aside.

4 Put the onion, garlic clove and 150ml/¼ pint/⅔ cup stock into a large pan. Bring to the boil and boil for about 5 minutes, or until the stock has reduced in volume. Reduce the heat and stir until the onion is softened and just beginning to colour.

5 Sprinkle the flour over the onion, then gradually stir in the remaining stock. Stir in the chopped, roasted pepper flesh and bring to the boil. Cover and simmer for a further 5 minutes.

6 Remove the pan from the heat and leave to cool slightly, then purée the mixture in a blender or food processor until smooth. Season to taste with salt and pepper. Return the soup to the pan and reheat gently until piping hot. Ladle into four soup bowls and garnish each with a sprinkling of diced peppers. Serve.

Energy 79kcal/330kJ; Protein 2.4g; Carbohydrate 16.3g, of which sugars 11.6g; Fat 0.8g, of which saturates 0.2g, of which polyunsaturates 0.4g; Cholesterol 0mg; Calcium 25mg; Fibre 3.2g; Sodium 8mg.

SPICY PUMPKIN SOUP ★

PUMPKIN IS POPULAR ALL OVER THE MEDITERRANEAN AND IT'S AN IMPORTANT INGREDIENT IN MIDDLE EASTERN COOKING. GINGER AND CUMIN GIVE THE SOUP ITS SPICY FLAVOUR.

SERVES FOUR

INGREDIENTS
  900g/2lb pumpkin, peeled and
    seeds removed
  10ml/2 tsp olive oil
  2 leeks, trimmed and sliced
  1 garlic clove, crushed
  5ml/1 tsp ground ginger
  5ml/1 tsp ground cumin
  900ml/1½ pints/3¾ cups chicken or
    vegetable stock
  salt and ground black pepper
  fresh coriander (cilantro) leaves,
    to garnish
  60ml/4 tbsp natural (plain) yogurt,
    to serve

1 Cut the pumpkin into chunks. Heat the oil in a large pan and add the leeks and garlic. Cook gently until softened.

2 Add the ginger and cumin and cook, stirring, for a further minute. Add the pumpkin and stock and season with salt and pepper. Bring to the boil, then reduce the heat and simmer for 30 minutes, or until the pumpkin is tender. Cool slightly, then process the soup, in batches if necessary, in a blender or food processor.

3 Gently reheat the soup in the rinsed out pan, then serve in warmed soup bowls, with a swirl of yogurt and a garnish of coriander leaves.

Energy 105kcal/441kJ; Protein 2.3g; Carbohydrate 12.5g, of which sugars 7.9g; Fat 3.6g, of which saturates 0.6g, of which polyunsaturates 0.6g; Cholesterol 0mg; Calcium 27mg; Fibre 2.3g; Sodium 61mg.

CHILLED TOMATO AND SWEET PEPPER SOUP ★

A RECIPE INSPIRED BY THE SPANISH GAZPACHO, WHERE RAW INGREDIENTS ARE COMBINED TO MAKE A CHILLED SOUP. IN THIS RECIPE THE INGREDIENTS ARE COOKED FIRST AND THEN CHILLED.

SERVES SIX

INGREDIENTS
  2 red (bell) peppers, halved
  10ml/2 tsp olive oil
  1 onion, finely chopped
  2 garlic cloves, crushed
  675g/1½lb ripe well-flavoured
    tomatoes
  150ml/¼ pint/⅔ cup red wine
  600ml/1 pint/2½ cups vegetable stock
  salt and ground black pepper
  chopped fresh chives, to garnish
For the croûtons
  2 slices day-old white bread,
    crusts removed
  15ml/1 tbsp olive oil

COOK'S TIP
Any juice that accumulates in the pan after grilling (broiling) the peppers, or in the bowl, should be stirred into the soup. It will add a delectable flavour.

1 Cut each pepper half into quarters and seed. Place skin side up on a grill (broiling) rack and cook until the skins have charred. Transfer to a bowl and cover with a plate.

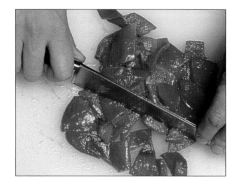

2 Heat the oil in a large non-stick pan. Add the onion and garlic, and cook until soft. Meanwhile, remove and discard the skin from the peppers and roughly chop the flesh. Chop the tomatoes.

3 Add the peppers and tomatoes to the pan, then cover and cook gently for 10 minutes. Add the wine and cook for a further 5 minutes, then add the stock, and salt and pepper, and simmer for 20 minutes.

4 To make the croûtons, cut the bread into small cubes. Heat the oil in a small, non-stick frying pan, add the bread and fry until golden. Drain on kitchen paper, cool, then store in an airtight container.

5 Process the soup in a blender or food processor until smooth. Pour into a clean glass or ceramic bowl and leave to cool thoroughly before chilling for at least 3 hours. When the soup is cold, season to taste.

6 Serve the soup in bowls, topped with the croûtons and garnished with chopped chives.

Energy 105kcal/441kJ; Protein 2.3g; Carbohydrate 12.5g, of which sugars 7.9g; Fat 3.6g, of which saturates 0.6g, of which polyunsaturates 0.6g; Cholesterol 0mg; Calcium 27mg; Fibre 2.3g; Sodium 61mg.

PLUM TOMATO ᴬᴺᴰ FRESH BASIL SOUP ★

A DELICIOUS, LOW-FAT SOUP FOR LATE SUMMER WHEN FRESH TOMATOES ARE AT THEIR RIPEST AND MOST FLAVOURSOME. SERVE WITH CRUSTY FRESH ITALIAN OR FRENCH BREAD, OR WARM SODA BREAD.

SERVES SIX

INGREDIENTS

15ml/1 tbsp olive oil
1 onion, finely chopped
900g/2lb ripe plum tomatoes, chopped
1 garlic clove, chopped
about 750ml/1¼ pints/3 cups
  chicken or vegetable stock
120ml/4fl oz/½ cup dry white wine
30ml/2 tbsp sun-dried tomato
  purée (paste)
30ml/2 tbsp shredded fresh basil
60ml/4 tbsp single (light) cream
salt and ground black pepper
fresh basil leaves, to garnish

VARIATION
This soup can also be served chilled. Pour into a container after straining, allow to cool to room temperature and then chill in the refrigerator for 4 hours.

1 Heat the oil in a large pan until hot. Add the onion and cook gently for about 5 minutes, stirring frequently, until softened but not brown.

2 Stir in the tomatoes and garlic, add the stock, wine and sun-dried tomato purée. Season to taste. Bring to the boil, then reduce the heat, partially cover the pan and simmer gently for 20 minutes, stirring occasionally to stop the tomatoes sticking to the pan base.

3 Process the soup with the shredded basil in a blender or food processor, then press through a sieve (strainer) into a clean pan.

4 Add the cream and heat through gently without boiling, stirring. Check the consistency and add a little more stock or water if necessary, then taste for seasoning. Pour into warmed bowls and garnish with basil leaves. Serve at once.

Energy 81kcal/338kJ; Protein 1.7g; Carbohydrate 6.1g, of which sugars 5.9g; Fat 4.2g, of which saturates 1.6g, of which polyunsaturates 0.5g; Cholesterol 6mg; Calcium 25mg; Fibre 1.7g; Sodium 24mg.

AVGOLEMONO ★

Energy 93kcal/388kJ; Protein 3.3g; Carbohydrate 10.2g, of which sugars 0.2g; Fat 4.3g, of which saturates 1.2g, of which polyunsaturates 0.5g; Cholesterol 151mg; Calcium 35mg; Fibre 0.4g; Sodium 9mg.

THIS IS A GREAT FAVOURITE IN GREECE AND IS A FINE EXAMPLE OF HOW A FEW INGREDIENTS CAN MAKE A MARVELLOUS DISH IF CAREFULLY CHOSEN AND COOKED. IT IS ESSENTIAL TO USE A WELL-FLAVOURED LOW-FAT STOCK. ADD AS LITTLE OR AS MUCH RICE AS YOU LIKE.

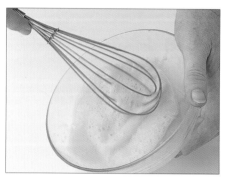

2 Whisk the egg yolks in a bowl, then add about 30ml/2 tbsp of the lemon juice, whisking constantly until the mixture is smooth and bubbly. Add a ladleful of soup and whisk again.

3 Remove the soup from the heat and slowly add the egg mixture, whisking all the time. The soup will turn a pretty lemon colour and will thicken slightly.

4 Taste and add more lemon juice, if necessary. Stir in the chopped parsley. Serve immediately, without reheating, garnished with lemon slices and parsley sprigs.

COOK'S TIP

The trick here is to add the egg mixture to the soup without it curdling. Avoid whisking the mixture into boiling liquid. It is safest to remove the soup from the heat entirely and then whisk in the mixture in a slow but steady stream. Do not reheat as curdling would be almost inevitable.

SERVES FOUR

INGREDIENTS
900ml/1½ pints/3¾ cups
 chicken stock
50g/2oz/¼ cup long grain rice,
 rinsed
3 egg yolks
30–60ml/2–4 tbsp lemon juice
30ml/2 tbsp finely chopped
 fresh parsley
salt and ground black pepper
lemon slices and parsley sprigs,
 to garnish

1 Pour the stock into a pan, bring to simmering point, then add the drained rice. Half-cover and cook for about 12 minutes, or until the rice is just tender. Season with salt and pepper.

ROASTED GARLIC AND BUTTERNUT SQUASH SOUP WITH TOMATO SALSA ★

THIS IS A WONDERFUL, RICHLY FLAVOURED LOW-FAT SOUP. A SPOONFUL OF THE HOT AND SPICY TOMATO SALSA GIVES BITE TO THE SWEET TASTE OF THE SQUASH AND GARLIC.

SERVES SIX

INGREDIENTS
  2 garlic bulbs, outer papery
    skin removed
  a few fresh thyme sprigs
  15ml/1 tbsp olive oil
  1 large butternut squash, halved
    and seeded
  2 onions, chopped
  5ml/1 tsp ground coriander
  1.2 litres/2 pints/5 cups vegetable or
    chicken stock
  30–45ml/2–3 tbsp chopped fresh
    oregano or marjoram
  salt and ground black pepper
For the salsa
  4 large ripe tomatoes, halved
    and seeded
  1 red (bell) pepper, seeded
  1 large fresh red chilli, halved
    and seeded
  15ml/1 tbsp extra virgin olive oil
  15ml/1 tbsp balsamic vinegar
  pinch of caster (superfine) sugar

1 Preheat the oven to 220°C/425°F/ Gas 7. Place the garlic bulbs on a piece of foil, add the thyme and drizzle over 7.5ml/1½ tsp of the oil, then fold the foil around the garlic bulbs to enclose them.

2 Transfer the foil parcel to a baking sheet with the butternut squash and lightly brush the squash with 10ml/2 tsp of the remaining olive oil. Place the tomatoes, red pepper and fresh chilli for the salsa on the baking sheet.

3 Roast the vegetables for 25 minutes, then remove the tomatoes, pepper and chilli. Reduce the oven temperature to 190°C/375°F/Gas 5 and roast the squash and garlic for a further 20–25 minutes, or until the squash is tender.

4 Heat the remaining oil in a large, heavy non-stick pan and cook the onions and ground coriander gently for about 10 minutes, or until softened and just beginning to brown.

5 Meanwhile, skin the pepper and chilli, then process them in a blender or food processor with the tomatoes and the olive oil for the salsa. Stir in the balsamic vinegar and seasoning to taste, adding a pinch of caster sugar, if necessary, to moderate the taste.

6 Squeeze the roasted garlic out of its papery skin into the onions and scoop the squash out of its skin, adding it to the pan too. Add the stock, 5ml/1 tsp salt and plenty of black pepper. Bring to the boil, then simmer for 10 minutes.

7 Stir in half the chopped oregano or marjoram and cool the soup slightly before processing it in a blender or food processor. Alternatively, use a wooden spoon to press the soup through a fine sieve (strainer) placed over a bowl.

8 Reheat the soup without allowing it to boil, then taste for seasoning before ladling it into warmed bowls. Top each with a spoonful of salsa and sprinkle with the remaining chopped oregano or marjoram. Serve immediately.

Energy 120kcal/502kJ; Protein 5g; Carbohydrate 15.7g, of which sugars 9.1g; Fat 4.6g, of which saturates 0.8g, of which polyunsaturates 0.6g; Cholesterol 0mg; Calcium 70mg; Fibre 4.6g; Sodium 10mg.

CATALAN POTATO AND BROAD BEAN SOUP ★

BROAD BEANS ARE ALSO KNOWN AS FAVA BEANS. WHILE THEY ARE IN SEASON FRESH BEANS ARE PERFECT, BUT CANNED OR FROZEN WILL MAKE AN IDEAL SUBSTITUTE FOR THIS FLAVOURFUL SOUP.

SERVES SIX

INGREDIENTS
  15ml/1 tbsp olive oil
  2 onions, chopped
  3 large floury potatoes, diced
  450g/1lb fresh broad (fava) beans
  1.75 litres/3 pints/7½ cups
    vegetable stock
  1 bunch fresh coriander (cilantro),
    finely chopped
  60ml/4 tbsp single (light) cream
  salt and ground black pepper
  fresh coriander (cilantro) leaves,
    to garnish

COOK'S TIP
Broad beans sometimes have a tough outer skin, particularly if they are large. To remove this, cook the beans briefly, peel off the skin, and add the tender centre part to the soup.

1 Heat the oil in a large pan, add the onions and cook, stirring occasionally, for 5 minutes, until soft but not brown.

2 Add the potatoes, beans (reserving a few for garnishing) and stock to the mixture in the pan and bring to the boil, then simmer for 5 minutes. Stir in the chopped coriander and simmer for a further 10 minutes. Remove the pan from the heat and cool slightly.

3 Process the mixture in batches in a blender or food processor until smooth, then return the soup to the rinsed-out pan.

4 Stir in the cream, season with salt and pepper, and reheat gently without boiling. Serve garnished with coriander leaves and the reserved beans.

Energy 181kcal/765kJ; Protein 8.6g; Carbohydrate 28g, of which sugars 4.6g; Fat 4.7g, of which saturates 1.7g, of which polyunsaturates 0.6g; Cholesterol 6mg; Calcium 82mg; Fibre 6.8g; Sodium 24mg.

SPANISH POTATO AND GARLIC SOUP ★

SERVED IN EARTHENWARE DISHES, THIS CLASSIC SPANISH SOUP REALLY IS ONE TO SAVOUR.

SERVES SIX

INGREDIENTS
  15ml/1 tbsp olive oil
  1 large onion, thinly sliced
  4 garlic cloves, crushed
  1 large potato, halved and cut into
    thin slices
  5ml/1 tsp paprika
  400g/14oz can chopped
    tomatoes, drained
  5ml/1 tsp chopped fresh
    thyme leaves
  900ml/1½ pints/3¾ cups
    vegetable stock
  5ml/1 tsp cornflour (cornstarch)
  salt and ground black pepper
  chopped fresh thyme leaves,
    to garnish

1 Heat the oil in a large pan. Add the onions, garlic, potato and paprika and cook for 5 minutes, or until the onions are softened, but not browned.

2 Add the tomatoes, thyme and stock. Bring to the boil, reduce the heat and simmer for 15–20 minutes until tender.

3 Blend the cornflour with a little water in a small bowl to form a paste, then stir into the soup. Simmer for 5 minutes, stirring, until the soup is thickened.

4 Break the potatoes up slightly. Season to taste. Sprinkle with the chopped thyme leaves to garnish.

Energy 74kcal/313kJ; Protein 1.6g; Carbohydrate 12.8g, of which sugars 4.8g; Fat 2.2g, of which saturates 0.4g, of which polyunsaturates 0.4g; Cholesterol 0mg; Calcium 17mg; Fibre 1.6g; Sodium 12mg.

MEDITERRANEAN FARMHOUSE SOUP ★

ROOT VEGETABLES FORM THE BASE OF THIS FLAVOURFUL, CHUNKY, MINESTRONE-STYLE SOUP.
YOU CAN VARY THE VEGETABLES ACCORDING TO WHAT YOU HAVE TO HAND.

SERVES SIX

INGREDIENTS

- 15ml/1 tbsp olive oil
- 1 onion, roughly chopped
- 3 carrots, cut into large chunks
- 175–200g/6–7oz turnips, cut into large chunks
- about 175g/6oz swede (rutabaga), cut into large chunks
- 400g/14oz can chopped Italian tomatoes
- 15ml/1 tbsp tomato purée (paste)
- 5ml/1 tsp dried mixed herbs
- 5ml/1 tsp dried oregano
- 50g/2oz/½ cup dried peppers, washed and thinly sliced (optional)
- 1.5 litres/2½ pints/6¼ cups vegetable stock or water
- 50g/2oz/½ cup dried small macaroni or conchiglie
- 400g/14oz can red kidney beans, rinsed and drained
- 30ml/2 tbsp chopped fresh flat leaf parsley
- salt and ground black pepper
- freshly grated Parmesan cheese, to serve (optional)

1 Heat the oil in a large non-stick pan, add the onion and cook over a low heat for about 5 minutes until softened. Add the fresh vegetables, tomatoes, tomato purée, herbs and peppers, if using. Season to taste. Pour in the stock or water and bring to the boil. Stir well, cover, reduce the heat and simmer for 30 minutes, stirring occasionally.

COOK'S TIP
Packets of dried Italian peppers are sold in supermarkets and delicatessens. They are piquant and firm with a "meaty" bite to them, which makes them ideal for adding to vegetarian soups.

2 Add the pasta and bring to the boil, stirring. Reduce the heat and simmer uncovered, stirring frequently, until the pasta is only just *al dente*: about 5 minutes or according to the instructions on the packet.

3 Stir in the beans. Heat through for 2–3 minutes, then remove from the heat and stir in the chopped parsley. Taste the soup for seasoning. Serve hot in warmed soup bowls, with grated Parmesan handed around separately, if you like.

Energy 154kcal/651kJ; Protein 7g; Carbohydrate 26.6g, of which sugars 10.3g; Fat 2.9g, of which saturates 0.4g, of which polyunsaturates 0.7g; Cholesterol 0mg; Calcium 106mg; Fibre 7.2g; Sodium 282mg.

PISTOU ★

A DELICIOUS CHUNKY VEGETABLE SOUP SERVED WITH TOMATO PESTO. SERVE IN SMALL PORTIONS AS AN APPETIZER, OR IN LARGER BOWLS WITH CRUSTY BREAD AS A FILLING LUNCH.

SERVES SIX

INGREDIENTS

  1 courgette (zucchini), diced
  1 small potato, diced
  1 shallot, chopped
  1 carrot, diced
  400g/14oz can chopped tomatoes
  1.2 litres/2 pints/5 cups vegetable
    stock
  50g/2oz green beans, cut into
    1cm/½in lengths
  50g/2oz/½ cup frozen petits pois
    (baby peas)
  50g/2oz/½ cup small pasta shapes
  30ml/2 tbsp pesto sauce
  10ml/2 tsp tomato purée (paste)
  salt and ground black pepper
  freshly grated Parmesan or Pecorino
    cheese, to serve (optional)

1 Place the courgette, potato, shallot, carrot and tomatoes in a large pan. Add the vegetable stock and season with salt and plenty of black pepper. Bring to the boil over a medium heat, then reduce the heat, cover the pan and simmer for 20 minutes.

2 Add the green beans and petits pois to the pan and bring the soup back to the boil. Boil the mixture briefly for about a minute.

VARIATIONS

• To strengthen the tomato flavour, try using tomato-flavoured spaghetti, broken into small lengths, instead of the small pasta shapes.
• Sun-dried tomato purée (paste) can be used instead of regular.

3 Add the pasta. Simmer the soup for a further 10 minutes, or until the pasta is tender. Taste and adjust the seasoning.

4 Ladle the soup into bowls. Mix together the pesto and tomato purée; stir a little into each serving. Sprinkle with grated cheese, if you like.

Energy 96kcal/406kJ; Protein 4.1g; Carbohydrate 15g, of which sugars 5.3g; Fat 2.7g, of which saturates 0.7g, of which polyunsaturates 0.5g; Cholesterol 2mg; Calcium 47mg; Fibre 2.5g; Sodium 37mg.

CANNELLINI BEAN SOUP ★

CAVOLO NERO IS A DARK GREEN CABBAGE WITH A NUTTY FLAVOUR, FROM SOUTHERN ITALY. IT IS IDEAL FOR THIS TRADITIONAL RECIPE. IT IS AVAILABLE IN MOST LARGE SUPERMARKETS, BUT IF YOU CAN'T GET IT, USE SAVOY CABBAGE INSTEAD. SERVE THE SOUP WITH WARM CRUSTY BREAD.

SERVES FOUR

INGREDIENTS

2 x 400g/14oz cans chopped
  tomatoes with herbs
250g/9oz cavolo nero leaves, rinsed
  and drained
400g/14oz can cannellini beans
20ml/4 tsp extra virgin olive oil
salt and ground black pepper

1 Pour the tomatoes into a large pan and add a can of cold water. Season with salt and pepper and bring to the boil, then reduce the heat to a simmer.

2 Roughly shred the cabbage leaves and add them to the pan. Partially cover the pan and simmer gently, stirring occasionally, for about 15 minutes, or until the cabbage is tender.

3 Drain and rinse the cannellini beans, add to the pan and warm through for a few minutes. Check and adjust the seasoning, then ladle the soup into bowls. Drizzle each portion with a little olive oil and serve.

Energy 155kcal/655kJ; Protein 8.2g; Carbohydrate 22.3g, of which sugars 10.4g; Fat 4.2g, of which saturates 0.7g, of which polyunsaturates 0.9g; Cholesterol 0mg; Calcium 60mg; Fibre 7.9g; Sodium 443mg.

PASTA, BEAN AND VEGETABLE SOUP ★

THIS IS A CALABRIAN SPECIALITY AND BY TRADITION LITERALLY ANYTHING EDIBLE CAN GO IN THIS SOUP. IN CALABRIA THEY INCLUDE A BEAN CALLED CICERCHIA THAT IS PECULIAR TO THE REGION. USE WHATEVER BEANS AND VEGETABLES ARE TO HAND.

SERVES SIX

INGREDIENTS

 75g/3oz/scant ½ cup dried
  brown lentils
 15g/½oz/¼ cup dried mushrooms
 15ml/1 tbsp olive oil
 1 carrot, diced
 1 celery stick, diced
 1 onion, finely chopped
 1 garlic clove, finely chopped
 a little chopped fresh flat leaf parsley
 a good pinch of crushed red chillies
  (optional)
 1.5 litres/2½ pints/6¼ cups
  vegetable stock
 150g/5oz/1 cup each canned red
  kidney beans, cannellini beans and
  chickpeas, rinsed and drained
 115g/4oz/1 cup dried small pasta
  shapes, such as rigatoni, penne or
  penne rigate
 salt and ground black pepper
 chopped flat leaf parsley, to garnish
 freshly grated Pecorino cheese,
  to serve (optional)

1 Put the lentils in a pan, add 475ml/ 16fl oz/2 cups water and bring to the boil over a high heat. Reduce the heat and simmer gently, stirring occasionally, for 15–20 minutes, or until tender. Soak the dried mushrooms in 175ml/6fl oz/ ¾ cup warm water for 20 minutes.

2 Tip the lentils into a sieve (strainer) to drain, then rinse under the cold tap. Drain the soaked mushrooms and reserve the soaking liquid. Finely chop the mushrooms and set aside.

3 Heat the oil in a large non-stick pan and add the carrot, celery, onion, garlic, chopped parsley and chillies, if using. Cook over a low heat, stirring constantly, for 5–7 minutes.

4 Add the stock, then the mushrooms and their soaking liquid. Bring to the boil, then add the beans, chickpeas and lentils, with salt and pepper to taste. Cover, and simmer gently for 20 minutes.

5 Add the pasta and bring the soup back to the boil, stirring. Simmer, stirring frequently, until the pasta is *al dente*: 7–8 minutes or according to the instructions on the packet. Season, then serve hot in soup bowls, garnished with chopped parsley. Sprinkle with grated Pecorino, if you like.

Energy 206kcal/874kJ; Protein 10.7g; Carbohydrate 36.7g, of which sugars 5g; Fat 2.9g, of which saturates 0.4g, of which polyunsaturates 0.6g; Cholesterol 0mg; Calcium 72mg; Fibre 6.4g; Sodium 306mg.

RIBOLLITA ★

This soup is rather like an Italian minestrone. It is based on tomatoes, but with beans instead of pasta. In Italy it is traditionally ladled over bread and a green vegetable.

SERVES EIGHT

INGREDIENTS
  350g/12oz well-flavoured tomatoes,
    preferably plum tomatoes
  15ml/1 tbsp extra virgin olive oil or
    sunflower oil
  2 onions, chopped
  2 carrots, sliced
  4 garlic cloves, crushed
  2 celery sticks, thinly sliced
  1 fennel bulb, trimmed and chopped
  2 large courgettes (zucchini),
    thinly sliced
  400g/14oz can chopped tomatoes
  15ml/1 tbsp pesto sauce
  900ml/1½ pints/3¾ cups
    vegetable stock
  400g/14oz can haricot (navy) or
    borlotti beans, drained
  salt and ground black pepper
To finish
  10ml/2 tsp extra virgin olive oil
  450g/1lb fresh young spinach
  8 small slices white bread
  Parmesan or Pecorino cheese
    shavings, to serve (optional)

1 To skin the tomatoes, plunge them into boiling water for 30 seconds, refresh in cold water and then peel off and discard the skins. Chop the tomato flesh and set it aside.

2 Heat the oil in a large non-stick pan. Add the onions, carrots, garlic, celery and fennel and cook gently for 10 minutes. Add the courgettes and cook for a further 2 minutes.

3 Stir in the chopped fresh and canned tomatoes, pesto, stock and beans, and bring to the boil. Reduce the heat, cover the pan and simmer gently for 25–30 minutes, or until the vegetables are completely tender and the stock is full of flavour. Season the soup with salt and pepper to taste.

4 To finish, heat the oil in a non-stick frying pan and cook the spinach for 2 minutes, or until wilted. Place a slice of bread in each serving bowl, top with the spinach and then ladle the soup over the spinach. Serve with a little Parmesan or Pecorino cheese to sprinkle on top, if you like.

Energy 154kcal/648kJ; Protein 7.9g; Carbohydrate 21.3g, of which sugars 8.3g; Fat 4.7g, of which saturates 0.7g, of which polyunsaturates 1g; Cholesterol 0mg; Calcium 156mg; Fibre 6.4g; Sodium 379mg.

CHICKPEA AND PARSLEY SOUP ★

Energy 142kcal/600kJ; Protein 8.3g; Carbohydrate 19.6g, of which sugars 1.7g; Fat 4g, of which saturates 0.5g, of which polyunsaturates 1.2g; Cholesterol 0mg; Calcium 76mg; Fibre 4.5g; Sodium 17mg.

THICK, TASTY AND COMFORTING, THIS LOW-FAT SOUP IS PERFECT FOR WINTRY EVENINGS, OR WHEN STORE CUPBOARD INGREDIENTS ARE ALL YOU'VE GOT.

SERVES SIX

INGREDIENTS

225g/8oz/1⅓ cups dried chickpeas, soaked overnight
1 small onion
1 bunch fresh parsley (about 40g/1½oz)
1.2 litres/2 pints/5 cups vegetable or chicken stock
juice of ½ lemon
salt and ground black pepper
lemon wedges and finely pared strips of rind, to garnish
crusty bread, to serve (optional)

1 Drain the chickpeas and rinse them under cold water. Cook them in a pan of rapidly boiling water for 10 minutes, then reduce the heat and simmer for 1–1½ hours, or until just tender. Drain.

2 Place the onion and parsley in a blender or food processor and process until finely chopped.

3 In a non-stick pan or flameproof casserole cook the onion mixture gently for 5 minutes, or until the onion is slightly softened.

4 Add the chickpeas, cook gently for 1–2 minutes, then add the stock. Season well with salt and pepper. Bring the soup to the boil, then reduce the heat, cover and simmer for 20 minutes, or until the chickpeas are soft.

5 Allow the soup to cool a little. Part-purée the soup in a blender or food processor, or by mashing the chickpeas fairly roughly with a fork, so that the soup is thick and still has plenty of texture.

6 Return the soup to a clean pan, add the lemon juice and adjust the seasoning, if necessary. Reheat gently and then serve, garnished with lemon wedges and finely pared lemon rind. Serve with crusty bread, if you like.

LENTIL SOUP WITH TOMATOES ★

A CLASSIC RUSTIC ITALIAN SOUP FLAVOURED WITH ROSEMARY, DELICIOUS SERVED WITH CRUSTY BREAD.

SERVES FOUR

INGREDIENTS
225g/8oz/1 cup dried green or
  brown lentils
10ml/2 tsp extra virgin olive oil
2 rindless lean back bacon rashers
  (strips), cut into small dice
1 onion, finely chopped
2 celery sticks, finely chopped
2 carrots, finely diced
2 rosemary sprigs, finely chopped
2 bay leaves
400g/14oz can chopped
  plum tomatoes
1.75 litres/3 pints/7½ cups
  vegetable stock
salt and ground black pepper
bay leaves and rosemary sprigs,
  to garnish

1 Place the lentils in a bowl and cover with cold water. Leave to soak for 2 hours. Rinse and drain well.

2 Heat the oil in a pan. Add the bacon and cook for 3 minutes, then stir in the onion and cook gently for 5 minutes, or until softened. Stir in the celery, carrots, rosemary, bay leaves and lentils and toss over the heat for 1 minute.

3 Add the tomatoes and stock and bring to the boil. Reduce the heat, partially cover the pan and simmer, stirring occasionally, for about 1 hour, or until the lentils are perfectly tender.

4 Remove and discard the bay leaves, add salt and pepper to taste and serve with a garnish of fresh bay leaves and rosemary sprigs.

Energy 256kcal/1083kJ; Protein 16.6g; Carbohydrate 39.1g, of which sugars 8.2g; Fat 4.8g, of which saturates 1.3g, of which polyunsaturates 1g; Cholesterol 7mg; Calcium 56mg; Fibre 5g; Sodium 241mg.

SUMMER MINESTRONE ★

THIS BRIGHTLY COLOURED, FRESH-TASTING, LOW-FAT SOUP MAKES THE MOST OF SUMMER VEGETABLES.

SERVES FOUR

INGREDIENTS
10ml/2 tsp olive oil
1 large onion, finely chopped
15ml/1 tbsp sun-dried tomato
   purée (paste)
450g/1lb ripe Italian plum tomatoes,
   peeled and finely chopped
225g/8oz green courgettes (zucchini),
   trimmed and roughly chopped
225g/8oz yellow courgettes (zucchini),
   trimmed and roughly chopped
3 waxy new potatoes, diced
2 garlic cloves, crushed
about 1.2 litres/2 pints/5 cups
   vegetable stock or water
60ml/4 tbsp shredded fresh basil
25g/1oz/¼ cup finely grated fresh
   Parmesan cheese
salt and ground black pepper

1 Heat the oil in a large, non-stick pan, add the onion and cook gently, stirring constantly, for about 5 minutes, or until softened. Stir in the sun-dried tomato purée, chopped tomatoes, courgettes, potatoes and garlic. Mix well and cook gently for 10 minutes, uncovered, shaking the pan frequently to stop the vegetables sticking to the base.

2 Add the stock or water. Bring to the boil, reduce the heat, partially cover the pan and simmer gently for 15 minutes, or until the vegetables are just tender. Add more stock or water if necessary.

3 Remove the pan from the heat and stir in the basil and half the cheese. Taste for seasoning. Serve hot, sprinkled with the remaining cheese.

Energy 160kcal/672kJ; Protein 7.6g; Carbohydrate 22.9g, of which sugars 10.3g; Fat 4.8g, of which saturates 1.8g, of which polyunsaturates 0.8g; Cholesterol 6mg; Calcium 147mg; Fibre 4.2g; Sodium 93mg.

PEA SOUP WITH GARLIC ★

IF YOU KEEP PEAS IN THE FREEZER, YOU CAN RUSTLE UP THIS DELICIOUS LOW-FAT SOUP IN MINUTES. IT HAS A WONDERFULLY SWEET TASTE AND SMOOTH TEXTURE AND IS GREAT SERVED WITH CRUSTY BREAD AND GARNISHED WITH MINT.

<u>SERVES SIX</u>

INGREDIENTS
    15g/½oz/1 tbsp butter
    1 garlic clove, crushed
    900g/2lb/8 cups frozen peas
    1.2 litres/2 pints/5 cups vegetable or
      chicken stock
    salt and ground black pepper
    fresh mint leaves, to garnish

1 Heat the butter in a large non-stick pan and add the garlic. Cook gently for 2–3 minutes, or until softened.

2 Add the peas. Cook for 1–2 minutes, then pour in the stock. Bring to the boil, reduce to a simmer, cover and cook for 5–6 minutes, or until tender.

3 Remove the pan from the heat and leave to cool slightly, then transfer the mixture to a blender or food processor and process, in batches if necessary, until smooth.

4 Return the soup to the rinsed-out pan and heat through gently, stirring. Season to taste with salt and black pepper. Ladle into warmed soup bowls to serve and garnish with mint leaves.

COOK'S TIPS
• When buying fresh garlic, choose plump bulbs with tightly packed cloves and dry skin.
• Avoid any garlic bulbs with soft, shrivelled cloves or green shoots.

Energy 143kcal/593kJ; Protein 10.4g; Carbohydrate 17g, of which sugars 3.5g; Fat 4.3g, of which saturates 1.8g, of which polyunsaturates 1.1g; Cholesterol 5mg; Calcium 32mg; Fibre 7.1g; Sodium 17mg.

BORLOTTI BEAN AND PASTA SOUP ★

A COMPLETE MEAL IN A BOWL, THIS IS A LOW-FAT VERSION OF A CLASSIC ITALIAN SOUP, COMPLETE WITH PASTA, VEGETABLES AND TOMATOES. TRADITIONALLY, THE PERSON WHO FINDS THE BAY LEAF IS HONOURED WITH A KISS FROM THE COOK.

SERVES FOUR

INGREDIENTS

   1 onion, chopped
   1 celery stick, chopped
   2 carrots, chopped
   15ml/1 tbsp olive oil
   1 bay leaf
   1 glass white wine (optional)
   1 litre/1¾ pints/4 cups
     vegetable stock
   400g/14oz can chopped tomatoes
   300ml/½ pint/1¼ cups passata
     (bottled strained tomatoes)
   175g/6oz/1½ cups dried pasta shapes,
     such as farfalle or conchiglie
   400g/14oz can borlotti
     beans, drained
   250g/9oz spinach, washed
     and drained
   salt and ground black pepper
   freshly grated Parmesan cheese,
     to serve (optional)

3 Add the pasta and beans, bring to the boil, and simmer for 8 minutes, or until the pasta is *al dente*. Stir to prevent the pasta from sticking.

4 Season to taste with salt and pepper. Remove and discard any thick stalks from the spinach and add it to the mixture. Cook for a further 2 minutes, then serve in heated soup bowls. Sprinkle with freshly grated Parmesan, if you like.

VARIATIONS

• This soup is also delicious with pieces of crispy cooked lean back bacon – simply add to the soup at the end of Step 3 and stir in.
• For vegetarians, you could use lightly cooked chunks of smoked or marinated tofu as an alternative to meat.

1 Place the chopped onion, celery and carrots in a large, non-stick pan with the olive oil. Cook over a medium heat, stirring occasionally, for about 5 minutes or until the vegetables soften.

2 Add the bay leaf, wine, if using, vegetable stock, tomatoes and passata, and bring to the boil. Reduce the heat and simmer for 10 minutes, or until the vegetables are just tender.

Energy 321kcal/1363kJ; Protein 15g; Carbohydrate 57.8g, of which sugars 12.7g; Fat 5g, of which saturates 0.8g, of which polyunsaturates 1.4g; Cholesterol 0mg; Calcium 166mg; Fibre 9.9g; Sodium 762mg.

SPICED MUSSEL SOUP ★

CHUNKY AND COLOURFUL, THIS TURKISH FISH SOUP IS LIKE A CHOWDER IN ITS CONSISTENCY. IT IS FLAVOURED WITH HARISSA SAUCE, AN INGREDIENT MORE FAMILIAR IN NORTH AFRICAN COOKING.

SERVES SIX

INGREDIENTS
  1.3–1.6kg/3–3½lb fresh mussels,
    in their shells
  150ml/¼ pint/⅔ cup white wine
  3 tomatoes
  15ml/1 tbsp olive oil
  1 onion, finely chopped
  2 garlic cloves, crushed
  2 celery sticks, thinly sliced
  bunch of spring onions (scallions),
    thinly sliced
  1 potato, diced
  7.5ml/1½ tsp harissa
  45ml/3 tbsp chopped fresh parsley
  ground black pepper, to taste
  thick low-fat natural (plain) yogurt,
    to serve (optional)

1 Scrub the mussels, discarding any that are damaged or any open ones that do not close when tapped with a knife.

2 Bring the wine to the boil in a pan. Add the mussels and cover with a lid. Cook for 4–5 minutes, or until the mussels have opened wide. Discard any that remain closed. Drain, reserving the cooking liquid. Set aside a few mussels for garnish, then shell the rest.

3 Skin the tomatoes and dice the flesh. Set aside. Heat the oil in a pan and cook the onion, garlic, celery and spring onions for 5 minutes. Add the mussels, reserved liquid, potato, harissa and tomatoes. Bring to the boil, then reduce the heat, cover and simmer gently for 25 minutes, until the potatoes break up.

4 Stir in the parsley and pepper and add the reserved mussels in their shells. Heat through for 1 minute. Serve hot with a spoonful of yogurt, if you like.

VARIATION
Use 3–4 shallots, finely chopped, in place of the standard onion.

Energy 127kcal/536kJ; Protein 12.5g; Carbohydrate 8g, of which sugars 2.8g; Fat 3.5g, of which saturates 0.6g, of which polyunsaturates 0.7g; Cholesterol 26mg; Calcium 152mg; Fibre 1.3g; Sodium 153mg.

GREEN LENTIL SOUP ★

LENTIL SOUP IS AN EASTERN MEDITERRANEAN CLASSIC, VARYING IN ITS SPICINESS ACCORDING TO REGION. RED OR PUY LENTILS MAKE AN EQUALLY GOOD SUBSTITUTE FOR THE GREEN LENTILS USED HERE. SERVE THIS FLAVOURFUL SOUP WITH FRESH CRUSTY BREAD.

SERVES SIX

INGREDIENTS
  225g/8oz/1 cup dried green lentils
  25ml/1½ tbsp olive oil
  3 onions, finely chopped
  2 garlic cloves, thinly sliced
  10ml/2 tsp cumin seeds, crushed
  1.5ml/¼ tsp ground turmeric
  600ml/1 pint/2½ cups chicken or
    vegetable stock
  30ml/2 tbsp roughly chopped fresh
    coriander (cilantro)
  salt and ground black pepper

COOK'S TIP
When using dried pulses such as lentils, tip them on to a shallow tray before use, and sift through them lightly using your fingertips to pick out any traces of grit. Remove any damaged lentils.

1 Put the lentils in a pan and cover with cold water. Bring to the boil and boil rapidly for 10 minutes. Remove the pan from the heat, drain the lentils and set aside.

2 Heat 15ml/1 tbsp of the oil in a non-stick pan and fry two of the onions with the garlic, cumin and turmeric for 3 minutes, stirring. Add the lentils, stock and 600ml/1 pint/2½ cups water. Bring to the boil, then reduce the heat, cover and simmer gently for 30 minutes, or until the lentils are soft.

3 Meanwhile, in a separate non-stick pan, fry the third onion in the remaining oil until golden. Remove the pan from the heat and set aside.

4 Use a potato masher to lightly mash the lentils and make the soup pulpy. Reheat gently and season to taste with salt and pepper. Pour the soup into warmed bowls. Stir the chopped coriander into the fried onion and sprinkle over the soup. Serve with warm crusty bread.

Energy 163kcal/688kJ; Protein 9.7g; Carbohydrate 25.2g, of which sugars 3.8g; Fat 3.3g, of which saturates 0.5g, of which polyunsaturates 0.5g; Cholesterol 0mg; Calcium 42mg; Fibre 2.8g; Sodium 17mg.

PROVENÇAL FISH SOUP ★

THE ADDITION OF RICE MAKES THIS A SUBSTANTIAL SOUP. BASMATI OR THAI RICE HAS THE BEST FLAVOUR, BUT ANY LONG GRAIN RICE COULD BE USED. IF YOU PREFER A STRONGER TOMATO FLAVOUR, REPLACE THE WHITE WINE WITH EXTRA PASSATA.

SERVES SIX

INGREDIENTS

450g/1lb fresh mussels in their shells
about 250ml/8fl oz/1 cup white wine
675–900g/1½–2lb mixed white fish
    fillets such as monkfish, plaice,
    flounder, cod or haddock
6 large fresh scallops (without shells)
15ml/1 tbsp olive oil
3 leeks, chopped
1 garlic clove, crushed
1 red (bell) pepper, seeded and cut
    into 2.5cm/1in pieces
1 yellow (bell) pepper, seeded and
    cut into 2.5cm/1in pieces
175g/6oz fennel bulb, cut into
    4cm/1½in pieces
400g/14oz can chopped tomatoes
150ml/¼ pint/⅔ cup passata
    (bottled strained tomatoes)
about 1 litre/1¾ pints/4 cups well-
    flavoured fish stock
generous pinch of saffron threads,
    soaked in 15ml/1 tbsp hot water
175g/6oz/scant 1 cup basmati
    rice, soaked
8 large fresh raw prawns (shrimp),
    peeled and deveined
salt and ground black pepper
30–45ml/2–3 tbsp fresh dill, to garnish

1 Clean the mussels, discarding any that do not close when tapped with a knife. Place them in a heavy pan. Add 90ml/6 tbsp of the wine, cover, bring to the boil over a high heat and cook for about 3 minutes, or until all the mussels have opened.

2 Strain the mussels, reserving the cooking liquid. Discard any mussels that have not opened. Set aside half the mussels in their shells for the garnish; shell the rest and put them in a bowl.

3 Cut the fish into 2.5cm/1in cubes. Detach the corals from the scallops and slice the white flesh into three or four pieces. Add the scallops to the fish and the corals to the shelled mussels.

4 Heat the oil in a non-stick pan and cook the leeks and garlic for 3–4 minutes, or until softened. Add the pepper chunks and fennel, and cook for a further 2 minutes, or until just softened.

COOK'S TIP
To make your own fish stock, place about 450g/1lb white fish trimmings – bones, heads, but not gills – in a large pan. Add a chopped onion, carrot, bay leaf, parsley sprig, 6 peppercorns and a piece of pared lemon rind. Pour in 1.2 litres/ 2 pints/5 cups water, bring to the boil, then simmer gently for 25–30 minutes. Strain through muslin (cheesecloth).

5 Add the tomatoes, passata, stock, saffron water, reserved mussel liquid and wine. Season and cook for 5 minutes. Drain the rice, stir it into the mixture, cover and simmer for 10 minutes.

6 Carefully stir in the white fish and cook over a low heat for 5 minutes. Add the prawns, cook for 2 minutes, then add the scallop corals and shelled mussels and cook for a further 2–3 minutes, or until all the fish is tender. Add a little extra white wine or stock, if needed. Spoon into warmed soup bowls, top with mussels in their shells and garnish with chopped dill. Serve.

Energy 352kcal/1481kJ; Protein 37.9g; Carbohydrate 33.3g, of which sugars 8.6g; Fat 4.6g, of which saturates 0.8g, of which polyunsaturates 1.3g; Cholesterol 117mg; Calcium 129mg; Fibre 4.5g; Sodium 208mg.

MEDITERRANEAN LEEK AND FISH SOUP WITH TOMATOES AND GARLIC ★

THIS HEARTY CHUNKY SOUP, WHICH IS ALMOST A STEW, MAKES A ROBUST AND WONDERFULLY AROMATIC DISH. SERVE IT WITH CRISP-BAKED CROÛTONS OR FRESH CRUSTY BREAD.

SERVES SIX

INGREDIENTS

2 large thick leeks
15ml/1 tbsp olive oil
5ml/1 tsp crushed coriander seeds
a good pinch of dried red chilli flakes
300g/11oz small salad potatoes,
  peeled and thickly sliced
400g/14oz can chopped tomatoes
600ml/1 pint/2½ cups fish stock
150ml/¼ pint/⅔ cup white wine
1 fresh bay leaf
1 star anise
strip of pared orange rind
good pinch of saffron threads
450g/1lb white fish fillets, such as
  monkfish, sea bass, cod or haddock
450g/1lb small squid, cleaned
250g/9oz fresh raw peeled prawns
  (shrimp)
30–45ml/2–3 tbsp chopped fresh flat
  leaf parsley
salt and ground black pepper

3 Add the potatoes and tomatoes, and pour in the stock and wine. Add the bay leaf, star anise, orange rind and saffron. Bring to the boil, then reduce the heat and partially cover the pan. Simmer for 20 minutes, or until the potatoes are tender. Taste and adjust the seasoning.

4 Cut the white fish fillets into chunks. Cut the squid sacs into rectangles and score a criss-cross pattern into them without cutting right through.

5 Add the fish to the soup and cook gently for 4 minutes. Add the prawns and cook for 1 minute. Add the squid and the reserved sliced white part of the leek and cook, stirring occasionally, for a further 2 minutes.

6 Finally, stir in the chopped parsley and serve immediately, ladling the soup into warmed bowls. Serve with toasted French bread slices or fresh crusty bread, if you like.

1 Slice the leeks, keeping the green tops separate from the white bottom pieces. Wash the leek slices thoroughly in a colander and drain them well. Set the white slices aside for later.

2 Heat the oil in a heavy non-stick pan over a low heat, then add the green leek slices, crushed coriander seeds and dried red chilli flakes. Cook, stirring occasionally, for 5 minutes.

Energy 249kcal/1051kJ; Protein 35.2g; Carbohydrate 13.3g, of which sugars 4.5g; Fat 4.7g, of which saturates 0.9g, of which polyunsaturates 1.3g; Cholesterol 285mg; Calcium 90mg; Fibre 3g; Sodium 223mg.

SOPA DE MARISCOS ★

THIS HEARTY MIXED SEAFOOD SOUP CONTAINS ALL THE COLOURS AND FLAVOURS OF THE MEDITERRANEAN AND IT IS LOW IN FAT TOO.

SERVES SIX

INGREDIENTS

675g/1½lb fresh raw prawns (shrimp), in the shell
900ml/1½ pints/3¾ cups cold water
1 onion, chopped
1 celery stick, chopped
1 bay leaf
15ml/1 tbsp olive oil
2 slices stale bread, crusts removed
1 small onion, finely chopped
1 large garlic clove, chopped
2 large tomatoes, halved
½ large green (bell) pepper, seeded and finely chopped
500g/1¼lb fresh cockles (small clams) or mussels in their shells, cleaned
juice of 1 lemon
45ml/3 tbsp chopped fresh parsley
5ml/1 tsp paprika
salt and ground black pepper

COOK'S TIP
Good fish and shellfish dishes are normally based on proper fish stock (including the juices saved from opening mussels). This is equivalent to the French *court bouillon*, and takes 30 minutes' simmering. The method used here is one of the quickest, because the prawn heads come off neatly, and the rest of the shells are simply added as they are removed.

1 Remove the heads from the prawns and put the heads in a pan with the cold water. Set aside the prawn bodies. Add the onion, celery and bay leaf and simmer for 20–25 minutes.

2 Meanwhile, peel the prawns, adding the shells to the stock as you go along.

3 Heat the oil in a wide, deep flameproof casserole and fry the bread slices quickly, then set aside. Add the onion to the pan and cook until soft, adding the garlic towards the end.

4 Scoop the seeds out of the tomatoes and discard. Chop the flesh and add to the casserole with the green pepper. Cook briefly, stirring occasionally.

5 Strain the stock into the casserole and bring to the boil. Check over the cockles or mussels, discarding any that are open or damaged.

6 Add half the cockles or mussels to the stock and simmer gently. When open, use a slotted spoon to transfer some of them out on to a plate. Remove the mussels or cockles from the shells and discard the shells. (You should end up having discarded about half of the shells.) Meanwhile, repeat the process to cook the remaining cockles or mussels.

7 Return the shelled cockles or mussels to the soup and add the prawns. Add the bread, torn into little pieces, and the lemon juice and chopped parsley. Simmer gently until the prawns are cooked.

8 Season to taste with paprika, salt and pepper and stir gently to dissolve the bread. Serve at once in soup bowls, providing a plate for the empty shells.

VARIATION
For a slightly thinner consistency, add a little extra water or white wine.

Energy 122kcal/518kJ; Protein 15.7g; Carbohydrate 8.4g, of which sugars 3.6g; Fat 3.2g, of which saturates 0.5g, of which polyunsaturates 0.6g; Cholesterol 128mg; Calcium 133mg; Fibre 1.5g; Sodium 784mg.

SALADS

The Mediterranean climate is ideal for growing many different vegetables, especially the salad varieties. Because they are grown in a sunny climate, they grow large and have an intense and delicious flavour. Best of all, salad vegetables are fat free. Choose from this appetizing selection of dishes for a tasty light lunch or supper.

SWEET AND SOUR ARTICHOKE SALAD ★

AGRODOLCE IS A SWEET-AND-SOUR SAUCE THAT WORKS PERFECTLY IN THIS TASTY SALAD.

SERVES FOUR

INGREDIENTS

6 small globe artichokes
juice of 1 lemon
10ml/2 tsp olive oil
2 onions, roughly chopped
175g/6oz/1 cup fresh or frozen broad
  (fava) beans (shelled weight)
175g/6oz/1½ cups fresh or frozen
  peas (shelled weight)
salt and ground black pepper
fresh mint leaves, to garnish
For the *salsa agrodolce*
  120ml/4fl oz/½ cup white
    wine vinegar
  15ml/1 tbsp caster (superfine) sugar
  handful of fresh mint leaves,
    roughly torn

1 Peel and discard the outer leaves from the artichokes, then cut the artichokes into quarters. Place them in a bowl of cold water with the lemon juice. Set aside.

2 Heat the oil in a large, non-stick pan, add the onions and cook gently until the onions are golden. Add the broad beans and stir, then drain the artichokes and add to the pan. Pour in about 300ml/ ½ pint/1¼ cups of water and cook, covered, for 10–15 minutes.

3 Add the peas, season with salt and pepper and cook, stirring occasionally, for a further 5 minutes, or until the vegetables are tender. Strain the mixture through a sieve, then place all the vegetables in a bowl. Leave to cool, then cover and chill in the refrigerator. Discard the cooking juices.

4 To make the *salsa agrodolce*, mix all the ingredients in a small pan. Heat gently, stirring, for 2–3 minutes, or until the sugar has dissolved, then simmer gently for about 5 minutes, stirring occasionally. Remove the pan from the heat and leave to cool. To serve, drizzle the salsa over the vegetables and garnish with fresh mint leaves.

Energy 138kcal/577kJ; Protein 8.6g; Carbohydrate 20.4g, of which sugars 10.1g; Fat 3g, of which saturates 0.4g, of which polyunsaturates 0.8g; Cholesterol 0mg; Calcium 157mg; Fibre 7.8g; Sodium 128mg.

MOROCCAN COOKED SALAD ★

THIS SALAD IS OFTEN SERVED WITH A MAIN COURSE. KEEPING IT FOR A DAY IMPROVES THE FLAVOUR.

SERVES SIX

INGREDIENTS
2 well-flavoured tomatoes, quartered
2 onions, chopped
½ cucumber, halved lengthways,
  seeded and sliced
1 green (bell) pepper, halved, seeded
  and chopped
30ml/2 tbsp lemon juice
30ml/2 tbsp olive oil
2 garlic cloves, crushed
30ml/2 tbsp chopped fresh coriander
salt and ground black pepper
sprigs of fresh coriander (cilantro),
  to garnish

1 Put the tomatoes, onions, cucumber and green pepper into a pan. Add 60ml/4 tbsp water and bring to the boil, then reduce the heat and simmer for 5 minutes. Remove the pan from the heat and leave to cool.

2 In a small bowl, whisk together the lemon juice, olive oil and garlic. Strain the vegetables, then transfer them to a bowl. Pour over the dressing, season with salt and pepper and stir in the chopped coriander. Serve at once, garnished with coriander sprigs.

Energy 67Kcal/279kJ; Protein 1.6g; Carbohydrate 6.5g, of which sugars 5.2g; Fat 4.1g, of which saturates 0.6g, of which polyunsaturates 0.5g; Cholesterol 0mg; Calcium 40mg; Fibre 2.1g; Sodium 10mg.

FENNEL, ORANGE AND ROCKET SALAD ★

THIS LIGHT AND REFRESHING SALAD IS IDEAL TO SERVE WITH SPICY FOODS.

SERVES SIX

INGREDIENTS
    2 oranges
    1 fennel bulb
    115g/4oz rocket (arugula) leaves
    50g/2oz/⅓ cup black olives
For the dressing
    30ml/2 tbsp extra virgin olive oil
    15ml/1 tbsp balsamic vinegar
    1 small garlic clove, crushed
    salt and ground black pepper

1 With a vegetable peeler, cut strips of rind from the oranges, leaving the pith behind, then cut the rind into thin julienne strips. Cook in a pan of boiling water for a few minutes. Drain and set aside. Peel the oranges, removing and discarding all the white pith. Slice them into thin rounds and discard any seeds.

2 Cut the fennel bulb in half lengthways and slice across the bulb as thinly as possible, preferably in a food processor fitted with a slicing disc or using a mandoline.

3 Combine the oranges and fennel in a serving bowl and toss with the rocket leaves.

4 In a small bowl, whisk together the oil, vinegar, garlic and seasoning and pour over the salad. Toss together to mix well, then leave to stand for a few minutes. Sprinkle with the black olives and julienne strips of orange rind and serve.

Energy 57kcal/235kJ; Protein 1.3g; Carbohydrate 4.3g, of which sugars 4.2g; Fat 3.9g, of which saturates 0.6g, of which polyunsaturates 0.4g; Cholesterol 0mg; Calcium 58mg; Fibre 1.8g; Sodium 32mg.

AUBERGINE, LEMON AND CAPER SALAD ★

THIS COOKED VEGETABLE SALAD IS A CLASSIC SICILIAN DISH, WHICH IS DELICIOUS SERVED AS AN ACCOMPANIMENT TO COLD LEAN MEATS, WITH COOKED PASTA OR SIMPLY WITH SOME GOOD CRUSTY BREAD. MAKE SURE THE AUBERGINE IS COOKED UNTIL IT IS MELTINGLY SOFT.

SERVES SIX

INGREDIENTS
    1 large aubergine (eggplant), about
        675g/1½lb
    30ml/2 tbsp olive oil
    grated rind and juice of 1 lemon
    30ml/2 tbsp capers, rinsed
    12 pitted green olives
    30ml/2 tbsp chopped fresh
        flat leaf parsley
    salt and ground black pepper

COOK'S TIPS
• This salad will taste even better when made the day before. Serve at room temperature. It will keep, covered, in the refrigerator, for up to a month.
• To enrich this dish to serve it on its own as a main course, add toasted pine nuts and shavings of Parmesan cheese. Serve with crusty bread.

1 Cut the aubergine into 2.5cm/1in cubes. Heat the olive oil in a large non-stick frying pan, add the aubergine cubes and cook over a medium heat for about 10 minutes, tossing regularly, until golden and softened. You may need to do this in two batches. Drain on kitchen paper and sprinkle with a little salt.

2 Place the aubergine cubes in a large serving bowl, toss with the lemon rind and juice, capers, olives and chopped parsley and season well with salt and pepper. Serve at room temperature.

Energy 61kcal/255kJ; Protein 1.3g; Carbohydrate 2.7g, of which sugars 2.5g; Fat 5g, of which saturates 0.8g, of which polyunsaturates 0.6g; Cholesterol 0mg; Calcium 33mg; Fibre 2.9g; Sodium 193mg.

Butter Bean, Tomato and Red Onion Salad ★

Serve this salad with toasted pitta bread for a fresh summer lunch, or as an accompaniment to lean meat cooked on a barbecue.

SERVES SIX

INGREDIENTS

2 x 400g/14oz cans butter (lima)
  beans, rinsed and drained
4 plum tomatoes, roughly chopped
1 red onion, thinly sliced
30ml/2 tbsp herb-infused
  olive oil
salt and ground black pepper

VARIATION

To make a tasty tuna salad, drain a 200g/7oz can tuna in brine, flake the flesh and stir into the bean salad.

1 Mix together the beans, tomatoes and onion in a large bowl. Season with salt and pepper.

2 Stir in the oil. Cover with clear film (plastic wrap) and chill for 20 minutes before serving.

Energy 156kcal/658kJ; Protein 8.6g; Carbohydrate 21.4g, of which sugars 4.9g; Fat 4.6g, of which saturates 0.7g, of which polyunsaturates 0.7g; Cholesterol 0mg; Calcium 31mg; Fibre 7.2g; Sodium 567mg.

MOROCCAN COOKED CARROT AND CUMIN SALAD ★

IN THIS LOW-FAT SALAD THE CARROTS ARE COOKED BEFORE BEING TOSSED IN VINAIGRETTE. CUMIN HAS A SPICY AROMA AND A PUNGENT FLAVOUR THAT GOES WELL WITH ROOT VEGETABLES.

SERVES SIX

INGREDIENTS
    4 carrots, thinly sliced
    1.5ml/¼ tsp ground cumin, or to taste
    60ml/4 tbsp low-fat or fat-free
      garlic-flavoured vinaigrette-style
      salad dressing
    30ml/2 tbsp chopped fresh coriander
      (cilantro) leaves, or a mixture of
      fresh coriander and fresh parsley
    salt and ground black pepper

COOK'S TIP
There is a good range of low-fat and fat-free salad dressings available – choose one to suit your taste.

1 Cook the carrots by either steaming or boiling them in a pan of lightly salted water, until they are just tender but not soft. Drain them, leave for a few minutes to dry and cool, then pour them into a mixing bowl.

2 Add the cumin, garlic salad dressing and chopped herbs. Season to taste and chill well before serving. Check the seasoning just before serving and add more ground cumin, salt or black pepper, if required.

Energy 19Kcal/81kJ; Protein 0.5g; Carbohydrate 3g, of which sugars 2.5g; Fat 0.7g, of which saturates 0.1g, of which polyunsaturates 0.1g; Cholesterol 0mg; Calcium 24mg; Fibre 0.8g; Sodium 10mg.

BULGUR WHEAT AND FRESH MINT SALAD ★

ALSO KNOWN AS CRACKED WHEAT, BURGHUL OR POURGOURI, BULGUR WHEAT HAS BEEN PARTIALLY COOKED, SO IT REQUIRES ONLY A SHORT SOAKING BEFORE SERVING.

SERVES FOUR

INGREDIENTS
250g/9oz/1½ cups bulgur wheat
4 tomatoes
4 small courgettes (zucchini), thinly
  sliced lengthways
4 spring onions (scallions), sliced on
  the diagonal
8 ready-to-eat dried apricots,
  chopped
40g/1½oz/⅓ cup raisins
juice of 1 lemon
30ml/2 tbsp tomato juice
45ml/3 tbsp chopped fresh mint
1 garlic clove, crushed
salt and ground black pepper
fresh mint sprig, to garnish

1 Put the bulgur wheat into a large bowl. Add enough cold water to come 2.5cm/1in above the top of the wheat. Leave to soak for 30 minutes. Drain well, squeezing out any excess water in a clean dish towel. Return to the bowl.

2 Meanwhile, plunge the tomatoes into boiling water for 1 minute and then into cold water. Slip off the skins. Halve the tomatoes, remove and discard the seeds and cores, and roughly chop the flesh.

3 Stir the chopped tomato flesh, courgettes, spring onions, apricots and raisins into the bulgur wheat.

4 Put the lemon and tomato juices, chopped mint, garlic and seasoning into a small bowl and whisk together with a fork. Pour over the salad and toss to mix well. Chill for at least 1 hour. Serve garnished with a sprig of mint.

Energy 223kcal/939kJ; Protein 6.9g; Carbohydrate 48.1g, of which sugars 15.9g; Fat 1.5g, of which saturates 0.2g, of which polyunsaturates 0.4g; Cholesterol 0mg; Calcium 61mg; Fibre 2.9g; Sodium 35mg.

MOROCCAN DATE, ORANGE AND CARROT SALAD ★

A COLOURFUL AND UNUSUAL SALAD WITH EXOTIC INGREDIENTS — FRESH DATES AND ORANGE FLOWER WATER — COMBINED WITH CRISP SALAD LEAVES, CARROTS, ORANGES AND TOASTED ALMONDS.

SERVES FOUR

INGREDIENTS

    1 Little Gem (Bibb) lettuce
    2 carrots, finely grated
    2 oranges
    115g/4oz fresh dates, stoned
      (pitted) and each cut lengthways
      into eighths
    25g/1oz/¼ cup toasted whole
      almonds, chopped
    30ml/2 tbsp lemon juice
    5ml/1 tsp caster (superfine) sugar
    1.5ml/¼ tsp salt
    15ml/1 tbsp orange flower water

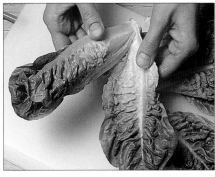

1 Separate the lettuce leaves, then rinse and drain them thoroughly. Arrange the lettuce in the bottom of a salad bowl or on individual serving plates. Place the grated carrot in a mound on top.

2 Peel and segment the oranges and arrange them around the carrot. Pile the dates on top, then sprinkle with the almonds. Mix together the lemon juice, sugar, salt and orange flower water and sprinkle over the salad. Serve chilled.

Energy 124Kcal/524kJ; Protein 3.1g; Carbohydrate 20.3g, of which sugars 19.9g; Fat 4g, of which saturates 0.4g, of which polyunsaturates 0.9g; Cholesterol 0mg; Calcium 77mg; Fibre 3.7g; Sodium 20mg.

BEETROOT WITH FRESH MINT ★

THIS SIMPLE AND DECORATIVE BEETROOT SALAD CAN BE SERVED AS PART OF A SELECTION OF SALADS, AS AN APPETIZER, OR AS AN ACCOMPANIMENT TO GRILLED LEAN MEATS.

SERVES SIX

INGREDIENTS
6 cooked beetroot (beets), peeled
30ml/2 tbsp balsamic vinegar
30ml/2 tbsp olive oil
1 bunch fresh mint, leaves stripped
  and thinly shredded
salt, to taste

VARIATION
To make Tunisian beetroot, add a little harissa to taste and substitute chopped fresh coriander (cilantro) for the shredded mint.

1 Slice the beetroot or cut into even-size dice with a sharp knife. Put the beetroot in a bowl. Add the balsamic vinegar, olive oil and a pinch of salt and toss together to combine.

2 Add half the thinly shredded mint to the salad and toss lightly until thoroughly combined. Chill the salad in the refrigerator for about 1 hour. Serve garnished with the remaining shredded mint leaves.

Energy 58kcal/240kJ; Protein 1.4g; Carbohydrate 4.8g, of which sugars 4.1g; Fat 3.8g, of which saturates 0.5g, of which polyunsaturates 0.4g; Cholesterol 0mg; Calcium 29mg; Fibre 0.9g; Sodium 53mg.

BLACK AND ORANGE SALAD ★

THIS DRAMATIC SALAD IS TYPICALLY MOROCCAN — THE DARK BLACK OLIVES CONTRASTING IN TASTE AND COLOUR WITH THE SWEET ORANGES, A FAVOURITE MOROCCAN FRUIT.

SERVES FOUR

INGREDIENTS

3 oranges
60g/2oz pitted black olives
15ml/1 tbsp chopped fresh
coriander (cilantro)
15ml/1 tbsp chopped fresh parsley
30ml/2 tbsp olive oil
15ml/1 tbsp lemon juice
2.5ml/½ tsp paprika
2.5ml/½ tsp ground cumin

COOK'S TIP
Use a sharp serrated knife to cut away the white pith from the orange flesh.

1 Cut away the peel and pith from the oranges and cut the flesh into wedges.

2 Place the oranges in a salad bowl and add the black olives, chopped coriander and parsley.

3 In a small bowl, whisk together the olive oil, lemon juice, paprika and cumin. Pour the dressing over the salad and toss gently to mix. Chill in the refrigerator for about 30 minutes before serving.

Energy 77Kcal/323kJ; Protein 1.5g; Carbohydrate 8g, of which sugars 7.9g; Fat 4.6g, of which saturates 0.7g, of which polyunsaturates 0.4g; Cholesterol 0mg; Calcium 74mg; Fibre 2.5g; Sodium 346mg.

CARROT AND ORANGE SALAD ★

THIS IS A WONDERFUL FRESH-TASTING MOROCCAN SALAD WITH A FABULOUS COMBINATION OF SWEET-TASTING FRUIT AND VEGETABLES. MOROCCANS WOULD TYPICALLY EAT THIS DISH BY ITSELF AT MIDDAY WITH A REFRESHING GLASS OF MINT TEA.

2 Peel the oranges with a sharp knife and cut into segments, catching the juice in a bowl.

3 In a small bowl, whisk together the olive oil, lemon juice and any orange juice. Season with a little salt and pepper to taste, and sugar if you like.

SERVES FOUR

INGREDIENTS
   450g/1lb carrots
   2 large oranges
   15ml/1 tbsp olive oil
   30ml/2 tbsp lemon juice
   pinch of granulated sugar (optional)
   30ml/2 tbsp chopped pistachio nuts
     or toasted pine nuts (optional)
   salt and ground black pepper

1 Trim and peel the carrots, then coarsely grate them into a large bowl.

4 In a small bowl mix the oranges with the carrots, pour the dressing over and toss to mix thoroughly. Arrange on plates and scatter over the pistachio nuts or pine nuts before serving, if you like.

Energy 101kcal/424kJ; Protein 1.8g; Carbohydrate 17.4g, of which sugars 16.8g; Fat 3.2g, of which saturates 0.5g, of which polyunsaturates 0.5g; Cholesterol 0mg; Calcium 75mg; Fibre 4.4g; Sodium 33mg.

COUSCOUS SALAD ★

THIS IS A SPICY LOW-FAT VARIATION ON THE CLASSIC MIDDLE EASTERN DISH KNOWN AS TABBOULEH, WHICH IS TRADITIONALLY MADE WITH BULGUR WHEAT, NOT COUSCOUS. THE INCLUSION OF PARSLEY AND MINT MEAN THAT IT IS STILL AS REFRESHING AND DELICIOUS SERVED WITH BREAD.

SERVES FOUR

INGREDIENTS
   15ml/1 tbsp olive oil
   5 spring onions (scallions), chopped
   1 garlic clove, crushed
   5ml/1 tsp ground cumin
   350ml/12fl oz/1½ cups
      vegetable stock
   175g/6oz/1 cup couscous
   2 tomatoes, peeled and chopped
   60ml/4 tbsp chopped fresh parsley
   60ml/4 tbsp chopped fresh mint
   1 fresh green chilli, seeded and
      finely chopped
   30ml/2 tbsp lemon juice
   salt and ground black pepper
   toasted pine nuts and grated lemon
      rind, to garnish
   crisp lettuce leaves, to serve

1 Heat the oil in a non-stick pan. Add the spring onions, garlic and cumin and cook, stirring, for 1 minute. Add the stock and bring to the boil.

2 Remove the pan from the heat, stir in the couscous, cover the pan and leave it to stand for 10 minutes, or until the couscous has swelled and all the liquid has been absorbed. If using instant couscous, follow the instructions on the packet.

3 Tip the couscous into a bowl. Stir in the tomatoes, chopped parsley and mint, chilli and lemon juice, with salt and pepper to taste. If possible, leave to stand in a cool place for up to 1 hour to allow the flavours to develop fully.

4 To serve, line a bowl with lettuce leaves and spoon the couscous salad into the centre. Sprinkle the toasted pine nuts and grated lemon rind over, to garnish.

COOK'S TIP
Wash your hands thoroughly after preparing fresh chillies (or wear disposable gloves), as chillies contain oils which will irritate the skin and eyes.

Energy 142Kcal/594kJ; Protein 3.7g; Carbohydrate 24.9g, of which sugars 2.4g; Fat 3.7g, of which saturates 0.5g, of which polyunsaturates 0.4g; Cholesterol 0mg; Calcium 57mg; Fibre 1.7g; Sodium 12mg.

WARM CHICKEN SALAD <u>WITH</u> SHALLOTS ★

SUCCULENT COOKED CHICKEN PIECES ARE COMBINED WITH VEGETABLES IN A LIGHT CHILLI DRESSING.

SERVES SIX

INGREDIENTS
  50g/2oz mixed salad leaves
  50g/2oz baby spinach leaves
  50g/2oz watercress
  30ml/2 tbsp chilli sauce
  30ml/2 tbsp dry sherry
  15ml/1 tbsp light soy sauce
  15ml/1 tbsp tomato ketchup
  10ml/2 tsp olive oil
  8 shallots, finely chopped
  1 garlic clove, crushed
  350g/12oz skinless, boneless chicken
    breast fillets, cut into thin strips
  1 red (bell) pepper, seeded and sliced
  175g/6oz mangetouts (snow peas),
    trimmed
  400g/14oz can baby corn, drained
    and halved
  275g/10oz can brown rice
  salt and ground black pepper
  fresh parsley sprig, to garnish

1 Place the mixed salad leaves, tearing up any large ones, and the spinach leaves on a serving dish. Add the watercress and toss to mix.

2 In a small bowl, mix together the chilli sauce, sherry, soy sauce and tomato ketchup, and set aside.

3 Heat the oil in a large non-stick frying pan or wok. Add the shallots and garlic and stir-fry over a medium heat for 1 minute.

4 Add the chicken strips to the pan and stir-fry for a further 4–5 minutes, or until the chicken pieces are nearly cooked.

5 Add the red pepper, mangetouts, baby corn and rice and stir-fry for 2–3 minutes.

6 Pour in the chilli sauce mixture and stir-fry for 2–3 minutes, or until hot and bubbling. Season to taste with salt and pepper. Spoon the chicken mixture over the salad leaves, toss together to mix and serve immediately, garnished with a sprig of parsley.

VARIATIONS
• Use other kinds of lean meat – such as turkey breast or rindless lean back bacon – in place of the chicken breast.
• Use rocket (arugula) leaves in place of the watercress. Use 275g/10oz (boiled) white or brown rice, if canned brown rice is not available.

Energy 194kcal/816kJ; Protein 19.1g; Carbohydrate 23g, of which sugars 7.2g; Fat 2.8g, of which saturates 0.5g, of which polyunsaturates 0.6g; Cholesterol 41mg; Calcium 40mg; Fibre 3.1g; Sodium 881mg.

ROCKET, PEAR AND PARMESAN SALAD ★

FOR A SOPHISTICATED START TO A LATE SUMMER'S MEAL WITH FRIENDS, TRY THIS SIMPLE ITALIAN SALAD OF SUCCULENT FRESH, RIPE PEARS, TASTY PARMESAN CHEESE AND AROMATIC LEAVES OF ROCKET. SERVE WITH FRESH ITALIAN BREAD OR CRISP TOASTS.

SERVES FOUR

INGREDIENTS

   3 ripe pears, such as Williams
     or Packhams
   10ml/2 tsp lemon juice
   15ml/1 tbsp hazelnut or walnut oil
   100g/4oz rocket (arugula) leaves
   25g/1oz fresh Parmesan cheese

1 Peel and core the pears and slice them thickly. Place in a bowl and moisten with lemon juice to keep the flesh white.

2 Combine the nut oil with the pears. Add the rocket leaves and toss to mix.

3 Divide the salad among four small plates and top each portion with shavings of Parmesan cheese. Season with ground black pepper and serve.

COOK'S TIPS
• You can grow your own rocket from early spring to late summer.
• You can also use watercress in place of rocket.

Energy 102Kcal/423kJ; Protein 0.9g; Carbohydrate 17.1g, of which sugars 17g; Fat 5g, of which saturates 1.6g, of which polyunsaturates 0g; Cholesterol 6.24mg; Calcium 38mg; Fibre 2.6g; Sodium 6mg.

SIDE DISHES

Throughout the Mediterranean side dishes
form an important element of everyday meals.
Included in this chapter are a delicious and
healthy selection of mainly vegetable-based
side dishes, including low-fat versions of
classics such as Spanish Patatas Bravas and
Ratatouille from Provence in France.

PATATAS BRAVAS ★

THERE ARE SEVERAL VARIATIONS ON THIS CHILLI AND POTATO DISH, BUT THE MOST IMPORTANT THING IS THE SPICING, WHICH IS MADE HOTTER STILL BY ADDING VINEGAR. THE CLASSIC VERSION IS MADE WITH FRESH TOMATO SAUCE FLAVOURED WITH GARLIC AND CHILLI.

2 Heat the oil in a large non-stick frying or sauté pan and fry the potatoes, turning them frequently, until golden.

3 Meanwhile, crush together the garlic, chillies and cumin using a mortar and pestle. Mix the paste with the paprika and wine vinegar, then add to the potatoes with the sliced pepper and cook, stirring, for 2 minutes. Sprinkle with salt, if using, and serve hot as a tapas dish or cold as a side dish.

SERVES FOUR

INGREDIENTS
675g/1½lb small new potatoes
25ml/1½ tbsp olive oil
2 garlic cloves, sliced
3 dried chillies, seeded
  and chopped
2.5ml/½ tsp ground cumin
10ml/2 tsp paprika
30ml/2 tbsp red or white
  wine vinegar
1 red or green (bell) pepper,
  seeded and sliced
coarse sea salt, for sprinkling
  (optional)

1 Scrub the potatoes and put them into a pan of salted water. Bring to the boil and cook for 10 minutes, or until almost tender. Drain and leave to cool slightly. Peel, if you like, then cut into chunks.

Energy 173kcal/728kJ; Protein 3.3g; Carbohydrate 30g, of which sugars 4.9g; Fat 5g, of which saturates 0.9g, of which polyunsaturates 0.6g; Cholesterol 0mg; Calcium 14mg; Fibre 2.4g; Sodium 20mg.

MOORS AND CHRISTIANS ★

MOROS Y CRISTIANOS IS MADE EVERY YEAR IN VALENCIA, SPAIN, AT A FESTIVAL CELEBRATING AN ANCIENT VICTORY OF THE CHRISTIANS OVER THE MOORS. THE BLACK BEANS REPRESENT THE LATTER, AND THE WHITE RICE THE FORMER. THIS IS AN ELEGANT LOW-FAT VERSION OF A TRADITIONAL DISH.

SERVES SIX

INGREDIENTS
  400g/14oz/2¼ cups black beans,
    soaked overnight
  1 onion, quartered
  1 carrot, sliced
  1 celery stick, sliced
  1 garlic clove, finely chopped
  1 bay leaf
  5ml/1 tsp paprika
  25ml/1½ tbsp olive oil
  juice of 1 orange
  300g/11oz/1½ cups long grain rice
  salt and cayenne pepper
For the garnish
  chopped fresh parsley
  thin wedges of orange
  sliced red onion

1 Put the beans in a large pan with the onion, carrot, celery, garlic and bay leaf and 1.75 litres/3 pints/7½ cups water. Bring to the boil and cook rapidly for 10 minutes, then reduce the heat and simmer for 1 hour, topping up the water if necessary. When the beans are almost tender, drain, discarding the vegetables. Return the beans to a clean pan.

2 Blend the paprika and oil with cayenne pepper to taste and stir into the beans with the orange juice. Top up with a little water, if necessary. Heat gently until barely simmering, then cover and cook for 10–15 minutes, or until the beans are completely tender. Remove from the heat and allow to stand in the liquid for 15 minutes. Season with salt to taste.

3 Meanwhile, cook the rice in a pan of boiling water until tender. Drain, then pack into a lightly buttered bowl or individual moulds and allow to stand for 10 minutes.

4 Unmould the rice on to a serving plate and arrange the black beans around the edge. Garnish with parsley, orange wedges and red onion slices.

Energy 431kcal/1815kJ; Protein 19.8g; Carbohydrate 79.7g, of which sugars 5g; Fat 4.4g, of which saturates 0.8g, of which polyunsaturates 0.8g; Cholesterol 0mg; Calcium 76mg; Fibre 6.2g; Sodium 18mg.

SOUR CUCUMBER WITH FRESH DILL ★

THIS IS HALF PICKLE, HALF SALAD, AND TOTALLY DELICIOUS SERVED WITH PUMPERNICKEL OR OTHER COARSE, DARK, FULL-FLAVOURED BREAD. CHOOSE SMOOTH-SKINNED, SMALLISH CUCUMBERS AS LARGER ONES TEND TO BE LESS TENDER. IF YOU CAN ONLY BUY A LARGE CUCUMBER, PEEL IT BEFORE SLICING.

SERVES FOUR

INGREDIENTS

   2 small cucumbers, thinly sliced
   3 onions, thinly sliced
   75–90ml/5–6 tbsp cider vinegar
   30–45ml/2–3 tbsp chopped fresh dill
   salt, to taste

VARIATION
For a sweet and sour mixture, add 45ml/ 3 tbsp caster (superfine) sugar with the cider vinegar in step 2.

1 Put the sliced cucumbers and onions into a large mixing bowl. Season the vegetables with salt and toss together until they are thoroughly combined. Leave the mixture to stand in a cool place for 5–10 minutes.

2 Add the cider vinegar, 30–45ml/ 2–3 tbsp cold water and the chopped dill to the cucumber and onion mixture. Toss all the ingredients together until well combined, then chill in the refrigerator for a few hours, or until ready to serve.

Energy 59kcal/243kJ; Protein 2.5g; Carbohydrate 11.7g, of which sugars 8.7g; Fat 0.5g, of which saturates 0g, of which polyunsaturates 0.1g; Cholesterol 0mg; Calcium 72mg; Fibre 2.9g; Sodium 11mg.

MARINATED COURGETTES ★

THIS IS A SIMPLE LOW-FAT VEGETABLE DISH THAT IS PREPARED ALL OVER ITALY USING THE BEST OF THE SEASON'S COURGETTES. IT HAS A LIGHT AND FRESH FLAVOUR. IT CAN BE EATEN HOT OR COLD AND IS A DELICIOUS ACCOMPANIMENT TO A MAIN COURSE.

SERVES SIX

INGREDIENTS
    4 courgettes (zucchini)
    30ml/2 tbsp extra virgin olive oil
    30ml/2 tbsp chopped fresh mint,
      plus whole leaves, to garnish
    30ml/2 tbsp white wine vinegar
    salt and ground black pepper

1 Cut the courgettes into thin slices using a sharp knife. Heat 15ml/1 tbsp of the oil in a large non-stick frying pan.

2 Fry the courgette slices in batches, for 4–6 minutes, or until tender and brown around the edges. Transfer the courgettes to a bowl. Season well with salt and pepper.

3 Heat the remaining oil in the pan, then add the chopped mint and vinegar and let it bubble for a few seconds. Stir into the courgettes. Set aside to marinate for 1 hour, then serve garnished with mint leaves.

Energy 60kcal/248kJ; Protein 2.7g; Carbohydrate 2.8g, of which sugars 2.3g; Fat 4.3g, of which saturates 0.7g, of which polyunsaturates 0.6g; Cholesterol 0mg; Calcium 49mg; Fibre 1.2g; Sodium 3mg.

ITALIAN PEPPER GRATIN ★

SERVE THIS SIMPLE BUT DELICIOUS LOW-FAT DISH AS A SIDE DISH, OR AS AN APPETIZER WITH A MIXED LEAF SALAD AND SOME GOOD CRUSTY BREAD TO MOP UP THE JUICES FROM THE PEPPERS.

SERVES 4

INGREDIENTS

2 red (bell) peppers
15ml/1 tbsp extra virgin olive oil
60ml/4 tbsp fresh white breadcrumbs
1 garlic clove, finely chopped
5ml/1 tsp capers
8 pitted black olives,
  roughly chopped
15ml/1 tbsp chopped fresh oregano
15ml/1 tbsp chopped fresh flat
  leaf parsley
salt and ground black pepper
fresh herbs, to garnish

1 Preheat the grill (broiler) to high. Lightly grease a small ovenproof dish and set aside. Place the peppers on a grill (broiling) rack and place under the hot grill. Turn occasionally until they are blackened and blistered all over. Remove from the heat and place in a plastic food bag. Seal and leave to cool.

2 Preheat the oven to 200°C/400°F/ Gas 6. When cool, skin the peppers. (Not under the tap as the water would wash away some of the delicious smoky flavour.) Halve the peppers lengthways and remove and discard the stalks, cores and seeds, then cut the flesh into thick strips.

3 Arrange the pepper strips in the prepared dish.

4 Sprinkle the remaining ingredients evenly on top, drizzle with the olive oil and add salt and pepper to taste. Bake in the oven for about 20 minutes, or until the breadcrumbs have browned. Garnish with fresh herbs and serve immediately.

COOK'S TIP
You could serve this dish as a light lunch for two.

Energy 110kcal/460kJ; Protein 2.7g; Carbohydrate 15.5g, of which sugars 5.8g; Fat 4.5g, of which saturates 0.7g, of which polyunsaturates 0.5g; Cholesterol 0mg; Calcium 44mg; Fibre 2.4g; Sodium 326mg.

MOJETE ★

THE SPANISH LOVE TO SCOOP UP COOKED VEGETABLES WITH BREAD, AND THE NAME OF THIS DISH, WHICH IS DERIVED FROM THE WORD MEANING TO DIP, REFLECTS THAT. PEPPERS, TOMATOES AND ONIONS ARE BAKED TOGETHER TO MAKE A COLOURFUL, LOW-FAT SOFT VEGETABLE DISH.

SERVES EIGHT

INGREDIENTS
2 red (bell) peppers
2 yellow (bell) peppers
1 red onion, sliced
2 garlic cloves, halved
50g/2oz/⅓ cup black olives
6 large ripe tomatoes, quartered
5ml/1 tsp soft light brown sugar
45ml/3 tbsp Amontillado sherry
3–4 fresh rosemary sprigs
25ml/1½ tbsp olive oil
salt and ground black pepper
fresh bread, to serve (optional)

1 Halve the peppers lengthways and remove and discard the stalks, cores and seeds. Cut each pepper lengthways into 12 even strips. Preheat the oven to 200°C/400°F/Gas 6.

2 Place the peppers, onion, garlic, olives and tomatoes in a large non-stick roasting pan. Sprinkle the vegetables with the sugar, then pour in the sherry. Season well with salt and pepper, cover with foil and bake in the oven for 45 minutes.

3 Remove the foil from the pan and stir the mixture well. Add the rosemary sprigs and drizzle with the olive oil. Return the pan to the oven and bake, uncovered, for a further 30 minutes, or until the vegetables are very tender. Serve hot or cold with plenty of chunks of fresh crusty bread, if you like.

COOK'S TIP
Spain is the world's chief olive producer, with half the crop being exported. Try to use good quality Spanish olives for this recipe. Choose unpitted ones as they have a better flavour.

Energy 76kcal/315kJ; Protein 1.4g; Carbohydrate 8.5g, of which sugars 8.1g; Fat 3.5g, of which saturates 0.6g, of which polyunsaturates 0.6g; Cholesterol 0mg; Calcium 18mg; Fibre 2.3g; Sodium 178mg.

SPICY ROASTED VEGETABLES ★

OVEN-ROASTING BRINGS OUT ALL THE FLAVOURS OF CHERRY TOMATOES, COURGETTES, ONION AND RED PEPPERS. SERVE THEM HOT WITH GRILLED LEAN MEAT OR FISH.

SERVES FOUR

INGREDIENTS

2–3 courgettes (zucchini)
1 Spanish (Bermuda) onion
2 red (bell) peppers
16 cherry tomatoes
2 garlic cloves, chopped
pinch of cumin seeds
5ml/1 tsp chopped fresh thyme or
  4–5 torn fresh basil leaves
25ml/1½ tbsp olive oil
juice of ½ lemon
5–10ml/1–2 tsp harissa or
  Tabasco sauce
fresh thyme sprigs, to garnish

COOK'S TIP

Harissa is a chilli paste, popular in northern Africa. It can be bought in jars or cans and contains pounded chillies, garlic, coriander, olive oil and seasoning.

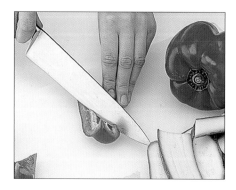

1 Preheat the oven to 220°C/425°F/Gas 7. Trim the courgettes and cut into long strips. Cut the onion into thin wedges. Cut the peppers into chunks, discarding the stalks, cores and seeds.

2 Place these vegetables in a cast-iron dish or non-stick roasting pan; add the tomatoes, garlic, cumin seeds and chopped thyme or torn basil leaves.

3 Sprinkle with the olive oil and toss to coat. Roast the mixture in the oven for 25–30 minutes, or until the vegetables are very soft and have begun to char slightly.

4 In a cup, mix the lemon juice with the harissa or Tabasco sauce. Stir into the vegetables, garnish with the thyme sprigs and serve immediately.

Energy 117kcal/484kJ; Protein 4.1g; Carbohydrate 14g, of which sugars 11.3g; Fat 5g, of which saturates 0.8g, of which polyunsaturates 0.8g; Cholesterol 0mg; Calcium 77mg; Fibre 3.4g; Sodium 9mg.

OKRA AND CORIANDER WITH TOMATOES ★

OKRA IS FREQUENTLY COMBINED WITH TOMATOES AND MILD SPICES IN MEDITERRANEAN COUNTRIES.
LOOK FOR FRESH OKRA THAT IS SOFT AND VELVETY, NOT DRY AND SHRIVELLED.

SERVES FOUR

INGREDIENTS
450g/1lb fresh tomatoes or
  400g/14oz can chopped tomatoes
450g/1lb okra
20ml/4 tsp olive oil
2 onions, thinly sliced
10ml/2 tsp coriander seeds, crushed
3 garlic cloves, crushed
2.5ml/½ tsp granulated sugar
finely grated rind and juice of
  1 lemon
salt and ground black pepper

COOK'S TIP
When okra pods are sliced, they ooze a sticky, somewhat mucilaginous liquid which, when cooked, acts as a thickener. It gives dishes a very distinctive texture, which not everyone appreciates. If the pods are left whole, however, as here, all you get is the delicious flavour.

1 If using fresh tomatoes, cut a cross in the base of each tomato, plunge them into a bowl of boiling water for 30 seconds, then refresh them in cold water. Peel off and discard the skins and roughly chop the tomato flesh. Set aside.

2 Trim off and discard any stalks from the okra and leave whole. Heat the oil in a non-stick frying pan and cook the onions and coriander seeds for 3–4 minutes, or until the onions are beginning to colour.

3 Add the okra and garlic to the pan and cook for 1 minute. Gently stir in the chopped fresh or canned tomatoes. Add the sugar, which will bring out the flavour of the tomatoes. Simmer gently for about 20 minutes, stirring once or twice, or until the okra is tender.

4 Stir in the lemon rind and juice, and add salt and pepper to taste, adding a little more sugar if necessary. Serve warm or cold.

Energy 88kcal/370kJ; Protein 4.1g; Carbohydrate 8.6g, of which sugars 7.7g; Fat 4.5g, of which saturates 0.9g, of which polyunsaturates 0.8g; Cholesterol 0mg; Calcium 192mg; Fibre 5.8g; Sodium 20mg.

VEGETABLES PROVENÇAL ★

*THE SUNSHINE FLAVOURS OF THE MEDITERRANEAN ARE CREATED IN THIS DELICIOUS LOW-FAT
VEGETABLE DISH, IDEAL FOR A SIDE DISH OR LUNCHTIME SNACK, SERVED WITH FRESH, CRUSTY
WHOLEMEAL BREAD. IT IS AN EXCELLENT DISH FOR VEGETARIANS.*

SERVES SIX

INGREDIENTS
  1 onion, sliced
  2 leeks, washed and sliced
  2 garlic cloves, crushed
  1 red (bell) pepper, seeded and sliced
  1 green (bell) pepper, seeded
    and sliced
  1 yellow (bell) pepper, seeded
    and sliced
  350g/12oz courgettes (zucchini), sliced
  225g/8oz/3 cups mushrooms, sliced
  400g/14oz can chopped tomatoes
  30ml/2 tbsp ruby port
  30ml/2 tbsp tomato purée (paste)
  15ml/1 tbsp tomato ketchup
  400g/14oz can chickpeas
  60g/2oz/pitted black olives
  45ml/3 tbsp chopped fresh
    mixed herbs
salt and ground black pepper
additional chopped fresh mixed
  herbs, to garnish

1 Put the onion, leeks, garlic, peppers, courgettes and mushrooms into a large pan.

2 Add the chopped tomatoes, port, tomato purée and tomato ketchup, and stir to mix well. Rinse and drain the chickpeas and add to the pan. Mix well.

3 Cover and bring to the boil, then reduce the heat and simmer gently for 20–30 minutes, or until the vegetables are cooked and tender but not overcooked. Stir carefully from time to time.

4 Remove the lid and increase the heat slightly for the last 10 minutes of the cooking time, to thicken the sauce.

5 Stir in the black olives, chopped mixed herbs and seasoning. Serve the vegetables either hot or cold, garnished with additional chopped mixed herbs.

Energy 173kcal/729kJ; Protein 9.5g; Carbohydrate 24.1g, of which sugars 12.5g; Fat 4.3g, of which saturates 0.7g, of which polyunsaturates 1.7g; Cholesterol 0mg; Calcium 96mg; Fibre 7.9g; Sodium 422mg.

BROAD BEANS WITH BACON ★

Energy 96kcal/401kJ; Protein 6.7g; Carbohydrate 7.8g, of which sugars 1.6g; Fat 3.9g, of which saturates 1.1g, of which polyunsaturates 0.6g; Cholesterol 7mg; Calcium 36mg; Fibre 3.9g; Sodium 198mg.

THIS IS A CLASSIC COMBINATION, HOWEVER, FOR A CHANGE, OR IF YOU'D LIKE TO SERVE THIS DISH TO VEGETARIANS, YOU CAN OMIT THE CHOPPED BACON AND SUBSTITUTE THE SAME QUANTITY OF DRAINED SUN-DRIED TOMATOES IN OIL — IT WILL BE EQUALLY DELICIOUS.

SERVES FOUR

INGREDIENTS
  10ml/2 tsp olive oil
  1 small onion, finely chopped
  1 garlic clove, finely chopped
  50g/2oz rindless lean smoked back
    bacon, roughly chopped
  225g/8oz broad (fava) beans (shelled
    weight), thawed if frozen
  5ml/1 tsp paprika
  15ml/1 tbsp sweet sherry
  salt and ground black pepper

COOK'S TIP
If you have time, remove the dull grey skins from the broad beans to reveal the bright green beans beneath.

1 Heat the oil in a non-stick frying pan and cook the onion, garlic and bacon over a fairly high heat for about 5 minutes, or until softened and browned.

2 Add the broad beans and paprika and stir-fry for 1 minute. Add the sherry, cover and cook for 5–10 minutes, or until the beans are tender. Season to taste with salt and pepper, then serve.

OVEN-ROASTED RED ONIONS ★

THE WONDERFUL TASTE OF THESE SWEET RED ONIONS IS ENHANCED STILL FURTHER WITH THE POWERFUL FLAVOURS OF FRESH ROSEMARY AND JUNIPER BERRIES, AND THE ADDED TANGY SWEETNESS FROM THE BALSAMIC VINEGAR.

SERVES FOUR

INGREDIENTS

4 large or 8 small red onions
25ml/1½ tbsp olive oil
6 juniper berries, crushed
8 small fresh rosemary sprigs
30ml/2 tbsp balsamic vinegar
salt and ground black pepper

VARIATION
Add a similar quantity of long, thin potato wedges to the onion. Use a larger dish so that the vegetables are still in one layer.

COOK'S TIP
To help hold back the tears during preparation, chill the onions first for about 30 minutes, and then remove the root end last. The root contains the largest concentration of the sulphuric compounds that make the eyes water.

1 Soak a clay onion baker in cold water for 15 minutes, then drain. If the base of the baker is glazed, only the lid will need to be soaked.

2 Trim and discard the roots from the onions and remove the skins, if you like. Cut the onions from the tip to the root, cutting the large onions into quarters and the small onions in half.

3 Lightly rub the onions with olive oil, salt and pepper and the juniper berries. Place the onions in the baker, inserting the rosemary in among the onions. Drizzle the remaining oil and vinegar over.

4 Cover and place in a cold oven. Set the oven to 200°C/400°F/Gas 6 and roast for 40 minutes. Remove the lid and roast for a further 10 minutes.

Energy 47kcal/194kJ; Protein 1.5g; Carbohydrate 9.9g, of which sugars 7.1g; Fat 0.3g, of which saturates 0g, of which polyunsaturates 0.1g; Cholesterol 0mg; Calcium 32mg; Fibre 1.8g; Sodium 4mg.

MARINATED MUSHROOMS ★

CHAMPIÑONES EN ESCABECHE *IS A GOOD WAY TO SERVE MUSHROOMS IN SUMMER, AND MAKES A REFRESHING LOW-FAT ALTERNATIVE TO THE EVER-POPULAR MUSHROOMS FRIED IN GARLIC. SERVE WITH PLENTY OF CRUSTY BREAD TO MOP UP THE DELICIOUS JUICES.*

SERVES FOUR

INGREDIENTS
    10ml/2 tsp olive oil
    1 small onion, very finely chopped
    1 garlic clove, finely chopped
    15ml/1 tbsp tomato purée (paste)
    50ml/2fl oz/¼ cup amontillado sherry
    50ml/2fl oz/¼ cup water
    2 cloves
    225g/8oz/3 cups button (white)
      mushrooms, trimmed
    salt and ground black pepper
    chopped fresh parsley, to garnish

VARIATION
In Spain, wild mushrooms, known as *setas*, are served in this way.

1 Heat the oil in a non-stick pan. Add the onion and garlic and cook until soft. Stir in the tomato purée, sherry, water and cloves and season with salt and black pepper. Bring to the boil, cover and simmer gently for 45 minutes, adding more water if it becomes too dry.

2 Add the mushrooms to the pan, then cover and simmer for about 5 minutes. Remove from the heat and allow to cool, still covered. Chill in the refrigerator overnight. Serve the mushrooms cold, sprinkled with the chopped parsley, to garnish.

Energy 44kcal/181kJ; Protein 1.4g; Carbohydrate 2.1g, of which sugars 1.7g; Fat 1.8g, of which saturates 0.3g, of which polyunsaturates 0.3g; Cholesterol 0mg; Calcium 9mg; Fibre 0.9g; Sodium 14mg.

BRAISED LETTUCE AND PEAS WITH MINT ★

BASED ON THE TRADITIONAL FRENCH WAY OF BRAISING PEAS WITH LETTUCE IN A LITTLE BUTTER,
THIS LOW-FAT DISH IS DELICIOUS WITH SIMPLY COOKED FISH OR GRILLED CHICKEN.

2 Toss the vegetables in the butter, then sprinkle in the sugar, 2.5ml/½ tsp salt and plenty of black pepper. Cover, then cook very gently for 5 minutes, stirring once.

3 Add the peas and mint sprigs to the pan. Toss the peas in the juices, then pour in the stock or water.

4 Cover the pan and cook over a gentle heat for a further 5 minutes, or until the peas are almost tender, then remove the lid from the pan. Increase the heat to high and cook, stirring occasionally, until the cooking liquid has reduced to a few tablespoons.

5 Stir in the remaining butter and adjust the seasoning. Transfer to a warmed serving dish and garnish with the extra mint. Serve immediately.

VARIATIONS
• Braise about 250g/9oz baby carrots with the lettuce.
• Use 1 lettuce, shredding it coarsely, and omit the fresh mint. Towards the end of cooking, stir in about 150g/5oz rocket (arugula) – preferably the slightly stronger-flavoured, wild variety – and cook briefly until just wilted.
• Cook 115g/4oz chopped lean smoked back bacon with 1 small chopped red or white onion in the butter. Use 1 bunch of spring onions and omit the mint. Stir in some chopped fresh flat leaf parsley before serving. This version is also very good with small, white summer turnips, braised with the lettuce.

SERVES SIX

INGREDIENTS
25g/1oz/2 tbsp butter
4 Little Gem (Bibb) lettuces, halved lengthways
2 bunches spring onions (scallions)
5ml/1 tsp granulated sugar
400g/14oz shelled peas (about 1kg/2¼lb in pods)
4–5 fresh mint sprigs, plus extra to garnish
120ml/4fl oz/½ cup light vegetable or chicken stock or water
salt and ground black pepper

1 Melt half the butter in a wide, heavy non-stick pan over a low heat. Add the lettuces and spring onions.

Energy 110kcal/455kJ; Protein 6.2g; Carbohydrate 10.8g, of which sugars 4.3g; Fat 5g, of which saturates 2.5g, of which polyunsaturates 0.9g; Cholesterol 9mg; Calcium 64mg; Fibre 4.2g; Sodium 32mg.

MEDITERRANEAN VEGETABLE PANCAKE ★

CRUNCHY GOLDEN BATTER SURROUNDS THESE VEGETABLES, MAKING THEM DELICIOUS AND FILLING. SERVE AS A SIDE DISH OR WITH SALAD AS A LIGHT LUNCH.

SERVES EIGHT

INGREDIENTS

   1 small aubergine (eggplant),
     trimmed, halved and thickly sliced
   1 egg
   115g/4oz/1 cup plain (all-purpose) flour
   300ml/½ pint/1¼ cups
     semi-skimmed (low-fat) milk
   30ml/2 tbsp fresh thyme,
     or 10ml/2 tsp dried
   1 red onion
   2 large courgettes (zucchini)
   1 red (bell) pepper
   1 yellow (bell) pepper
   30ml/2 tbsp sunflower oil
   30ml/2 tbsp freshly grated
     Parmesan cheese (optional)
   salt and ground black pepper
   fresh herbs, to serve

1 Place the aubergine slices in a colander, sprinkle generously with salt and leave for 10 minutes. Drain, rinse well and pat dry on kitchen paper.

2 Meanwhile, beat the egg in a bowl, then gradually beat in the flour and a little milk to make a smooth, thick paste. Gradually blend in the rest of the milk, add the thyme and seasoning to taste and stir until smooth. Leave the batter in a cool place until required. Preheat the oven to 220°C/425°F/Gas 7.

COOK'S TIP
It is essential to get the fat in the dish really hot before adding the batter, which should sizzle slightly as it goes in. If the fat is not hot enough, the batter will not rise well. Use a non-stick roasting pan.

3 Quarter the onion, trim and slice the courgettes, and seed and quarter the peppers. Put the oil in a non-stick roasting pan and heat in the oven until hot. Add the prepared vegetables, toss in the oil to coat thoroughly and return to the oven for 20 minutes.

4 Give the batter another whisk, then pour it over the vegetables. Return the pan to the oven for 30 minutes. When puffed up and golden, reduce the heat to 190°C/375°F/Gas 5 for 10–15 minutes, or until crisp around the edges. Sprinkle with Parmesan, if using, and herbs; serve.

Energy 124kcal/522kJ; Protein 5.1g; Carbohydrate 17.7g, of which sugars 6.3g; Fat 4.2g, of which saturates 0.7g, of which polyunsaturates 0.8g; Cholesterol 25mg; Calcium 90mg; Fibre 2.2g; Sodium 29mg.

Courgettes in Tomato Sauce ★

This richly flavoured Mediterranean dish can be served hot or cold as a side dish.
Cut the courgettes into fairly thick slices, so that they stay slightly crunchy.

SERVES FOUR

INGREDIENTS

15ml/1 tbsp extra virgin olive oil
  or sunflower oil
1 onion, chopped
1 garlic clove, chopped
4 courgettes (zucchini),
  thickly sliced
400g/14oz can chopped tomatoes
2 tomatoes, skinned, seeded
  and chopped
5ml/1 tsp vegetable bouillon powder
15ml/1 tbsp tomato purée (paste)
salt and ground black pepper

1 Heat the oil in a heavy non-stick pan, add the onion and garlic and sauté, stirring occasionally, for 5 minutes, or until the onion is softened. Add the courgettes and cook, stirring occasionally, for a further 5 minutes.

2 Add the canned and fresh tomatoes, bouillon powder and tomato purée. Stir well, then simmer for 10–15 minutes, or until the sauce is thickened and the courgettes are just tender. Season to taste with salt and pepper and serve.

Energy 77kcal/320kJ; Protein 3.2g; Carbohydrate 8.2g, of which sugars 7.7g; Fat 3.7g, of which saturates 0.7g, of which polyunsaturates 0.8g; Cholesterol 0mg; Calcium 41mg; Fibre 2.7g; Sodium 24mg.

RATATOUILLE ★

A HIGHLY VERSATILE TOMATO AND MIXED VEGETABLE STEW FROM PROVENCE IN FRANCE, RATATOUILLE IS DELICIOUS SERVED WARM OR COLD. THIS LOW-FAT VERSION IS FULL OF FLAVOUR TOO!

SERVES SIX

INGREDIENTS

900g/2lb ripe plum tomatoes
30ml/2 tbsp olive oil
2 onions, thinly sliced
2 red and 1 yellow (bell) peppers,
  seeded and cut into chunks
1 large aubergine (eggplant), cut
  into chunks
2 courgettes (zucchini), sliced
4 garlic cloves, crushed
2 bay leaves
15ml/1 tbsp chopped fresh thyme
salt and ground black pepper

1 Plunge the tomatoes into boiling water for 30 seconds, then refresh in cold water. Peel away and discard the skins, then roughly chop the flesh.

2 Heat 10ml/2 tsp of the olive oil in a large, heavy non-stick pan and gently cook the onions for 5 minutes. Stir them constantly so that they do not brown, as this will adversely affect their flavour and make them bitter, but cook them until they are just transparent.

3 Add the peppers to the onions and cook for a further 2 minutes. Using a slotted spoon, transfer the onions and peppers to a plate and set them aside.

4 Add a further 10ml/2 tsp oil and the aubergine to the pan and cook gently for 5 minutes. Add the remaining oil and the courgettes, and cook for 3 minutes. Lift out the courgettes and aubergine and set them aside.

5 Add the garlic and tomatoes to the pan with the bay leaves and chopped thyme, and a little salt and pepper. Cook gently until the tomatoes have softened and are turning pulpy.

6 Return all the vegetables to the pan and cook gently, stirring frequently, for about 15 minutes, or until fairly pulpy but retaining a little texture. Adjust the seasoning to taste. Serve warm or cold.

Energy 120kcal/503kJ; Protein 4.1g; Carbohydrate 15.4g, of which sugars 14.4g; Fat 5g, of which saturates 0.9g, of which polyunsaturates 1.1g; Cholesterol 0mg; Calcium 48mg; Fibre 5.3g; Sodium 20mg.

ROASTED PLUM TOMATOES ᴬᴺᴰ GARLIC ★

THESE ARE SO SIMPLE TO PREPARE YET TASTE ABSOLUTELY WONDERFUL. USE A LARGE, SHALLOW EARTHENWARE DISH THAT WILL ALLOW THE TOMATOES TO SEAR AND CHAR IN A HOT OVEN.

SERVES FOUR

INGREDIENTS
   8 plum tomatoes, halved
   12 garlic cloves
   20ml/4 tsp extra virgin olive oil
   3 bay leaves
   salt and ground black pepper
   45ml/3 tbsp fresh oregano leaves,
     to garnish

COOK'S TIP
Use ripe plum tomatoes for this recipe as they keep their shape and do not fall apart when roasted at such a high temperature. Leave the stalks on, if possible.

1 Preheat the oven to 230°C/450°F/ Gas 8. Select an ovenproof dish that will hold all the tomatoes snugly in a single layer. Place the tomatoes in the dish and push the whole, unpeeled garlic cloves between them.

2 Lightly brush the tomatoes with the oil, add the bay leaves and sprinkle black pepper over the top. Bake in the oven for about 45 minutes, until the tomatoes have softened and are sizzling in the dish. They should be charred around the edges. Season with salt and a little more black pepper, if needed. Garnish with oregano leaves and serve at once.

Energy 70kcal/294kJ; Protein 1.8g; Carbohydrate 7.8g, of which sugars 7.8g; Fat 3.8g, of which saturates 0.7g, of which polyunsaturates 0.8g; Cholesterol 0mg; Calcium 18mg; Fibre 2.5g; Sodium 23mg.

GREEN BEANS WITH TOMATOES ★

THIS IS A REAL SUMMER FAVOURITE, USING THE BEST RIPE PLUM TOMATOES AND FRENCH BEANS. USE CRUSTY FRENCH BREAD TO MOP UP THE JUICES OF THIS FLAVOURFUL SALAD.

SERVES FOUR

INGREDIENTS

5ml/1 tsp olive oil
1 large onion, thinly sliced
2 garlic cloves, finely chopped
6 large ripe plum tomatoes, skinned,
  seeded and coarsely chopped
150ml/¼ pint/⅔ cup dry white wine
450g/1lb French (green) beans,
  sliced in half lengthways
16 pitted black olives
10ml/2 tsp lemon juice
salt and ground black pepper

COOK'S TIPS

• French (green) beans need little preparation and now that they are grown without the string you simply trim them.
• When choosing, make sure that they snap easily – this is a sign of freshness.

1 Heat the oil in a large, non-stick frying pan. Add the onion and garlic and cook for about 5 minutes, or until the onion is softened but not brown.

2 Add the chopped tomatoes, white wine, French beans, olives and lemon juice and cook over a gentle heat, stirring occasionally, for a further 20 minutes, or until the sauce is thickened and the beans are tender. Season to taste with salt and pepper and serve immediately.

Energy 122kcal/511kJ; Protein 4g; Carbohydrate 12.2g, of which sugars 10.4g; Fat 4.1g, of which saturates 0.7g, of which polyunsaturates 1.1g; Cholesterol 0mg; Calcium 78mg; Fibre 5.3g; Sodium 469mg.

MOROCCAN BRAISED CHICKPEAS ★

THIS SWEET AND SPICY VEGETARIAN DISH IS A REAL TREAT THAT GOES WELL WITH A LIGHT EVENING MEAL. SERVE IT HOT OR COLD AS A TASTY AND NUTRITIOUS SIDE DISH.

SERVES SIX

INGREDIENTS
  250g/9oz/1½ cups dried chickpeas,
    soaked overnight in cold water
  15ml/1 tbsp olive oil
  2 onions, cut into wedges
  10ml/2 tsp ground cumin
  1.5ml/¼ tsp ground turmeric
  1.5ml/¼ tsp cayenne pepper
  15ml/1 tbsp ground coriander
  5ml/1 tsp ground cinnamon
  300ml/½ pint/1¼ cups
    vegetable stock
  2 carrots, sliced
  115g/4oz/½ cup ready-to-eat dried
    apricots, halved
  50g/2oz/scant ½ cup raisins
  25g/1oz/¼ cup flaked (sliced)
    almonds (optional)
  30ml/2 tbsp chopped fresh
    coriander (cilantro)
  30ml/2 tbsp chopped fresh flat
    leaf parsley
  salt and ground black pepper

1 Soak a bean clay pot in cold water for 20 minutes, then drain. Place the chickpeas in a pan with plenty of cold water. Bring to the boil and boil rapidly for 10 minutes, then drain and place the chickpeas in the bean pot, cover with lukewarm water and cover with the lid.

COOK'S TIP
The cooking time for the chickpeas will vary depending on their age – if old, they could take a further 30 minutes.

2 Place in a cold (unheated) oven and set the temperature to 200°C/400°F/Gas 6. Cook for 1 hour, then reduce the oven temperature to 160°C/325°F/Gas 3. Cook for a further 1 hour, or until the chickpeas are tender.

3 Meanwhile, heat the olive oil in a non-stick frying pan, add the onions and cook for about 6 minutes, or until softened. Add the cumin, turmeric, cayenne pepper, coriander and cinnamon and cook for 2–3 minutes. Stir in the stock, carrots, apricots, raisins and almonds and bring to the boil.

4 Drain the chickpeas and return them to the clay pot, add the spicy vegetable mixture and stir to mix. Cover and return to the oven for 30 minutes.

5 Season with salt and pepper, lightly stir in half the chopped coriander and parsley and serve sprinkled with the remainder.

Energy 205kcal/865kJ; Protein 10.1g; Carbohydrate 33.3g, of which sugars 12.8g; Fat 4.4g, of which saturates 0.5g, of which polyunsaturates 1.4g; Cholesterol 0mg; Calcium 107mg; Fibre 6.6g; Sodium 34mg.

OKRA AND TOMATO TAGINE ★

A SPICY VEGETARIAN DISH THAT IS DELICIOUS SERVED EITHER WITH OTHER VEGETABLE DISHES OR AS A SIDE DISH TO ACCOMPANY A LOW-FAT MEAT TAGINE.

SERVES FOUR

INGREDIENTS
350g/12oz small okra
5–6 tomatoes
2 small onions
2 garlic cloves, crushed
1 fresh green chilli, seeded
5ml/1 tsp paprika
a small handful of fresh coriander
   (cilantro) leaves
15ml/1 tbsp olive oil
juice of 1 lemon
120ml/4fl oz/½ cup water

1 Preheat the oven to 190°C/375°F/ Gas 5. Trim the okra, then cut the pods into 1cm/½in lengths. Set aside.

2 Skin the tomatoes, remove the seeds, then roughly chop the flesh. Set aside. Chop one of the onions, place in a food processor with the garlic, spices and 60ml/4 tbsp water and blend to a paste.

3 Slice the second onion. Heat the oil in a flameproof casserole and sauté the onion for 5–6 minutes, or until it turns golden brown. Transfer 30ml/2 tbsp sautéed onions to a plate and set aside.

4 Reduce the heat and pour the onion and coriander paste over the sautéed onions. Cook for 1–2 minutes, stirring frequently, then add the okra, tomatoes and lemon juice. Pour in the water and stir well to mix. Cover tightly and transfer to the oven. Bake for about 15 minutes, until the okra is tender.

5 Transfer the tagine to a serving dish, sprinkle with the reserved sautéed onion rings and serve immediately.

VARIATION
Canned, chopped tomatoes can be used instead of the fresh tomatoes in this recipe – simply add the contents of a 200g/7oz can with the okra in step 4.

COOK'S TIP
To skin fresh tomatoes easily, cut a small cross in the base of each tomato. Plunge the tomatoes into a bowl of boiling water for 30 seconds, then refresh them in cold water. The tomato skins should now peel off easily.

Energy 89kcal/372kJ; Protein 4.1g; Carbohydrate 9.4g, of which sugars 8.1g; Fat 4.2g, of which saturates 0.8g, of which polyunsaturates 0.8g; Cholesterol 0mg; Calcium 182mg; Fibre 5.8g; Sodium 23mg.

VEGETARIAN

Vegetarian dishes play an important part
in a low-fat Mediterranean diet, providing
nutritious, substantial and flavourful
meals that all the family will enjoy.
Choose from healthy hotpots, tempting
tagines, stuffed and roast vegetables, and
lighter versions of favourites such as
Vegetable Moussaka and Lasagne.

ROASTED SQUASH ★★★

GEM SQUASH HAS A SWEET, SUBTLE FLAVOUR THAT CONTRASTS WELL WITH OLIVES AND SUN-DRIED
TOMATOES IN THIS RECIPE. THE RICE ADDS SUBSTANCE WITHOUT CHANGING ANY OF THE FLAVOURS.

2 Mix together the rice, tomatoes, olives, goat's cheese, olive oil and chopped basil in a bowl.

3 Divide the rice mixture evenly between the squash and place them in a shallow non-stick baking tin (pan) or ovenproof dish, just large enough to hold the squash side by side.

4 Cover with foil and bake in the oven for 45–50 minutes, or until the squash are tender when pierced with a skewer. Garnish with basil sprigs and serve with a green salad, if you like.

SERVES TWO

INGREDIENTS
  4 whole gem squashes
  225g/8oz/2 cups cooked white
    long grain rice
  75g/3oz/1½ cups sun-dried
    tomatoes, chopped
  40g/1½ oz/⅓ cup pitted black
    olives, chopped
  50g/2oz/¼ cup soft goat's cheese
  10ml/2 tsp olive oil
  15ml/1 tbsp chopped fresh basil
    leaves, plus basil sprigs,
    to serve
  green salad, to serve (optional)

1 Preheat the oven to 180°C/350°F/ Gas 4. Trim away the base of each squash, slice off the top and scoop out and discard the seeds.

Energy 419kcal/1766kJ; Protein 15.7g; Carbohydrate 58.2g, of which sugars 18.4g; Fat 15g, of which saturates 6.6g, of which polyunsaturates 1.4g; Cholesterol 23mg; Calcium 359mg; Fibre 11.1g; Sodium 605mg.

PROVENÇAL STUFFED PEPPERS ★★★

THIS COLOURFUL MEDITERRANEAN DISH CREATES A TASTY LOW-FAT VEGETARIAN MEAL, IDEAL SERVED WITH A MIXED BABY LEAF SALAD AND CRUSTY BREAD.

SERVES FOUR

INGREDIENTS
    10ml/1 tsp olive oil
    1 red onion, sliced
    1 courgette (zucchini), diced
    115g/4oz mushrooms, sliced
    1 garlic clove, crushed
    400g/14oz can chopped tomatoes
    15ml/1 tbsp tomato purée (paste)
    40g/1½oz/scant ⅓ cup pine nuts
    30ml/2 tbsp chopped fresh basil
    4 large (bell) peppers
    50g/2oz/½ cup finely grated
        fresh Parmesan or half-fat Red
        Leicester cheese
    salt and ground black pepper
    fresh basil leaves, to garnish

1 Preheat the oven to 180°C/350°F/Gas 4. Heat the oil in a non-stick pan, add the onion, courgette, mushrooms and garlic and cook gently, stirring occasionally, for 3 minutes.

2 Stir in the tomatoes and tomato purée, then bring to the boil and simmer uncovered, stirring occasionally, for 10–15 minutes, or until thickened slightly. Remove from the heat and stir in the pine nuts, chopped basil and seasoning.

COOK'S TIP
Leave the root end intact when slicing or dicing an onion. This will prevent the release of the strong juices and fumes that can cause eyes to water.

3 Cut the peppers in half lengthways and seed them. Blanch in a pan of boiling water for 3 minutes. Drain.

VARIATION
Use the vegetable sauce to stuff other vegetables, such as large courgettes or baby aubergines (eggplants), in place of the peppers.

4 Place the pepper halves, cut side up, in a shallow, ovenproof dish and fill with the vegetable mixture.

5 Cover the dish with foil and bake in the oven for 20 minutes. Remove the foil, sprinkle each pepper with a little grated cheese and bake, uncovered, for a further 5–10 minutes, or until the cheese is melted and bubbling. Garnish with basil leaves and serve at once.

Energy 223kcal/930kJ; Protein 10.4g; Carbohydrate 16.9g, of which sugars 15.9g; Fat 13.1g, of which saturates 3.5g, of which polyunsaturates 5g; Cholesterol 13mg; Calcium 190mg; Fibre 5g; Sodium 155mg.

BAKED CHEESE POLENTA WITH TOMATO SAUCE ★★★

POLENTA, OR CORNMEAL, IS A STAPLE FOOD IN ITALY THAT IS ALSO LOW IN FAT. IT IS COOKED LIKE A SORT OF PORRIDGE, AND EATEN SOFT, OR SET, CUT INTO SHAPES THEN BAKED OR GRILLED.

SERVES FOUR

INGREDIENTS

5ml/1 tsp salt
250g/9oz/2¼ cups quick-cook polenta
5ml/1 tsp paprika
2.5ml/½ tsp freshly grated nutmeg
10ml/2 tsp olive oil
1 large onion, finely chopped
2 garlic cloves, crushed
2 x 400g/14oz cans chopped tomatoes
15ml/1 tbsp tomato purée (paste)
5ml/1 tsp granulated sugar
salt and ground black pepper
75g/3oz/¾ cup Gruyère cheese, finely grated

1 Lightly grease an ovenproof dish and set aside. Line a 28 x 18cm/11 x 7in baking tin (pan) with clear film (plastic wrap). In a pan, bring 1 litre/1¾ pints/4 cups water to the boil with the salt.

2 Pour in the polenta in a steady stream and cook, stirring continuously, for 5 minutes. Beat in the paprika and nutmeg, then pour the mixture into the prepared tin and smooth the surface. Leave to cool.

3 Heat the oil in a non-stick pan and cook the onion and garlic until soft. Add the tomatoes, tomato purée and sugar. Season with salt and pepper. Bring to the boil, then reduce the heat and simmer for 20 minutes.

4 Meanwhile, preheat the oven to 200°C/400°F/Gas 6. Turn out the polenta on to a chopping board, and cut into 5cm/2in squares. Place half the squares in the prepared dish. Spoon over half the tomato sauce, and sprinkle with half the cheese. Repeat the layers. Bake in the oven for about 25 minutes, or until golden. Serve hot.

Energy 380kcal/1590kJ; Protein 15.2g; Carbohydrate 55.8g, of which sugars 9.5g; Fat 10.4g, of which saturates 4.3g, of which polyunsaturates 0.7g; Cholesterol 19mg; Calcium 250mg; Fibre 3.9g; Sodium 724mg.

RICH TOMATO AND MEDITERRANEAN VEGETABLE HOT-POT ★★

HERE'S A ONE-DISH MEDITERRANEAN MEAL THAT'S SUITABLE FOR FEEDING LARGE NUMBERS OF PEOPLE. IT'S LOW IN FAT, LIGHTLY SPICED AND HAS PLENTY OF GARLIC — WHO COULD REFUSE?

SERVES FOUR

INGREDIENTS

30ml/2 tbsp extra virgin olive oil or sunflower oil
1 large onion, chopped
2 small–medium aubergines (eggplants), cut into small cubes
4 courgettes (zucchini), cut into small chunks
2 red, yellow or green (bell) peppers, seeded and chopped
115g/4oz/1 cup fresh or frozen peas
115g/4oz green beans
200g/7oz can flageolet or small cannellini beans, rinsed and drained
450g/1lb new or salad potatoes, peeled and cubed
2.5ml/½ tsp ground cinnamon
2.5ml/½ tsp ground cumin
5ml/1 tsp paprika
4–5 tomatoes, skinned
400g/14oz can chopped tomatoes
30ml/2 tbsp chopped fresh parsley
3–4 garlic cloves, crushed
350ml/12fl oz/1½ cups stock
salt and ground black pepper
black olives, to garnish
fresh parsley, to garnish

1 Preheat the oven to 190°C/375°F/ Gas 5. Heat 15ml/1 tbsp of the oil in a heavy non-stick pan, and sauté the onion until golden. Add the aubergines, sauté for 3 minutes, then add the courgettes, peppers, peas, beans and potatoes, and stir in the spices and seasoning. Cook, stirring constantly, for 3 minutes.

2 Cut the fresh tomatoes in half and scoop out and discard the seeds. Chop the tomatoes finely and place them in a bowl. Stir in the canned tomatoes with the chopped parsley, garlic and the remaining olive oil. Spoon the aubergine mixture into a shallow ovenproof dish and level the surface.

3 Pour the stock over the aubergine mixture and then spoon the prepared tomato mixture over the top.

4 Cover the dish with foil and bake in the oven for 30–45 minutes, or until the vegetables are tender. Serve hot, garnished with black olives and parsley.

Energy 320kcal/1346kJ; Protein 13.4g; Carbohydrate 50.3g, of which sugars 22.8g; Fat 8.7g, of which saturates 1.6g, of which polyunsaturates 2.1g; Cholesterol 0mg; Calcium 105mg; Fibre 13.2g; Sodium 251mg.

Spinach with Beans, Raisins and Pine Nuts ★★★

THIS DISH IS TRADITIONALLY MADE WITH CHICKPEAS, BUT CAN ALSO BE MADE WITH HARICOT BEANS AS HERE. USE EITHER DRIED OR CANNED BEANS.

SERVES FOUR

INGREDIENTS
115g/4oz/⅔ cup haricot (navy) beans, soaked overnight, or 400g/14oz can, drained
30ml/2 tbsp olive oil
1 thick slice white bread
1 onion, chopped
3–4 tomatoes, skinned, seeded and chopped
2.5ml/½ tsp ground cumin
450g/1lb fresh spinach leaves
5ml/1 tsp paprika
1 garlic clove, halved
25g/1oz/3 tbsp raisins
15g/½oz pine nuts, toasted
salt and ground black pepper

1 Cook the dried beans in a pan of boiling water for about 1 hour, or until tender. Drain and set aside.

2 Heat 10ml/2 tsp of the oil in a frying pan and fry the bread until golden. Transfer to a plate and set aside.

3 Sauté the onion in a further 10ml/ 2 tsp of the oil over a gentle heat, until soft but not brown, then add the tomatoes and cumin and continue cooking over a gentle heat.

4 Wash the spinach thoroughly, removing any tough stalks. Heat the remaining oil in a large, non-stick pan, stir in the paprika and then add the spinach and 45ml/3 tbsp water. Cover and cook for a few minutes, or until the spinach has wilted.

5 Add the onion and tomato mixture to the spinach and stir in the haricot beans, then season with salt and pepper.

6 Place the garlic and fried bread in a blender or food processor and process until smooth. Stir the bread mixture into the spinach and bean mixture, together with the raisins. Add 175ml/6fl oz/ ¾ cup water and then cover and simmer very gently for 20–30 minutes, adding more water, if necessary.

7 Place the spinach mixture on a warmed serving plate and sprinkle with toasted pine nuts. Serve hot with Moroccan bread or other fresh bread.

Energy 251kcal/1051kJ; Protein 11.4g; Carbohydrate 28.2g, of which sugars 11g; Fat 11g, of which saturates 1.3g, of which polyunsaturates 3.6g; Cholesterol 0mg; Calcium 259mg; Fibre 7g; Sodium 217mg.

RED PEPPER RISOTTO ★

THIS DELICIOUS ITALIAN RISOTTO CREATES A FLAVOURFUL AND LOW-FAT SUPPER OR MAIN-COURSE DISH, IDEAL SERVED WITH A MIXED LEAF SALAD AND FRESH ITALIAN BREAD.

SERVES FOUR

INGREDIENTS

3 large red (bell) peppers
10ml/2 tsp olive oil
3 large garlic cloves, thinly sliced
400g/14oz can chopped tomatoes
225g/8oz can chopped tomatoes
2 bay leaves
about 1.2–1.5 litres/2–2½ pints/
   5–6¼ cups vegetable stock
450g/1lb/2¼ cups arborio rice or
   long grain brown rice
6 fresh basil leaves, shredded
salt and ground black pepper

1 Preheat the grill (broiler) to high. Put the peppers in a grill (broiling) pan and grill (broil) until the skins are blackened and blistered all over. Transfer the peppers to a bowl, cover with a clean, damp dish towel and leave for 10 minutes. Peel off and discard the skins, then slice the peppers, discarding the cores and seeds. Set aside.

2 Heat the oil in a wide, shallow, non-stick pan. Add the garlic and tomatoes and cook gently, stirring occasionally, for 5 minutes, then add the prepared pepper slices and the bay leaves. Stir well, then cook gently, stirring occasionally, for 15 minutes.

3 Pour the vegetable stock into a separate large, heavy pan and heat it to simmering point. Stir the rice into the vegetable mixture and cook for about 2 minutes, then add two or three ladlefuls of the hot stock. Cook, stirring occasionally, until all the stock has been absorbed into the rice.

4 Continue to add stock, making sure each addition has been absorbed before adding the next. When the rice is tender, season to taste.

5 Remove the pan from the heat, cover and leave to stand for 10 minutes. Remove and discard the bay leaves, then stir in the shredded basil. Serve.

Energy 490kcal/2052kJ; Protein 10.9g; Carbohydrate 103.8g, of which sugars 13.6g; Fat 3.1g, of which saturates 0.5g, of which polyunsaturates 0.7g; Cholesterol 0mg; Calcium 44mg; Fibre 3.9g; Sodium 20mg.

VEGETABLE PAELLA ★

THIS LOW-FAT RECIPE MAKES A DELICIOUS VEGETARIAN VERSION OF THE TRADITIONAL, SEAFOOD-BASED PAELLA; A GOOD CHOICE TO RING THE CHANGES.

SERVES SIX

INGREDIENTS

1 onion, chopped
2 garlic cloves, crushed
225g/8oz leeks, washed and sliced
3 celery sticks, chopped
1 red (bell) pepper, seeded and sliced
2 courgettes (zucchini), sliced
175g/6oz brown cap (cremini)
  mushrooms, sliced
400g/14oz can cannellini beans
175g/6oz/1½ cups frozen peas
450g/1lb/2¼ cups long grain
  brown rice
900ml/1½ pints/3¾ cups
  vegetable stock
60ml/4 tbsp dry white wine
a few saffron threads
225g/8oz cherry tomatoes, halved
45–60ml/3–4 tbsp fresh mixed herbs
salt and ground black pepper
celery leaves and cherry tomatoes,
  to garnish
lemon wedges, to serve

1 Put the onion, garlic, leeks, celery, red pepper, courgettes and mushrooms in a large pan and mix together.

VARIATIONS
• Use 1 orange or yellow (bell) pepper in place of a red pepper.
• Use red onions or shallots in place of leeks.
• Use canned black-eyed beans (peas) in place of cannellini beans.

2 Rinse and drain the cannellini beans. Add them to the pan with the peas, rice, stock, wine and saffron threads.

3 Cover and bring to the boil, then reduce the heat and simmer, uncovered, stirring occasionally, for about 35 minutes, or until almost all the liquid has been absorbed and the rice is tender.

4 Stir in the tomatoes. Chop the herbs and add them to the pan. Season to taste. Serve the paella immediately, garnished with celery leaves and cherry tomatoes and accompanied by lemon wedges for squeezing.

Energy 388kcal/1646kJ; Protein 13.5g; Carbohydrate 78.8g, of which sugars 7.5g; Fat 3.6g, of which saturates 0.9g, of which polyunsaturates 1.5g; Cholesterol 0mg; Calcium 57mg; Fibre 8.5g; Sodium 299mg.

CHICKPEA TAGINE ★

A TAGINE IS A TYPE OF MOROCCAN STEW ORIGINALLY PREPARED BY LONG SIMMERING OVER AN OPEN FIRE. SERVE THIS FLAVOURFUL TAGINE WITH FRESH CRUSTY BREAD.

SERVES SIX

INGREDIENTS

150g/5oz/¾ cup dried chickpeas, soaked overnight and drained, or 2 x 400g/14oz cans chickpeas, rinsed and drained
15ml/1 tbsp sunflower oil or extra virgin olive oil
1 large onion, chopped
1 garlic clove, crushed or chopped (optional)
400g/14oz can chopped tomatoes
200g/7oz fresh tomatoes, skinned and puréed
5ml/1 tsp ground cumin
350ml/12fl oz/1½ cups vegetable stock
¼ preserved lemon
30ml/2 tbsp chopped fresh coriander (cilantro)

1 If using dried chickpeas, cook in a pan with plenty of boiling water for 1–1½ hours, or until tender. Drain.

2 Skin the chickpeas by placing them in a bowl of cold water and rubbing them between your fingers – the skins will rise to the surface.

3 Heat the oil in a large non-stick pan or flameproof casserole and cook the onion and garlic, if using, for 8–10 minutes, or until golden.

4 Stir in the canned and puréed fresh tomatoes and cumin, then add the stock and stir well. Cook for 10 minutes.

5 Add the chickpeas and simmer, uncovered, for a further 30–40 minutes.

6 Rinse the preserved lemon and cut away the flesh and pith. Cut the peel into slivers and stir into the chickpeas along with the chopped coriander. Serve immediately.

Energy 122kcal/516kJ; Protein 5.9g; Carbohydrate 16.5g, of which sugars 5.2g; Fat 4.1g, of which saturates 0.6g, of which polyunsaturates 1.3g; Cholesterol 0mg; Calcium 44mg; Fibre 4.2g; Sodium 157mg.

LENTIL FRITTATA ★★

THROUGHOUT THE MEDITERRANEAN A VARIETY OF THICK, VEGETABLE OMELETTES ARE COOKED.
THIS TASTY SUPPER DISH COMBINES GREEN LENTILS, RED ONIONS, BROCCOLI AND CHERRY TOMATOES.

SERVES SIX

INGREDIENTS
    75g/3oz/scant ½ cup green lentils
    225g/8oz small broccoli florets
    2 red onions, halved and thickly sliced
    15ml/1 tbsp olive oil
    8 eggs
    45ml/3 tbsp water
    45ml/3 tbsp chopped fresh mixed
      herbs, such as oregano, parsley,
      tarragon and chives, plus extra
      sprigs to garnish
    175g/6oz cherry tomatoes, halved
    salt and ground black pepper

1 Place the lentils in a pan, cover with cold water and bring to the boil, then reduce the heat and simmer for 25 minutes until tender. Add the broccoli, return to the boil and cook for 1 minute.

VARIATIONS
Use green beans, halved, in place of broccoli florets. Use standard white onions in place of red onions.

2 Meanwhile place the onion slices and olive oil in a shallow earthenware dish or cazuela about 23–25cm/9–10in in diameter, and place in a cold (unheated) oven. Set the oven to 200°C/400°F Gas 6 and cook for 25 minutes.

3 In a bowl, whisk together the eggs, water, a pinch of salt and plenty of black pepper. Stir in the chopped herbs and set aside.

4 Drain the lentils and broccoli and stir into the onions. Add the cherry tomatoes and sir gently to combine.

5 Pour the egg mixture evenly over the vegetables. Reduce the oven temperature to 190°C/375°F/Gas 5. Return the dish to the oven and cook for 10 minutes, then push the mixture into the centre of the dish using a spatula, allowing the raw egg mixture in the centre to flow to the edges.

6 Return the dish to the oven and cook the frittata for a further 15 minutes, or until it is just set. Garnish with sprigs of fresh herbs and serve warm, cut into thick wedges.

Energy 182kcal/761kJ; Protein 14.2g; Carbohydrate 14.1g, of which sugars 5.7g; Fat 8.2g, of which saturates 2.2g, of which polyunsaturates 1.2g; Cholesterol 254mg; Calcium 99mg; Fibre 3.2g; Sodium 108mg.

VEGETABLE COUSCOUS ★★

A North African favourite that is perfect for cool summer evenings, this spicy dish makes an excellent low-fat meal for vegetarians.

SERVES 4

INGREDIENTS

15ml/1 tbsp olive oil
1 onion, chopped
2 garlic cloves, crushed
5ml/1 tsp ground cumin
5ml/1 tsp paprika
400g/14oz can chopped tomatoes
300ml/½ pint/1¼ cups
  vegetable stock
1 cinnamon stick
generous pinch of saffron threads
4 baby aubergines (eggplants), quartered
8 baby courgettes (zucchini), trimmed
8 baby carrots
225g/8oz/1⅓ cups couscous
425g/15oz can chickpeas, rinsed
  and drained
175g/6oz/¾ cup pitted prunes
45ml/3 tbsp chopped fresh parsley
45ml/3 tbsp chopped fresh
  coriander (cilantro)
10–15ml/2–3 tsp harissa
salt, to taste

1 Heat the oil in a large non-stick pan. Add the onion and garlic and cook gently for 5 minutes, or until soft. Add the cumin and paprika and cook, stirring, for 1 minute.

2 Add the tomatoes, stock, cinnamon stick, saffron threads, aubergines, courgettes and carrots. Season with salt. Bring to the boil, then reduce the heat, cover and cook for 20 minutes until the vegetables are just tender.

3 Line a steamer, metal sieve (strainer) or colander with a double thickness of muslin (cheesecloth) and set aside. Soak the couscous according to the instructions on the packet. Add the chickpeas and prunes to the vegetables and cook for 5 minutes. Fork the couscous to break up any lumps and spread it in the prepared steamer. Place on top of the vegetables, cover, and cook for 5 minutes, or until hot.

4 Stir the chopped parsley and coriander into the vegetables. Heap the couscous on to a warmed serving plate. Using a slotted spoon, arrange the vegetables on top. Spoon over a little sauce and toss gently to combine. Stir the harissa into the remaining sauce and serve separately.

Energy 397kcal/1671kJ; Protein 14.8g; Carbohydrate 71.5g, of which sugars 26g; Fat 7.6g, of which saturates 1g, of which polyunsaturates 2.2g; Cholesterol 0mg; Calcium 137mg; Fibre 12g; Sodium 253mg.

TAGINE OF BUTTER BEANS, CHERRY TOMATOES AND OLIVES ★★

SERVE THIS HEARTY AND HEALTHY MOROCCAN BUTTER BEAN DISH ON ITS OWN, OR WITH A LEAFY SALAD AND FRESH CRUSTY BREAD AS A MAIN MEAL.

SERVES FOUR

INGREDIENTS
  115g/4oz/⅔ cup butter (lima) beans,
    soaked overnight
  15ml/1 tbsp olive oil
  1 onion, chopped
  2–3 garlic cloves, crushed
  25g/1oz fresh root ginger, peeled
    and chopped
  pinch of saffron threads
  16 cherry tomatoes
  generous pinch of granulated sugar
  handful of fleshy black olives, pitted
  5ml/1 tsp ground cinnamon
  5ml/1 tsp paprika
  small bunch of chopped fresh
    flat leaf parsley
  salt and ground black pepper

1 Rinse the beans and place them in a large pan with plenty of fresh water. Bring to the boil and boil for about 10 minutes, then reduce the heat and simmer gently for 1–1½ hours, or until tender. Drain the beans and refresh under cold water.

2 Heat the olive oil in a heavy non-stick pan. Add the onion, garlic and ginger, and cook for about 10 minutes, or until softened but not browned. Stir in the saffron threads, followed by the cherry tomatoes and a sprinkling of sugar.

3 Continue to cook and as the tomatoes begin to soften, stir in the butter beans. When the tomatoes have heated through, stir in the olives, cinnamon and paprika. Season to taste with salt and pepper and sprinkle over the chopped parsley. Serve immediately.

COOK'S TIP
If you are in a hurry, you could use two 400g/14oz cans of butter (lima) beans for this tagine. Make sure you rinse the beans well and drain before adding them, as canned beans tend to be salty.

Energy 177kcal/742kJ; Protein 7.3g; Carbohydrate 18.8g, of which sugars 4.4g; Fat 8.7g, of which saturates 1.2g, of which polyunsaturates 1.6g; Cholesterol 0mg; Calcium 82mg; Fibre 5.2g; Sodium 861mg.

PARMIGIANA DI MELANZANE ★★

THIS FLAVOURSOME ITALIAN DISH CAN BE SERVED AS A VEGETARIAN MAIN COURSE, OR AS AN ACCOMPANIMENT TO LEAN MEAT OR CHICKEN DISHES.

SERVES EIGHT

INGREDIENTS
900g/2lb aubergines (eggplants),
    sliced lengthways
30ml/2 tbsp olive oil
600ml/1 pint/2½ cups garlic and
    herb passata (bottled strained
    tomatoes)
115g/4oz/1¼ cups freshly grated
    Parmesan cheese
salt and ground black pepper

COOK'S TIP
Choose good-quality fresh Parmesan cheese (Parmigiano Reggiano is the best of Italy's Parmesan cheeses) for this recipe. Avoid the pre-grated long-life Parmesan cheeses, which are inferior in quality and flavour.

1 Preheat the grill (broiler) to high. Lightly brush the aubergine slices with the oil and season with salt and pepper to taste. Arrange the aubergine slices in a single layer on a grill (broiling) pan and grill (broil) for 4–5 minutes on each side, or until golden and tender. (You will have to do this in batches.)

VARIATION
For a delicious variation, layer a few artichoke hearts between the slices of aubergine.

2 Preheat the oven to 190°C/375°F/ Gas 5. Spoon a little passata into a large baking dish. Arrange a single layer of aubergine slices over the top and sprinkle with some grated Parmesan. Repeat the layers of passata, aubergine and Parmesan, until all the ingredients have been used up, finishing with a good sprinkling of Parmesan.

3 Bake in the oven for 20–25 minutes, or until golden and bubbling. Serve piping hot.

Energy 117kcal/490kJ; Protein 7.3g; Carbohydrate 4.7g, of which sugars 4.5g; Fat 7.9g, of which saturates 3.5g, of which polyunsaturates 0.6g; Cholesterol 14mg; Calcium 191mg; Fibre 2.7g; Sodium 332mg.

STUFFED TOMATOES AND PEPPERS ★★

*COLOURFUL PEPPERS AND TOMATOES MAKE PERFECT CONTAINERS FOR VARIOUS VEGETABLE STUFFINGS.
THIS LOW-FAT RICE AND HERB VERSION FROM GREECE USES TYPICALLY GREEK INGREDIENTS.*

2 Halve the peppers lengthways, leaving the cores intact. Scoop out and discard the seeds. Brush the peppers with 10ml/2 tsp of the oil and bake in the oven on a baking sheet for 15 minutes. Place the peppers and tomatoes cut side up in a shallow ovenproof dish and season with salt and pepper. Set aside.

3 Heat the remaining oil in a non-stick frying pan and cook the onions for 5 minutes. Add the garlic and chopped almonds and cook for a further 1 minute.

4 Remove the pan from the heat and stir in the rice, chopped tomatoes, chopped mint and parsley, and sultanas. Season well with salt and pepper, then spoon the mixture into the tomatoes and peppers.

SERVES FOUR

INGREDIENTS

2 large ripe tomatoes
1 green (bell) pepper
1 yellow or orange (bell) pepper
20ml/4 tsp olive oil
2 onions, chopped
2 garlic cloves, crushed
25g/1oz/¼ cup blanched
  almonds, chopped
75g/3oz/scant ½ cup long grain rice,
  boiled and drained
15g/½ oz chopped fresh mint
15g/½ oz chopped fresh parsley
25g/1oz sultanas (golden raisins)
15g/½ oz ground almonds
salt and ground black pepper
chopped fresh mixed herbs, to garnish

1 Preheat the oven to 190°C/375°F/Gas 5. Cut the tomatoes in half and scoop out the pulp and seeds using a teaspoon. Leave the tomatoes to drain on kitchen paper with cut sides down. Roughly chop the tomato pulp and seeds. Set aside.

5 Pour 150ml/¼ pint/⅔ cup boiling water around the tomatoes and peppers and bake, uncovered, in the oven for 20 minutes. Sprinkle with the ground almonds. Return to the oven and bake for a further 20 minutes, or until turning golden. Serve garnished with chopped mixed herbs.

Energy 234kcal/981kJ; Protein 5.7g; Carbohydrate 32.5g, of which sugars 14.5g; Fat 9.9g, of which saturates 1.2g, of which polyunsaturates 1.9g; Cholesterol 0mg; Calcium 71mg; Fibre 3.6g; Sodium 14mg.

CLASSIC MIXED MUSHROOM RISOTTO ★★

A CLASSIC RISOTTO OF MIXED MUSHROOMS, HERBS AND FRESH PARMESAN CHEESE, THIS IS BEST SIMPLY SERVED WITH A MIXED LEAF SALAD TOSSED IN A LIGHT FAT-FREE DRESSING.

SERVES FOUR

INGREDIENTS
    15ml/1 tbsp olive oil
    4 shallots, finely chopped
    2 garlic cloves, crushed
    10g/¼oz dried porcini mushrooms,
      soaked in 150ml/¼ pint/⅔ cup hot
      water for 20 minutes
    450g/1lb mixed mushrooms, such
      as closed cup, chestnut and field
      (portabello) mushrooms, sliced
    250g/9oz/1¼ cups long grain rice
    900ml/1½ pints/3¾ cups well-
      flavoured vegetable stock
    30–45ml/2–3 tbsp chopped fresh
      flat leaf parsley
    50g/2oz/⅔ cup freshly grated
      Parmesan cheese
    salt and ground black pepper

1 Heat the oil in a large pan, then add the shallots and garlic and cook gently for 5 minutes, stirring continuously.

2 Drain the porcini, reserving their liquid, and chop roughly. Add all the mushrooms to the pan with the porcini soaking liquid, the rice and 300ml/ ½ pint/1¼ cups of the stock.

3 Bring to the boil, then reduce the heat and simmer uncovered, stirring frequently, until all the liquid has been absorbed. Add a ladleful of hot stock and stir until it has been absorbed.

4 Continue cooking and adding the hot stock, a ladleful at a time, stirring frequently, until the rice is cooked and creamy but *al dente*. This should take about 35 minutes and it may not be necessary to add all the stock.

5 Season to taste with salt and pepper, then stir in the chopped parsley and grated Parmesan and serve at once. Alternatively, sprinkle the Parmesan over the risotto just before serving.

Energy 328kcal/1386kJ; Protein 11.7g; Carbohydrate 52.8g, of which sugars 2.1g; Fat 9.3g, of which saturates 3.5g, of which polyunsaturates 1.3g; Cholesterol 13mg; Calcium 189mg; Fibre 3.2g; Sodium 148mg.

VEGETABLE MOUSSAKA ★★★

THIS IS A REALLY FLAVOURSOME, LOW-FAT VEGETARIAN ALTERNATIVE TO CLASSIC MEAT MOUSSAKA. SERVE IT WITH WARM BREAD AND A GLASS OR TWO OF RUSTIC RED WINE.

SERVES SIX

INGREDIENTS

450g/1lb aubergines
  (eggplants), sliced
115g/4oz/½ cup dried whole
  green lentils
600ml/1 pint/2½ cups
  vegetable stock
1 bay leaf
225g/8oz fresh tomatoes
25ml/1½ tbsp olive oil
1 onion, sliced
1 garlic clove, crushed
225g/8oz/3 cups mushrooms, sliced
400g/14oz can chickpeas, rinsed
  and drained
400g/14oz can chopped tomatoes
30ml/2 tbsp tomato purée (paste)
10ml/2 tsp dried basil
300ml/½ pint/1¼ cups low-fat
  natural (plain) yogurt
3 eggs
50g/2oz/½ cup half-fat mature
  (sharp) Cheddar cheese, grated
salt and ground black pepper
fresh flat leaf parsley sprigs,
  to garnish

1 Sprinkle the aubergine slices with salt and place in a colander. Cover and leave over a sink for 30 minutes to allow any bitter juices to be extracted.

VARIATIONS

• Use brown cap (cremini), closed cup or button (white) mushrooms, or a mixture, for this recipe.
• Use canned borlotti, flageolet or cannellini beans in place of chickpeas.

2 Meanwhile, place the lentils, stock and bay leaf in a pan. Cover, bring to the boil and simmer for about 20 minutes, or until the lentils are just tender. Drain well and keep warm.

3 If you like, skin the fresh tomatoes, then roughly chop them.

4 Heat 10ml/2 tsp of the oil in a large, non-stick pan, add the onion and garlic, and cook, stirring, for 5 minutes. Stir in the lentils, mushrooms, chickpeas, fresh and canned tomatoes, tomato purée, basil and 45ml/3 tbsp water. Bring to the boil, cover and simmer gently for 10 minutes.

5 Preheat the oven to 180°C/350°F/ Gas 4. Rinse the aubergine slices, drain and pat dry. Heat the remaining oil in a non-stick frying pan and fry the slices in batches for 3–4 minutes, turning once.

6 Season the lentil mixture. Layer the aubergines and lentils in an ovenproof dish, starting with aubergines and finishing with the lentil mixture.

7 Beat together the yogurt, eggs and salt and pepper, and pour the mixture into the dish. Sprinkle with cheese and bake in the oven for 45 minutes. Serve, garnished with parsley sprigs.

Energy 285kcal/1202kJ; Protein 20.2g; Carbohydrate 29.6g, of which sugars 9.8g; Fat 10.5g, of which saturates 2.7g, of which polyunsaturates 2.2g; Cholesterol 99mg; Calcium 240mg; Fibre 7.5g; Sodium 306mg.

SPEEDY LASAGNE <u>WITH</u> MIXED MUSHROOMS ★★

THIS SIMPLE-TO-ASSEMBLE LOW-FAT VEGETARIAN VERSION OF LASAGNE REQUIRES NEITHER BAKING NOR THE LENGTHY PREPARATION OF VARIOUS SAUCES AND FILLINGS, BUT IS NO LESS DELICIOUS.

2 Heat the olive oil in a large, heavy non-stick frying pan and sauté the soaked mushrooms over a high heat for 5 minutes, or until the edges are slightly crisp. Reduce the heat, then add the garlic and fresh mushrooms, and sauté for a further 5 minutes, or until tender, stirring occasionally.

3 Add the wine and cook for 5–7 minutes, or until reduced. Stir in the tomatoes, sugar and seasoning and cook over a medium heat for about 5 minutes, or until thickened.

4 Meanwhile, cook the lasagne according to the instructions on the packet, until it is *al dente*. Drain lightly – the pasta should still be moist.

SERVES FOUR

INGREDIENTS
  40g/1½oz/¾ cup dried porcini
    mushrooms
  20ml/4 tsp olive oil
  1 large garlic clove, chopped
  375g/13oz mixed mushrooms,
    including brown cap (cremini),
    field (portabello), shiitake and
    wild varieties, roughly sliced
  175ml/6fl oz/¾ cup dry white wine
  90ml/6 tbsp canned chopped tomatoes
  2.5ml/½ tsp granulated sugar
  8 fresh lasagne sheets
  40g/1½oz/½ cup freshly grated
    Parmesan cheese
  salt and ground black pepper
  fresh basil leaves, to garnish

1 Place the porcini mushrooms in a bowl and cover with boiling water. Leave to soak for 15 minutes, then drain and rinse. Set aside.

5 To serve, spoon a little of the mushroom sauce on to each of four warm serving plates. Place a sheet of lasagne on top and spoon a quarter of the remaining mushroom sauce over each serving. Sprinkle with some Parmesan and top with another pasta sheet. Sprinkle with black pepper and more Parmesan and garnish with basil leaves. Serve immediately.

Energy 117kcal/487kJ; Protein 5.8g; Carbohydrate 1.3g, of which sugars 1.2g; Fat 6.8g, of which saturates 2.6g, of which polyunsaturates 0.7g; Cholesterol 10mg; Calcium 131mg; Fibre 1.3g; Sodium 118mg.

FUSILLI ^{WITH} TOMATO ^{AND} BALSAMIC VINEGAR SAUCE ★★

THIS IS A MODERN ITALIAN-STYLE RECIPE. THE INTENSE, SWEET-SOUR FLAVOUR OF BALSAMIC VINEGAR GIVES A PLEASANT KICK TO A SAUCE MADE WITH CANNED TOMATOES.

SERVES SIX

INGREDIENTS

   2 x 400g/14oz cans chopped Italian
     plum tomatoes
   2 sun-dried tomatoes in oil, drained
     and thinly sliced
   2 garlic cloves, crushed
   30ml/2 tbsp olive oil
   5ml/1 tsp granulated sugar
   350g/12oz/3 cups fresh or
     dried fusilli
   45ml/3 tbsp balsamic vinegar
   salt and ground black pepper
   a rocket (arugula) salad and
     coarsely shaved Pecorino cheese,
     to serve (optional)

COOK'S TIP
Remember, the cooking time for fresh and dried pasta is different – a shorter cooking time for fresh pasta – so follow the packet instructions carefully.

1 Put the canned and sun-dried tomatoes in a medium pan with the garlic, olive oil and sugar. Add salt and pepper to taste. Bring to the boil, stirring, then reduce the heat and simmer for about 30 minutes, or until reduced.

2 Meanwhile, cook the pasta in a pan of salted boiling water, according to the instructions on the packet.

3 Add the balsamic vinegar to the tomato sauce and stir to mix evenly. Cook for 1–2 minutes, then remove from the heat and adjust the seasoning to taste.

4 Drain the pasta and turn it into a warmed serving bowl. Pour the sauce over the pasta and toss well. Serve immediately, with a rocket salad and a little shaved Pecorino, if you like.

Energy 255kcal/1082kJ; Protein 7.9g; Carbohydrate 47.4g, of which sugars 6.1g; Fat 5.1g, of which saturates 0.8g, of which polyunsaturates 1g; Cholesterol 0mg; Calcium 24mg; Fibre 3g; Sodium 14mg.

CONCHIGLIE ^{WITH} ROASTED VEGETABLES ★★

*NOTHING COULD BE SIMPLER — OR MORE DELICIOUS — THAN TOSSING FRESHLY COOKED PASTA WITH
ROASTED VEGETABLES. THE FLAVOUR IS SUPERB AND THIS DISH IS LOW IN FAT TOO!*

SERVES SIX

INGREDIENTS

1 red (bell) pepper, seeded and cut
   into 1cm/½in squares
1 yellow or orange (bell) pepper,
   seeded and cut into 1cm/½in
   squares
1 small aubergine (eggplant),
   roughly diced
2 courgettes (zucchini), roughly diced
30ml/2 tbsp extra virgin olive oil
15ml/1 tbsp chopped fresh
   flat leaf parsley
5ml/1 tsp dried oregano or marjoram
250g/9oz baby Italian plum
   tomatoes, hulled and halved
   lengthways
2 garlic cloves, roughly chopped
350–400g/12–14oz/3–3½ cups
   dried conchiglie
salt and ground black pepper
4–6 fresh marjoram or oregano
   flowers, to garnish

1 Preheat the oven to 190°C/375°F/
Gas 5. Rinse the prepared peppers,
aubergine and courgettes in a colander
under cold running water, drain well,
then put the vegetables in a large,
non-stick roasting pan.

2 Drizzle the olive oil over the
vegetables and sprinkle with the
chopped fresh and dried herbs. Add
salt and pepper to taste and toss to
mix well. Roast in the oven for about
30 minutes, stirring two or three times.

3 Stir the halved tomatoes and
chopped garlic into the vegetable
mixture, then roast for a further
20 minutes, stirring once or twice.
Meanwhile, cook the pasta according
to the instructions on the packet.

4 Drain the pasta and tip it into a
warmed serving bowl. Add the roasted
vegetables and any cooking juices
and toss well. Serve the hot pasta and
vegetables in warmed bowls, sprinkling
each portion with a few herb flowers,
to garnish.

Energy 281kcal/1188kJ; Protein 9.8g; Carbohydrate 50.8g, of which sugars 9.1g; Fat 5.7g, of which saturates 0.9g, of which polyunsaturates 1.2g; Cholesterol 0mg; Calcium 63mg; Fibre 5.1g; Sodium 13mg.

SPAGHETTI WITH FRESH TOMATO SAUCE ★★

THE HEAT FROM THE PASTA RELEASES THE DELICIOUS FLAVOURS OF THIS SAUCE. USE TRULY RIPE PLUM TOMATOES, AS THE AROMATIC QUALITY OF GOOD TOMATOES IMPROVES THE FLAVOUR OF THIS SAUCE.

SERVES FOUR

INGREDIENTS
675g/1½lb ripe Italian
    plum tomatoes or sweet
    cherry tomatoes
20ml/4 tsp extra virgin olive oil
    or sunflower oil
1 onion, finely chopped
350g/12oz fresh or dried spaghetti
a small handful fresh basil leaves
salt and ground black pepper
coarsely shaved Parmesan cheese,
    to serve (optional)

COOK'S TIPS
• The Italian plum tomatoes called San Marzano are the best variety to use. When fully ripe, they have thin skins that peel off easily.
• In Italy, cooks often make this sauce in bulk in the summer months and freeze it for later use. Let it cool, then freeze in usable quantities in rigid containers. Thaw before reheating.

1 With a sharp knife, cut a cross in the base end of each tomato. Plunge the tomatoes, a few at a time, into a bowl of boiling water. Leave for 30 seconds or so, then lift them out with a slotted spoon and drop them into a bowl of cold water. Drain well. The skin will have begun to peel back from the crosses. Remove it entirely.

2 Place the tomatoes on a chopping board and cut into quarters, then eighths, and chop as finely as possible.

3 Heat the oil in a large non-stick pan, add the onion and cook over a low heat, stirring frequently, for about 5 minutes, or until softened and lightly coloured.

4 Add the tomatoes, season with salt and pepper to taste, bring to a simmer, then reduce the heat to low and cover the pan with a lid. Cook, stirring occasionally, for 30–40 minutes, or until the mixture is thick.

5 Meanwhile, cook the pasta in a separate pan, according to the instructions on the packet. Shred the basil leaves finely, or tear them into small pieces.

6 Remove the sauce from the heat, stir in the shredded basil and adjust the seasoning to taste. Drain the pasta, then tip the spaghetti into a warmed bowl, pour the sauce over and toss to mix well. Serve immediately, sprinkled with shaved fresh Parmesan, if you like.

Energy 360kcal/1531kJ; Protein 11.9g; Carbohydrate 71.3g, of which sugars 9g; Fat 5.1g, of which saturates 0.8g, of which polyunsaturates 1.3g; Cholesterol 0mg; Calcium 38mg; Fibre 4.4g; Sodium 18mg.

PASTA <u>WITH</u> GREEN PESTO SAUCE ★★★

TRADITIONALLY MADE WITH LASHINGS OF OLIVE OIL, THIS SIMPLE PESTO SAUCE IS STILL FULL OF FLAVOUR BUT RELATIVELY LOW IN FAT. SERVED WITH HOT PASTA, IT CREATES A TASTY SUPPER DISH.

2 Meanwhile, put half the basil and half the parsley, the garlic clove, pine nuts and curd cheese into a blender or food processor fitted with a metal blade and process until smooth.

3 Add the remaining basil and parsley, together with the Parmesan cheese and seasoning. Process until the herbs are finely chopped, and the mixture is well combined.

4 Toss the hot pasta with the pesto and serve on warmed plates. Garnish with basil sprigs.

SERVES FOUR

INGREDIENTS
225g/8oz/2 cups dried pasta such as spirals or bows
50g/2oz/1 cup fresh basil leaves
25g/1oz/½ cup fresh parsley sprigs
1 garlic clove, crushed
25g/1oz/¼ cup pine nuts
115g/4oz/½ cup curd (farmer's) cheese
30ml/2 tbsp freshly grated Parmesan cheese
salt and ground black pepper
a few sprigs fresh basil, to garnish

1 Cook the pasta in a large pan of lightly salted boiling water for 8–10 minutes, or until *al dente*. Drain well.

Energy 314kcal/1322kJ; Protein 15.4g; Carbohydrate 43.5g, of which sugars 3.6g; Fat 10.3g, of which saturates 3.4g, of which polyunsaturates 3.2g; Cholesterol 14mg; Calcium 176mg; Fibre 2.7g; Sodium 216mg.

VEGETABLE AND MACARONI BAKE ★★

A WELCOME CHANGE FROM MACARONI CHEESE, THIS FLAVOURFUL LOW-FAT RECIPE IS EXCELLENT SERVED WITH A SELECTION OF STEAMED FRESH VEGETABLES.

SERVES SIX

INGREDIENTS
225g/8oz/2¼ cups dried
  whole-wheat (wholemeal) macaroni
225g/8oz leeks, washed and sliced
45ml/3 tbsp vegetable stock
225g/8oz broccoli florets
50g/2oz/¼ cup half-fat spread
50g/2oz/½ cup plain (all-purpose)
  wholemeal (whole-wheat) flour
900ml/1½ pints/3¾ cups
  skimmed milk
150g/5oz/1¼ cups grated half-fat
  mature (sharp) Cheddar cheese
5ml/1 tsp prepared English
  (hot) mustard
350g/12oz can corn kernels
25g/1oz/½ cup fresh wholemeal
  (whole-wheat) breadcrumbs
30ml/2 tbsp chopped fresh parsley
2 tomatoes, cut into eighths
salt and ground black pepper

4 Remove the pan from the heat, add 115g/4oz/1 cup of the cheese and stir until it has melted and is well blended with the white sauce.

5 Add the macaroni, leeks, broccoli, mustard, drained corn kernels and seasoning and mix well. Transfer the mixture to an ovenproof dish.

6 Mix the remaining cheese, breadcrumbs and chopped parsley together and sprinkle this mixture evenly over the top. Arrange the tomatoes on top and then bake in the oven for about 30–40 minutes, or until bubbling and golden brown on top. Serve immediately.

1 Preheat the oven to 200°C/400°F/ Gas 6. Cook the macaroni in a large pan of lightly salted, boiling water for about 10 minutes, or until just tender. Drain well and keep warm.

2 Meanwhile, cook the leeks in the stock in a separate pan for about 10 minutes, or until tender, then strain and set aside. Blanch the broccoli in boiling water for 2 minutes, drain and set aside.

3 Put the half-fat spread, flour and milk in a pan. Heat gently, whisking continuously, until the sauce comes to the boil and thickens. Simmer gently for 3 minutes, stirring.

Energy 415kcal/1753kJ; Protein 23.2g; Carbohydrate 62.2g, of which sugars 15.9g; Fat 10g, of which saturates 4.5g, of which polyunsaturates 1.5g; Cholesterol 17mg; Calcium 454mg; Fibre 4.3g; Sodium 463mg.

TAGLIATELLE WITH BROCCOLI AND SPINACH ★★

THIS IS AN EXCELLENT VEGETARIAN SUPPER DISH. IT IS NUTRITIOUS AND FILLING, AND NEEDS NO ACCOMPANIMENT. IF YOU LIKE, YOU CAN USE TAGLIATELLE FLECKED WITH HERBS.

SERVES FOUR

INGREDIENTS
  2 heads broccoli
  450g/1lb fresh spinach,
    stalks removed
  freshly grated nutmeg, to taste
  450g/1lb fresh or dried
    egg tagliatelle
  30ml/2 tbsp extra virgin olive oil
  juice of ½ lemon, or to taste
  salt and ground black pepper
  freshly grated Parmesan cheese,
    to serve (optional)

2 Add salt to the water in the steamer and fill the steamer pan with boiling water, then add the pasta and cook according to the instructions on the packet. Meanwhile, chop the broccoli and spinach in the colander.

3 Drain the pasta. Heat the oil in the pasta pan, add the pasta and chopped vegetables and toss over a medium heat until evenly mixed. Sprinkle in the lemon juice and plenty of black pepper, then taste and add more lemon juice, salt and nutmeg, if you like. Serve immediately, sprinkled with black pepper and freshly grated Parmesan, if you like.

1 Put the broccoli in the basket of a steamer, cover and steam over a pan of boiling water for 10 minutes. Add the spinach to the broccoli, cover and steam for a further 4–5 minutes, or until both are tender. Towards the end of the cooking time, sprinkle the vegetables with freshly grated nutmeg and salt and pepper to taste. Transfer the vegetables to a colander and set aside.

VARIATIONS
• If you like, add a sprinkling of crushed dried chillies to the dish with the black pepper in Step 3.
• To add both texture and protein, garnish the finished dish with one or two handfuls of toasted pine nuts. They are often served with broccoli and spinach in Italy. (Remember though, the addition of pine nuts will increase the fat content of the dish.)

Energy 520kcal/2199kJ; Protein 24.4g; Carbohydrate 88.3g, of which sugars 8g; Fat 10g, of which saturates 1.5g, of which polyunsaturates 2.8g; Cholesterol 0mg; Calcium 318mg; Fibre 10.2g; Sodium 175mg.

RIGATONI WITH TOMATOES AND MUSHROOMS ★★

THIS IS A GOOD SAUCE TO MAKE FROM STORE-CUPBOARD INGREDIENTS BECAUSE IT DOESN'T RELY ON ANYTHING FRESH, APART FROM THE SHALLOTS AND HERBS. IT IS PERFECT FOR A LOW-FAT END-OF-WEEK MEAL WHEN YOU HAVE RUN OUT OF FOOD AND ENERGY FOR COOKING.

SERVES FOUR

INGREDIENTS
2 x 15g/½ oz packets dried
 wild mushrooms
175ml/6fl oz/¾ cup warm water
10ml/2 tsp olive oil
2 shallots, finely chopped
2 garlic cloves, crushed
a few sprigs fresh marjoram,
 chopped, plus extra to garnish
1 handful fresh flat leaf
 parsley, chopped
15g/½oz/1 tbsp cold butter
400g/14oz can chopped tomatoes
400g/14oz/3½ cups dried rigatoni
25g/1oz/⅓ cup freshly grated
 Parmesan cheese
salt and ground black pepper

1 Put the dried mushrooms in a bowl, pour the warm water over to cover and soak for 15–20 minutes. Tip into a fine sieve (strainer) set over a bowl and squeeze the mushrooms with your fingers to release as much liquid as possible. Reserve the mushrooms and the strained liquid.

2 Heat the oil in a non-stick frying pan and cook the shallots, garlic and chopped herbs over a low heat, stirring frequently, for about 5 minutes. Add the butter and soaked mushrooms, and stir until the butter has melted. Season well with salt and pepper.

3 Stir in the tomatoes and the reserved liquid from the soaked mushrooms. Bring to the boil, then reduce the heat, cover and simmer, stirring occasionally, for about 20 minutes. Meanwhile, cook the pasta according to the instructions on the packet.

4 Taste the sauce and adjust the seasoning. Drain the pasta, reserving some of the cooking water, and tip the pasta into a warmed large bowl. Add the sauce and the grated Parmesan and toss to mix. Add a little cooking water if you prefer a runnier sauce. Serve immediately, garnished with marjoram sprigs. Serve with more Parmesan cheese, which can be handed around separately, if you like.

VARIATION
If you have a bottle of wine open, red or white, add a splash when you add the canned tomatoes.

Energy 438kcal/1857kJ; Protein 15.8g; Carbohydrate 78.8g, of which sugars 7.6g; Fat 8.9g, of which saturates 3.8g, of which polyunsaturates 1.3g; Cholesterol 14mg; Calcium 137mg; Fibre 4.7g; Sodium 108mg.

LINGUINE WITH SUN-DRIED TOMATOES ★

CHOOSE PLAIN SUN-DRIED TOMATOES FOR THIS SAUCE, INSTEAD OF THOSE PRESERVED IN OIL, AS THEY WILL INCREASE THE FAT CONTENT. SERVE WITH A MIXED BABY LEAF SALAD FOR A TASTY SUPPER.

SERVES FOUR

INGREDIENTS
1 garlic clove, crushed
1 celery stick, thinly sliced
115g/4oz/2 cups sun-dried tomatoes, finely chopped
90ml/6 tbsp red wine
8 fresh ripe plum tomatoes
350g/12oz dried linguine
salt and ground black pepper
basil, to garnish

1 Put the garlic, celery, sun-dried tomatoes and wine into a pan, and cook gently for 15 minutes.

2 Meanwhile, plunge the plum tomatoes into a separate pan of boiling water for 30 seconds, then transfer the tomatoes to a pan of cold water. Drain, then slip off their skins. Halve them, remove and discard the seeds and cores, and roughly chop the flesh.

3 Add the tomato flesh to the pan and simmer for a further 5 minutes. Season to taste.

4 Meanwhile, cook the linguine in a large pan of lightly salted boiling water for 8–10 minutes, or until *al dente*. Drain well.

5 Return the pasta to the pan, add half the tomato sauce and toss to mix well. Serve immediately on warmed plates, topped with the remaining sauce.

COOK'S TIP
Add shavings of Parmesan for extra flavour, if you like.

Energy 346kcal/1471kJ; Protein 11.8g; Carbohydrate 70.5g, of which sugars 8.6g; Fat 2.1g, of which saturates 0.4g, of which polyunsaturates 1.1g; Cholesterol 0mg; Calcium 39mg; Fibre 4.4g; Sodium 25mg.

MEDITERRANEAN VEGETABLE LASAGNE ★★

LAYERS OF TASTY VEGETABLE SAUCE AND PASTA, TOPPED WITH A WHITE SAUCE AND SPRINKLED WITH CHEESE, COMBINE TO CREATE THIS DELICIOUS, LOW-FAT LASAGNE, IDEAL FOR VEGETARIANS.

SERVES SIX

INGREDIENTS
   1 small aubergine (eggplant)
   1 large onion, finely chopped
   2 garlic cloves, crushed
   150ml/¼ pint/⅔ cup vegetable stock
   225g/8oz mushrooms, sliced
   400g/14oz can chopped tomatoes
   30ml/2 tbsp tomato purée (paste)
   150ml/¼ pint/⅔ cup red wine
   1.5ml/¼ tsp ground ginger
   5ml/1 tsp mixed dried herbs
   25g/1oz/2 tbsp half-fat spread
   25g/1oz/¼ cup plain (all-purpose)
      flour
   300ml/½ pint/1¼ cups
      semi-skimmed (low-fat) milk
   large pinch of freshly grated nutmeg
   10–12 sheets lasagne
   200g/7oz cottage cheese
   1 egg, beaten
   15g/½oz freshly grated
      Parmesan cheese
   25g/1oz half-fat mature (sharp)
      Cheddar cheese, grated
   salt and ground black pepper

1 Trim the aubergine and cut it into 2.5cm/1in cubes; set aside. Put the onion and garlic into a pan with the stock, cover and cook for about 5 minutes, or until tender.

2 Add the aubergine, mushrooms, tomatoes, tomato purée, wine, ginger, herbs and seasoning. Bring to the boil, then reduce the heat, cover and cook for 15–20 minutes. Remove the lid, increase the heat and cook rapidly until the liquid is reduced by half.

3 Meanwhile, make the white sauce. Put the half-fat spread, flour, milk and nutmeg into a pan. Whisk continuously over a gentle heat, until thickened and smooth. Season to taste.

4 Preheat the oven to 200°C/400°F/ Gas 6. Spoon about a quarter of the vegetable mixture into the base of a 30 x 20 x 5cm/12 x 8 x 2in ovenproof dish. Cover with a layer of lasagne sheets and a quarter of the white sauce.

5 Repeat with two more layers, then cover with the cottage cheese. Beat the egg into the remaining white sauce and pour evenly over the top. Sprinkle with the combined grated Parmesan and Cheddar cheeses.

6 Bake in the oven for 25–30 minutes, or until the top is golden brown. Serve immediately.

Energy 348kcal/1470kJ; Protein 18.1g; Carbohydrate 50.9g, of which sugars 11.2g; Fat 7.5g, of which saturates 3.2g, of which polyunsaturates 1.3g; Cholesterol 44mg; Calcium 217mg; Fibre 4.4g; Sodium 234mg.

FISH AND SHELLFISH

White fish and many types of shellfish are naturally low in fat and form an important part of a healthy low-fat eating plan. Oily fish, although containing more fat, also provide many valuable nutrients in a healthy diet, and the Mediterranean is an abundant source of a wide variety of fish and shellfish, ideal for creating many delicious and nutritious dishes. Choose from tempting recipes such as Roast Monkfish with Garlic, Sea Bass in a Salt Crust and Moroccan Fish Tagine.

MUSSELS WITH A PARSLEY CRUST ★★★

MUSSELS, KNOWN AS MEJILLONES IN SPAIN, GROW TO AN ENORMOUS SIZE IN A VERY SHORT TIME, WITHOUT BECOMING TOUGH. HERE THEY ARE GRILLED WITH A DELICIOUSLY LIGHT, FRAGRANT TOPPING (WHICH HELPS TO PREVENT THE MUSSELS FROM BECOMING OVERCOOKED) TO CREATE A TASTY LUNCH OR SUPPER DISH.

SERVES TWO

INGREDIENTS

    450g/1lb fresh mussels in their shells
    45ml/3 tbsp water
    15ml/1 tbsp melted butter
    10ml/2 tsp olive oil
    25g/1oz/⅓ cup freshly grated
      Parmesan cheese
    30ml/2 tbsp chopped fresh parsley
    2 garlic cloves, finely chopped
    2.5ml/½ tsp coarsely ground
      black pepper
    crusty bread, to serve (optional)

COOK'S TIPS

• Steaming the mussels produces about 250ml/8fl oz/1 cup wonderful shellfish stock that can be used in other fish and shellfish recipes. Once the mussels have been steamed, remove them from the pan and leave the broth liquor to cool, then store it in a sealed container in the refrigerator or freezer.

• Combining fish and shellfish stock is the backbone of many Spanish fish dishes such as hake with green sauce. It is said that the stock from one shellfish makes the best sauce for another.

1 Scrub the mussels thoroughly, scraping off any barnacles with a round-bladed knife and pulling out the gritty beards. Sharply tap any open mussels and discard any that fail to close or whose shells are broken.

2 Place the mussels in a large pan and add the water. Cover the pan with a lid and steam for about 5 minutes, or until the mussel shells have opened.

3 Drain the mussels well and discard any that remain closed. Carefully snap off the top shell from each mussel, leaving the actual flesh still attached to the bottom shell.

4 Balance the shells in a flameproof dish, packing them closely together to make sure that they stay level.

5 Preheat the grill (broiler) to high. Put the melted butter, olive oil, grated Parmesan cheese, chopped parsley, garlic and black pepper in a small bowl and mix well to combine.

6 Spoon a small amount of the cheese and garlic mixture on top of each mussel and gently press down with the back of the spoon.

7 Grill (broil) the mussels for about 2 minutes, or until they are sizzling and golden. Serve the mussels in their shells, with fresh bread, if you like, and a mixed salad.

COOK'S TIP

Give your guest one of the discarded top shells of the mussels. They can be used as a little spoon to free the body from the shell of the next. Scoop up the mussel in the empty shell and tip the shellfish and topping into your mouth.

Energy 190kcal/792kJ; Protein 16g; Carbohydrate 0.3g, of which sugars 0.3g; Fat 13.9g, of which saturates 6.6g, of which polyunsaturates 1g; Cholesterol 53mg; Calcium 274mg; Fibre 0.5g; Sodium 300mg.

OVEN-BAKED PLAICE PROVENÇAL ★

RE-CREATE THE TASTE OF THE MEDITERRANEAN WITH THIS SIMPLE BUT TASTY LOW-FAT FISH CASSEROLE.

SERVES FOUR

INGREDIENTS
    4 large plaice fillets
    2 small red onions
    120ml/4fl oz/½ cup vegetable stock
    60ml/4 tbsp dry red wine
    1 garlic clove, crushed
    2 courgettes (zucchini), sliced
    1 yellow (bell) pepper, seeded
     and sliced
    400g/14oz can chopped tomatoes
    15ml/1 tbsp chopped fresh thyme
    salt and ground black pepper

VARIATION
Use standard onions and white wine,
in place of red onions and red wine.

1 Preheat the oven to 180°C/350°F/
Gas 4. Skin the plaice with a sharp
knife by laying it skin side down.
Holding the tail end, push the knife
between the skin and flesh in a sawing
movement. Hold the knife at a slight
angle with the blade towards the skin.

2 Cut each onion into eight wedges.
Put into a heavy pan with the stock.
Cover, bring to the boil, then reduce
the heat and simmer for 5 minutes.
Uncover and continue to cook, stirring
occasionally, until the stock has
reduced entirely. Add the wine and
garlic to the pan and continue to cook
until the onions are soft.

3 Add the courgettes, yellow pepper,
tomatoes and chopped thyme and
season to taste. Simmer for 3 minutes.
Spoon the sauce into a large casserole.

4 Fold each plaice fillet in half and
place on top of the sauce. Cover and
bake in the oven for 15–20 minutes,
or until the fish is opaque and cooked.
Serve immediately.

Energy 156kcal/659kJ; Protein 20.3g; Carbohydrate 11.7g, of which sugars 10.3g; Fat 2.4g, of which saturates 0.5g, of which polyunsaturates 0.8g; Cholesterol 42mg; Calcium 94mg; Fibre 3.3g; Sodium 134mg.

MUSSELS STEAMED IN WHITE WINE ★

THIS IS THE EASIEST WAY TO SERVE THE SMALL TENDER MUSSELS, BOUCHOTS, WHICH ARE FARMED ALONG MUCH OF THE FRENCH COASTLINE. SERVE WITH PLENTY OF CRUSTY FRENCH BREAD TO DIP IN THE WINE AND ONION JUICES.

SERVES FOUR

INGREDIENTS

2kg/4½lb fresh mussels in
their shells
300ml/½ pint/1¼ cups dry white wine
4–6 large shallots, finely chopped
1 fresh or dried bouquet garni
freshly ground black pepper

1 Discard any broken mussels and those with open shells that refuse to close when tapped. Under cold running water, scrape the mussel shells with a knife to remove any barnacles and pull out the stringy "beards". Soak the mussels in several changes of cold water for at least 1 hour.

2 In a large, heavy, flameproof casserole, combine the wine, shallots, bouquet garni and plenty of black pepper. Bring to the boil over a medium-high heat and cook for 2 minutes.

3 Add the mussels and cook, tightly covered, for 5 minutes, shaking and tossing the pan occasionally, or until the mussels open. Discard any mussels that do not open.

4 Remove and discard the bouquet garni. Using a slotted spoon, divide the mussels among warmed soup plates. Tilt the casserole a little and hold for a few seconds to allow any sand to settle to the bottom.

5 Spoon or pour the cooking liquid over the mussels, dividing it evenly, then serve at once with fresh crusty French bread.

VARIATION
Use 2 small or 1 large red or standard onion(s) in place of the shallots.

Energy 189kcal/799kJ; Protein 26.4g; Carbohydrate 2.4g, of which sugars 1.9g; Fat 3.1g, of which saturates 0.5g, of which polyunsaturates 1g; Cholesterol 60mg; Calcium 308mg; Fibre 0.4g; Sodium 319mg.

HERB-MARINATED MONKFISH
WITH TOMATO COULIS ★★

*A LIGHT BUT WELL-FLAVOURED DISH, PERFECT FOR SUMMERTIME EATING AND ENJOYING AL FRESCO
WITH A GLASS OR TWO OF CHILLED, FRUITY WINE.*

SERVES FOUR

INGREDIENTS
    30ml/2 tbsp olive oil
    finely grated rind and juice of
        1 lime
    30ml/2 tbsp chopped mixed
        fresh herbs
    5ml/1 tsp Dijon mustard
    4 skinless, boneless monkfish fillets
    salt and ground black pepper
    fresh herb sprigs, to garnish
For the coulis
    4 ripe plum tomatoes, skinned
        and chopped
    1 garlic clove, chopped
    10ml/2 tsp olive oil
    15ml/1 tbsp tomato purée (paste)
    30ml/2 tbsp chopped fresh oregano
    5ml/1 tsp soft light brown sugar

1 Place the oil, lime rind and juice, chopped herbs, mustard and salt and pepper in a small bowl and whisk together until thoroughly mixed.

2 Place the monkfish fillets in a shallow, non-metallic container and pour over the lime mixture. Turn the fish several times in the marinade to coat it all over. Cover and chill in the refrigerator for 1–2 hours.

3 Meanwhile, make the coulis. Place all the coulis ingredients in a blender or food processor and process until smooth. Season to taste with salt and pepper, then cover and chill until required.

4 Preheat the oven to 180°C/350°F/ Gas 4. Using a fish slice or metal spatula, place each fish fillet on a sheet of baking parchment paper big enough to hold it in a parcel.

5 Spoon a little marinade over each piece of fish. Gather the paper loosely over the fish and fold over the edges to secure the parcel tightly. Place on a baking sheet.

6 Bake in the oven for 20–30 minutes, or until the fish fillets are cooked, tender and just beginning to flake.

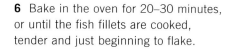
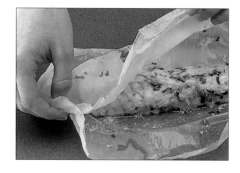

7 Carefully unwrap the parcels and serve the fish fillets immediately, with a little of the chilled coulis served alongside. Garnish with a few fresh herb sprigs.

COOK'S TIP
The coulis can be served hot, if you prefer. Simply make the coulis as directed in the recipe, then pour it into a small pan and heat gently, stirring occasionally, until almost boiling.

Energy 186kcal/784kJ; Protein 24.5g; Carbohydrate 4.7g, of which sugars 4.7g; Fat 7.9g, of which saturates 1.3g, of which polyunsaturates 0.9g; Cholesterol 21mg; Calcium 21mg; Fibre 1.1g; Sodium 45mg.

TUNA, COURGETTE AND PEPPER FRITTATA ★★★

THIS NUTRITIOUS ITALIAN-STYLE OMELETTE IS QUICK AND EASY TO MAKE. SERVE IT SIMPLY, WITH A MIXED LEAF SALAD FOR A TASTY LUNCH OR SUPPER.

SERVES FOUR

INGREDIENTS

15ml/1 tbsp sunflower oil
1 onion, chopped
1 courgette (zucchini), thinly sliced
1 red (bell) pepper, seeded and sliced
4 eggs
30ml/2 tbsp semi-skimmed
  (low-fat) milk
200g/7oz can tuna in brine or water,
  drained and flaked
10ml/2 tsp dried herbes de Provence
50g/2oz/½ cup grated half-fat Red
  Leicester or Cheddar cheese
salt and ground black pepper
mixed leaf salad, to serve

1 Heat half the oil in a shallow, non-stick pan, add the onion, courgette and red pepper and cook, stirring frequently, for 5 minutes.

2 Beat the eggs with the milk in a small bowl. Heat the remaining oil in a heavy, non-stick omelette pan. Add the cooked onion, courgette and red pepper, flaked tuna and dried herbs, and season well with salt and pepper.

3 Pour the egg mixture evenly into the frying pan over the vegetable mixture and cook over a medium heat until the eggs are beginning to set. Pull the sides into the middle to allow the uncooked egg to run on to the pan, then continue cooking undisturbed until the frittata is golden underneath. Meanwhile, preheat the grill (broiler) to medium.

4 Sprinkle the cheese over the top of the frittata and grill (broil) until the cheese has melted and the top is golden.

VARIATIONS
• Use 25g/1oz/⅓ cup freshly grated Parmesan cheese in place of Red Leicester or Cheddar cheese.
• Use canned pink or red salmon in place of tuna.

Energy 214kcal/894kJ; Protein 23.9g; Carbohydrate 5.2g, of which sugars 4.7g; Fat 11.1g, of which saturates 3.4g, of which polyunsaturates 2.7g; Cholesterol 222mg; Calcium 166mg; Fibre 1.4g; Sodium 320mg.

ROAST MONKFISH <u>WITH</u> GARLIC ★★

THIS COMBINATION OF MONKFISH AND SWEET ROASTED GARLIC IS SUPERB. FOR A CONTRAST IN COLOUR, SERVE IT WITH STEAMED VIBRANT GREEN OR FRENCH BEANS, SERVED PLAIN.

SERVES FOUR

INGREDIENTS
    1kg/2¼lb monkfish tail, skinned
    14 fat garlic cloves
    5ml/1 tsp fresh thyme leaves
    30ml/2 tbsp olive oil
    juice of 1 lemon
    2 bay leaves
    salt and ground black pepper

1 Preheat the oven to 220°C/425°F/ Gas 7. Remove any membrane from the monkfish tail and cut out the central bone. Peel 2 garlic cloves and cut them into thin slivers. Sprinkle a quarter of these and half the thyme leaves over the cut side of the fish, then close it up and use fine kitchen string to tie it into a neat shape, like a boned piece of meat. Pat dry with kitchen paper.

2 Make incisions on either side of the fish and push in the remaining garlic slivers. Heat half the olive oil in a frying pan which can safely be used in the oven. When the oil is hot, put in the monkfish and brown it all over for about 5 minutes, or until evenly coloured. Season with salt and pepper, sprinkle with lemon juice and the remaining thyme leaves.

3 Tuck the bay leaves under the monkfish, arrange the remaining (unpeeled) garlic cloves around it and drizzle the remaining olive oil over the fish and the garlic. Transfer the frying pan to the oven and roast the monkfish for 20–25 minutes, or until the flesh is cooked through.

4 Place on a warmed serving dish with the garlic and some green beans. To serve, remove the string and cut the monkfish into 2cm/¾in thick slices.

COOK'S TIPS
• The garlic heads can be used whole.
• When serving the monkfish, invite each guest to pop out the soft garlic pulp with a fork and spread it over the monkfish.
• Use monkfish fillets, if you prefer.

Energy 259kcal/1091kJ; Protein 45.7g; Carbohydrate 4.1g, of which sugars 0.4g; Fat 6.7g, of which saturates 1.1g, of which polyunsaturates 0.8g; Cholesterol 40mg; Calcium 27mg; Fibre 1g; Sodium 51mg.

SEA BASS IN A SALT CRUST ★

BAKING FISH IN A CRUST OF SEA SALT ENHANCES THE FLAVOUR AND BRINGS OUT THE TASTE OF THE SEA. IT IS ALSO AN EASY AND LOW-FAT METHOD OF COOKING A WHOLE FISH. IN SPAIN THE GILT-HEAD BREAM IS THE FISH MOST OFTEN USED, BUT ANY FIRM FISH, SUCH AS GREY MULLET AND STRIPED BASS, CAN BE COOKED THIS WAY. BREAK OPEN THE CRUST AT THE TABLE TO RELEASE THE GLORIOUS AROMA.

SERVES FOUR

INGREDIENTS
    1 sea bass, about 1kg/2¼lb,
      gutted and scaled
    1 sprig each fresh fennel, rosemary
      and thyme
    mixed peppercorns
    2kg/4½lb coarse sea salt
    seaweed or samphire, to garnish
    lemon slices, to serve

COOK'S TIP
In the Mediterranean, fish in salt are often baked whole and ungutted. But supermarkets elsewhere always sell them gutted, so use the opportunity to add flavourings inside.

1 Preheat the oven to 240°C/475°F/Gas 9. Fill the cavity of the sea bass with the fennel, rosemary and thyme sprigs and grind over some of the mixed peppercorns.

2 Spread half the salt in a shallow baking tray and lay the sea bass on it.

3 Cover the fish all over with a 1cm/½in layer of salt, pressing it down firmly. Bake in the oven for 30 minutes, or until the salt coagulates and is beginning to colour.

4 Leave the fish on the baking tray; garnish with seaweed or samphire. Bring the fish to the table in its salt crust. Use a sharp knife to break open the crust. Serve.

COOK'S TIP
Once baked, the salt sticks to the fish skin, and brings it off. Scrape back the layer of salt and lift out the top fillet in sections. Snip the backbone with scissors and lift out. Discard the herbs and remove the bottom fillet pieces. Add a lemon slice to each plate.

Energy 150kcal/632kJ; Protein 29g; Carbohydrate 0g, of which sugars 0g; Fat 3.8g, of which saturates 0.6g, of which polyunsaturates 0.9g; Cholesterol 120mg; Calcium 196mg; Fibre 0g; Sodium 2069mg.

BACALAO <u>WITH</u> SPICY TOMATOES ★★

SALT COD IS A POPULAR INGREDIENT IN SPAIN, NOT JUST A LENTEN NECESSITY. IT IS THE SALT THAT MAKES THE FISH SO CHARACTERFUL, SO DON'T OVERSOAK IT FOR THIS TRADITIONAL RECIPE. LOOK OUT FOR A LOIN PIECE, WHICH HAS VERY LITTLE WASTE; IF YOU CAN'T FIND ONE, BUY A LARGER PIECE TO ENSURE YOU HAVE ENOUGH ONCE ANY VERY DRY BITS HAVE BEEN REMOVED.

SERVES FOUR

INGREDIENTS
    400g/14oz salt cod loin, soaked
      in cold water for 24 hours
    15ml/1 tbsp olive oil
    1 large onion, chopped
    2 garlic cloves, finely chopped
    1½ green (bell) peppers, seeded
      and chopped
    500g/1¼lb ripe tomatoes, skinned
      and chopped, or a 400g/14oz
      can chopped tomatoes
    15ml/1 tbsp tomato purée (paste)
    15ml/1 tbsp clear honey
    1.5ml/¼ tsp dried thyme
    2.5ml/½ tsp cayenne pepper
    juice of ½ lemon (optional)
    2 potatoes
    45ml/3 tbsp stale breadcrumbs
    30ml/2 tbsp finely chopped
      fresh parsley
    salt and ground black pepper

1 Drain the salt cod and place it in a pan. Pour over enough water to cover generously and bring to the boil. Remove the pan from the heat as soon as the water boils, then set aside until cold.

2 Heat the oil in a non-stick pan. Sauté the onion for 5 minutes, then add the garlic. Add the chopped peppers and tomatoes, and cook gently to form a sauce. Stir in the tomato purée, honey, dried thyme, cayenne, black pepper and a little salt. Taste for seasoning: a little lemon juice will make it tangier.

3 Halve the potatoes lengthways and cut them into slices just thicker than a coin. Drain the fish, reserving the cooking water.

4 Preheat the grill (broiler) to medium with a shelf 15cm/6in below it. Bring the reserved fish cooking water to the boil and cook the potatoes for about 8 minutes. Do not add extra salt.

5 Remove the skin and bones from the cod, and pull it into small natural flakes. Spoon one-third of the tomato sauce into a flameproof casserole, top with the potatoes, fish and the remaining sauce. Combine the breadcrumbs and chopped parsley and sprinkle over the top. Place under the grill for 10 minutes. Serve.

Energy 351kcal/1484kJ; Protein 38.1g; Carbohydrate 40.6g, of which sugars 16g; Fat 5.1g, of which saturates 0.9g, of which polyunsaturates 1.2g; Cholesterol 59mg; Calcium 93mg; Fibre 5g; Sodium 517mg.

BAKED SEA BASS WITH FENNEL ★★★

SEA BASS HAS A WONDERFUL FLAVOUR, BUT CHEAPER ALTERNATIVES, SUCH AS SNAPPER OR BREAM, CAN BE USED. SERVE WITH CRISPLY COOKED GREEN BEANS FOR A LIGHT AND FLAVOURFUL LUNCH.

SERVES FOUR

INGREDIENTS

4 fennel bulbs, trimmed
4 tomatoes, skinned and diced
8 canned anchovy fillets, drained and
  halved lengthways
a large pinch of saffron threads,
  soaked in 30ml/2 tbsp hot water
150ml/¼ pint/⅔ cup chicken or
  fish stock
2 red or yellow (bell) peppers, seeded
  and each cut into 12 strips
4 garlic cloves, chopped
15ml/1 tbsp chopped fresh marjoram
25ml/1½ tbsp olive oil
1 sea bass, about 1.8–2kg/4–4½lb,
  scaled and cleaned
salt and ground black pepper
chopped fresh parsley, to garnish

1 Preheat the oven to 200°C/400°F/ Gas 6. Quarter the fennel bulbs lengthways. Cook in a pan of lightly salted boiling water for 5 minutes, until barely tender. Drain, then arrange in a shallow ovenproof dish. Season with pepper, and set aside.

2 Spoon the tomatoes and anchovy strips on top of the fennel. Stir the saffron and its soaking water into the stock and pour the mixture over the tomatoes. Lay the strips of pepper alongside the fennel and sprinkle with the garlic and marjoram. Drizzle 10ml/ 2 tsp of the olive oil over the peppers and season with salt and pepper. Bake the vegetables in the oven for 15 minutes.

3 Season the prepared sea bass inside and out and lay it on top of the fennel and pepper mixture. Drizzle the remaining olive oil over the fish and bake for a further 30–40 minutes, or until the sea bass flesh comes away easily from the bone when tested with the point of a sharp knife. Serve at once, garnished with chopped parsley.

Energy 296kcal/1241kJ; Protein 38.7g; Carbohydrate 12.3g, of which sugars 11.9g; Fat 10.5g, of which saturates 1.6g, of which polyunsaturates 1.9g; Cholesterol 144mg; Calcium 308mg; Fibre 7.2g; Sodium 391mg.

GRILLED HAKE ^{WITH} LEMON ^{AND} CHILLI ★★

CHOOSE FIRM HAKE FILLETS, AS THICK AS POSSIBLE FOR THIS RECIPE. THIS IS AN IDEAL RECIPE IF YOU ARE COUNTING CALORIES, BECAUSE IT IS LOW IN FAT.

SERVES FOUR

INGREDIENTS
 4 hake fillets, about 150g/5oz each
 25ml/1½ tbsp olive oil
 finely grated rind and juice of
  1 unwaxed lemon
 15ml/1 tbsp crushed chilli flakes
 salt and ground black pepper

COOK'S TIP
The rind or zest is the outermost part of citrus fruits such as lemons. For the purest flavour, the zest must be removed from the lemon without a trace of the bitter white pith underneath. Use a zester or a stainless steel potato peeler, or rub the fruit carefully against the finest cutter on a grater to achieve finely grated rind or zest.

1 Preheat the grill (broiler) to high. Brush the hake fillets all over with the olive oil and place them skin side up on a baking sheet.

2 Grill (broil) the fish for 4–5 minutes, until the skin is crispy, then carefully turn them over using a fish slice or metal spatula.

3 Sprinkle the fillets with the lemon rind and chilli flakes and season with salt and black pepper.

4 Grill the fillets for a further 2–3 minutes, or until the hake is cooked through. (Test using the point of a sharp knife; the flesh should flake.) Squeeze over the lemon juice just before serving.

Energy 176kcal/738kJ; Protein 27g; Carbohydrate 0g, of which sugars 0g; Fat 7.6g, of which saturates 1.1g, of which polyunsaturates 1.1g; Cholesterol 35mg; Calcium 21mg; Fibre 0g; Sodium 150mg.

FISH WITH ANISEED TOMATO SAUCE ★★

THIS DELICIOUS LOW-FAT DISH IS PERFECT FOR A DINNER PARTY, AS THE WHITE FLESH OF THE FISH CONTRASTS WITH THE STRIKING RED OF THE SAUCE. THE PASTIS IN THE SAUCE ADDS A SURPRISE TO THE RANGE OF FLAVOURS, AND WILL GIVE YOUR GUESTS A MEAL TO REMEMBER.

SERVES FOUR

INGREDIENTS
    4 white fish cutlets, about
      150g/5oz each
    150ml/¼ pint/⅔ cup fish stock and/
      or dry white wine, for poaching
    1 bay leaf
    a few black peppercorns
    a strip of pared lemon rind
    fresh parsley and lemon wedges,
      to garnish
For the tomato sauce
    400g/14oz can chopped tomatoes
    1 garlic clove
    15ml/1 tbsp sun-dried tomato
      purée (paste)
    15ml/1 tbsp pastis or other aniseed-
      flavoured liqueur
    15ml/1 tbsp drained capers
    12–16 pitted black olives
    salt and ground black pepper

1 Make the sauce. Heat the chopped tomatoes in a pan with the whole garlic clove. Stir in the sun-dried tomato purée.

2 Measure the pastis or other liqueur into the pan, then add the capers and olives. Season to taste with salt and pepper. Heat all the ingredients together for 5 minutes, stirring occasionally, to blend the flavours.

3 Place the fish in a frying pan, pour over the stock and/or wine and add the flavourings. Cover and simmer for 10 minutes, or until the fish flakes easily.

4 Using a slotted spoon, transfer the fish to a heated dish. Strain the stock into the tomato sauce and boil to reduce slightly. Season the sauce, pour it over the fish and serve immediately. Garnish with parsley and lemon wedges.

Energy 187kcal/783kJ; Protein 28.7g; Carbohydrate 3.6g, of which sugars 3.6g; Fat 5.5g, of which saturates 0.9g, of which polyunsaturates 1.2g; Cholesterol 69mg; Calcium 45mg; Fibre 2.2g; Sodium 952mg.

TURBOT IN PARCHMENT ★★

COOKING IN PARCHMENT PARCELS IS NOT NEW, BUT IT IS AN IDEAL WAY TO PREPARE FISH. SERVE THIS LOW-FAT DISH BY PLACING EACH PARCEL ON A PLATE AND LET EACH PERSON OPEN THEIR OWN PARCEL TO SAVOUR THE AROMA. BOILED NEW POTATOES ARE A GOOD ACCOMPANIMENT.

SERVES FOUR

INGREDIENTS

2 carrots, cut into thin julienne strips
2 courgettes (zucchini), cut into thin julienne strips
2 leeks, washed and cut into thin julienne strips
1 fennel bulb, cut into thin julienne strips
2 tomatoes, skinned, seeded and diced
30ml/2 tbsp chopped fresh dill, tarragon or chervil
4 turbot fillets (about 200g/7oz each), cut in half
20ml/4 tsp olive oil
60ml/4 tbsp white wine or fish stock
salt and ground black pepper

1 Preheat the oven to 190°C/375°F/Gas 5.

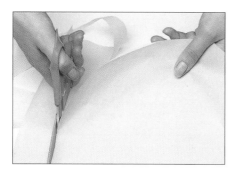

2 Cut four pieces of baking parchment, about 45cm/18in long. Fold each piece in half and cut into a heart shape.

3 Open the paper hearts. Arrange one quarter of each of the vegetables next to the fold of each heart. Sprinkle with salt and pepper and half of the chopped herbs.

COOK'S TIP
Cooking fish and vegetables in paper creates a softer, more tender result, as the food within the package is steamed and baked at the same time.

4 Arrange two pieces of turbot fillet over each bed of vegetables, overlapping the thin end of one piece and the thicker end of the other. Sprinkle the remaining chopped herbs, the olive oil and wine or stock evenly over the fish.

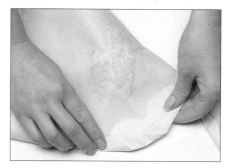

5 Fold the top half of one of the paper hearts over the fish and vegetables and, beginning at the rounded end, fold the edges of the paper over, twisting and folding to form an airtight packet. Repeat with the remaining three.

6 Slide the parcels on to one or two baking sheets and bake for 10 minutes, or until the paper is lightly browned and well puffed. Slide each parcel on to a warmed plate and serve immediately.

Energy 286kcal/1200kJ; Protein 39.7g; Carbohydrate 10.6g, of which sugars 9.6g; Fat 9.6g, of which saturates 2.1g, of which polyunsaturates 2.1g; Cholesterol 0mg; Calcium 171mg; Fibre 5.6g; Sodium 161mg.

FARFALLE <u>WITH</u> TASTY TUNA SAUCE ★

A QUICK AND SIMPLE LOW-FAT DISH THAT MAKES A GOOD AND ECONOMICAL WEEKDAY SUPPER IF YOU HAVE CANNED TOMATOES AND TUNA IN THE STORE CUPBOARD.

SERVES FOUR

INGREDIENTS

 10ml/2 tsp olive oil
 1 small onion, finely chopped
 1 garlic clove, finely chopped
 400g/14oz can chopped Italian
  plum tomatoes
 45ml/3 tbsp dry white wine
 8–10 pitted black olives, cut into rings
 10ml/2 tsp chopped fresh oregano or
  5ml/1 tsp dried oregano, plus extra
  fresh oregano to garnish
 400g/14oz/3½ cups dried farfalle
 200g/7oz can tuna in brine or
  spring water
 salt and black pepper

1 Heat the olive oil in a non-stick frying pan, add the onion and garlic and cook gently for 2–3 minutes, or until the onion is soft and golden.

2 Add the canned tomatoes and bring to the boil, then add the white wine and simmer for a minute or so. Stir in the olives and chopped fresh or dried oregano, with salt and pepper to taste, then cover and cook, stirring occasionally, for 20–25 minutes.

3 Meanwhile, cook the pasta in a large pan of salted boiling water according to the instructions on the packet.

4 Drain the canned tuna and flake it with a fork. Add the tuna to the tomato sauce with about 60ml/4 tbsp of the water used for cooking the pasta. Adjust the seasoning to taste.

5 Drain the cooked pasta well and tip it into a warmed large serving bowl. Pour the tuna sauce over the top and toss to mix. Serve immediately, garnished with sprigs of oregano.

VARIATIONS
• Use chopped fresh marjoram or mixed herbs in place of oregano.
• Use canned pink or red salmon, pilchards or sardines, in place of tuna.
• Use other dried pasta shapes, such as fusilli or penne, in place of farfalle.

Energy 443kcal/1881kJ; Protein 24.7g; Carbohydrate 78.5g, of which sugars 7.3g; Fat 4.8g, of which saturates 0.8g, of which polyunsaturates 1.3g; Cholesterol 26mg; Calcium 45mg; Fibre 4.3g; Sodium 342mg.

PASTA <u>WITH</u> TOMATOES <u>AND</u> SHELLFISH ★★

*COLOURFUL, DELICIOUS AND LOW IN FAT, THIS DISH IS IDEAL FOR A DINNER PARTY. THE TOMATO
SAUCE IS QUITE RUNNY, SO SERVE IT WITH CRUSTY BREAD AND SPOONS AS WELL AS FORKS.*

SERVES FOUR

INGREDIENTS
    25ml/1½ tbsp olive oil
    1 small onion, chopped
    1 garlic clove, crushed
    ½ fresh red chilli, seeded
      and chopped
    200g/7oz can chopped tomatoes
    30ml/2 tbsp chopped fresh flat
      leaf parsley
    400g/14oz fresh clams in their shells
    400g/14oz fresh mussels in
      their shells
    60ml/4 tbsp dry white wine
    400g/14oz/3½ cups dried trenette
      or spaghetti
    a few fresh basil leaves
    90g/3½oz cooked, peeled prawns
      (shrimp), thawed and thoroughly
      dried if frozen
    salt and ground black pepper
    lemon wedges and chopped fresh herbs,
      such as parsley or thyme, to garnish

1 Heat 10ml/2 tsp of the oil in a non-stick frying pan. Add the onion, garlic and chilli, and cook over a medium heat, stirring constantly, for 1–2 minutes. Stir in the tomatoes, half the chopped parsley and pepper to taste. Bring to the boil, then reduce the heat, cover and simmer for 15 minutes.

2 Meanwhile, scrub the clams and mussels under cold running water. Discard any that are open and that do not close when sharply tapped against the work surface.

3 Heat the remaining oil in a large pan. Add the clams and mussels with the remaining chopped parsley and toss over a high heat for a few seconds. Pour in the wine, then cover tightly. Cook, shaking the pan frequently, for about 5 minutes, or until the clams and mussels have opened.

4 Transfer the clams and mussels to a bowl, discarding any shellfish that have failed to open. Strain the cooking liquid and set aside. Reserve 8 clams and 4 mussels for the garnish, then remove the rest from their shells.

5 Cook the pasta according to the instructions on the packet. Meanwhile, add 120ml/4fl oz/½ cup of the reserved shellfish liquid to the tomato sauce. Add the basil, prawns, shelled clams and mussels to the sauce. Season.

6 Drain the cooked pasta and tip it into a warmed serving bowl. Add the tomato sauce and toss well to mix. Serve in individual bowls, sprinkled with chopped herbs and garnished with lemon wedges and the reserved clams and mussels in their shells.

Energy 473kcal/2004kJ; Protein 24.7g; Carbohydrate 77.3g, of which sugars 5.8g; Fat 8.3g, of which saturates 1.2g, of which polyunsaturates 1.6g; Cholesterol 68mg; Calcium 124mg; Fibre 3.6g; Sodium 339mg.

MONKFISH WITH TOMATO AND OLIVE SAUCE ★★

THIS DISH COMES FROM THE COAST OF CALABRIA IN SOUTHERN ITALY. GARLIC-FLAVOURED MASHED POTATO IS DELICIOUS WITH ITS ROBUST SAUCE.

2 Heat the oil and butter in a non-stick pan until foaming, add the monkfish pieces and sauté over a medium heat until they just change colour. Remove to a plate, set aside and keep warm.

3 Add the onion to the juices in the casserole and cook gently, stirring frequently, for about 5 minutes until softened. Add the passata, the reserved cooking liquid from the mussels and the tomato purée. Season to taste with salt and pepper. Bring to the boil, stirring, then reduce the heat, cover and simmer, stirring occasionally, for 20 minutes.

SERVES FOUR

INGREDIENTS
450g/1lb fresh mussels in their
  shells, scrubbed
a few fresh basil leaves, plus extra
  to garnish
2 garlic cloves, roughly chopped
300ml/½ pint/1¼ cups dry white wine
15ml/1 tbsp olive oil
15g/½oz/1 tbsp butter
900g/2lb monkfish fillets, skinned
  and cut into large chunks
1 onion, finely chopped
500g/1¼lb jar passata (bottled
  strained tomatoes)
15ml/1 tbsp sun-dried tomato
  purée (paste)
115g/4oz/1 cup pitted black olives
salt and ground black pepper

1 Put the mussels in a flameproof casserole with some basil leaves, the garlic and the wine. Cover and bring to the boil, then reduce the heat and simmer, shaking the pan frequently for 5 minutes. Remove the mussels, discarding any that fail to open. Strain the cooking liquid and reserve.

4 Pull off and discard the top shells from the mussels. Add the monkfish pieces to the tomato sauce and cook gently for 5 minutes. Gently stir in the olives and a few more basil leaves, then taste and adjust the seasoning. Place the mussels in their half shells on top of the sauce, cover the pan and heat the mussels through for 1–2 minutes. Serve at once, garnished with basil.

Energy 303kcal/1280kJ; Protein 42.4g; Carbohydrate 4.3g, of which sugars 4.3g; Fat 7.9g, of which saturates 1.4g, of which polyunsaturates 1.3g; Cholesterol 45mg; Calcium 118mg; Fibre 2.1g; Sodium 773mg.

CHARGRILLED SQUID ★★

IF YOU LIKE YOUR FOOD HOT, CHOP SOME OF THE CHILLI SEEDS WITH THE FLESH. IF NOT, CUT THE CHILLIES IN HALF, SCRAPE OUT THE SEEDS AND DISCARD THEM BEFORE CUTTING THE FLESH.

SERVES TWO

INGREDIENTS
   2 whole prepared squid, with
      tentacles
   75ml/5 tbsp olive oil
   30ml/2 tbsp balsamic vinegar
   2 fresh red chillies, finely chopped
   60ml/4 tbsp dry white wine
   salt and ground black pepper
   hot cooked risotto rice
   fresh parsley sprigs, to garnish

3 Cut the squid bodies into diagonal strips. Pile the hot risotto rice in the centre of heated soup plates and top with the strips of squid, arranging them criss-cross fashion. Keep hot.

4 Place the chopped tentacles and chillies in a pan and toss over a medium heat for 2 minutes. Stir in the wine until hot, then drizzle over the squid and rice. Garnish with the parsley sprigs and serve at once.

1 Make a lengthways cut down the body of each squid, then open the body out flat. Score the flesh on both sides of the bodies in a criss-cross pattern with the tip of a sharp knife. Chop the tentacles. Place all the squid in a china or glass dish. Whisk the oil and vinegar in a small bowl. Add salt and pepper to taste and pour over the squid. Cover and leave to marinate for about 1 hour.

2 Heat a ridged cast-iron pan until hot. Add the body of one of the squid. Cook over a medium heat for 2–3 minutes, pressing the squid with a fish slice or metal spatula to keep it flat. Repeat on the other side. Cook the other squid body in the same way. Discard the marinade.

COOK'S TIP
Squid is best eaten as soon as it is cooked, so that it has a melt-in-the-mouth texture. If left, it tends to become too chewy.

Energy 231kcal/974kJ; Protein 30.9g; Carbohydrate 2.6g, of which sugars 0.2g; Fat 8.9g, of which saturates 1.6g, of which polyunsaturates 1.7g; Cholesterol 450mg; Calcium 29mg; Fibre 0g; Sodium 221mg.

SPICY SEAFOOD AND MUSSEL STEW ★★

THIS MEDITERRANEAN SPICY SEAFOOD DISH IS SERVED WITH HERBY BROWN RICE TO CREATE A
FLAVOURFUL MEAL THAT ALL THE FAMILY WILL ENJOY.

SERVES FOUR

INGREDIENTS

    10ml/2 tsp olive oil
    1 onion, chopped
    1 garlic clove, crushed
    2 celery sticks, chopped
    1 red (bell) pepper, seeded and diced
    5ml/1 tsp each ground coriander,
      ground cumin and ground ginger
    2.5ml/½ tsp hot chilli powder
    2.5ml/½ tsp garam masala
    30ml/2 tbsp plain (all-purpose)
      wholemeal (whole-wheat) flour
    300ml/½ pint/1¼ cups each fish
      stock and dry white wine
    225g/8oz can chopped tomatoes
    225g/8oz mushrooms, sliced
    450g/1lb frozen cooked, shelled
      mixed seafood, thawed
    175g/6oz/1 cup frozen corn kernels
    225g/8oz fresh mussels
    225g/8oz/generous 1 cup long grain
      brown rice
    30–45ml/2–3 tbsp chopped mixed
      fresh herbs
    salt and ground black pepper
    fresh flat leaf parsley sprigs,
      to garnish

2 Add the ground spices and cook, stirring, for 1 minute, then add the flour and cook, continuing to stir, for a further 1 minute.

3 Gradually stir in the stock and wine, then add the tomatoes and mushrooms. Bring to the boil, stirring continuously, then cover and simmer, stirring occasionally, for 20 minutes.

4 Stir in the rest of the seafood, corn kernels and mussels and cook, stirring occasionally, for a further 10–15 minutes until hot.

5 Meanwhile, cook the brown rice in a large pan of lightly salted boiling water for about 35 minutes, or until just tender.

6 Rinse the cooked rice in fresh boiling water and drain thoroughly, then toss the rice together with the chopped mixed herbs. Finally, season the stew to taste and serve on a bed of the herbed rice. Garnish with fresh parsley sprigs and serve immediately.

1 Heat the oil in a large, non-stick pan. Add the onion, garlic, celery and red pepper and cook, stirring occasionally, for 5 minutes.

Energy 483kcal/2043kJ; Protein 29.3g; Carbohydrate 71.4g, of which sugars 12.4g; Fat 5.6g, of which saturates 1.2g, of which polyunsaturates 1.6g; Cholesterol 219mg; Calcium 224mg; Fibre 6.4g; Sodium 360mg.

SLOW-COOKED SKATE <u>WITH</u> TOMATO SAUCE ★

THE CLASSIC WAY OF SERVING SKATE IS WITH A BROWNED BUTTER SAUCE, BUT HERE IT IS COOKED IN
A SLOW-COOKER WITH TOMATOES, OLIVES, ORANGE AND A DASH OF PERNOD. IF TIME ALLOWS, SOAK
THE SKATE IN SALTED WATER FOR A FEW HOURS BEFORE COOKING, TO FIRM UP THE FLESH.

3 Meanwhile, rinse the skate wings under cold water and pat dry on kitchen paper. Sprinkle the flour on a large, flat dish and season well with salt and pepper. Coat each skate wing in the flour, shaking off any excess, then place the skate wings on top of the tomato sauce.

4 Re-cover the ceramic cooking pot and reduce the temperature to low. Cook for 1½–2 hours, or until the skate is cooked and flakes easily.

5 Place the fish on to warmed serving plates and spoon over the sauce. Sprinkle over the basil leaves and serve with a wedge of lime for squeezing.

SERVES FOUR

INGREDIENTS
  10ml/2 tsp olive oil
  1 small onion, finely chopped
  2 fresh thyme sprigs
  grated rind of ½ orange
  15ml/1 tbsp Pernod
  400g/14oz can chopped tomatoes
  50g/2oz/½ cup stuffed green olives
  1.5ml/¼ tsp caster (superfine) sugar
  4 small skate wings
  plain (all-purpose) flour, for coating
  salt and ground black pepper
  15ml/1 tbsp fresh basil leaves,
    to garnish
  lime wedges, to serve

COOK'S TIP
Pernod gives this dish a deliciously distinctive taste of aniseed, but if you don't like the flavour, use 15ml/1 tbsp vermouth instead.

1 Heat the oil in a non-stick pan, add the onion and cook gently for 10 minutes. Stir in the thyme and orange rind and cook for 1 minute. Stir in the Pernod, tomatoes, olives, sugar and a little salt and pepper, and heat until just below boiling point.

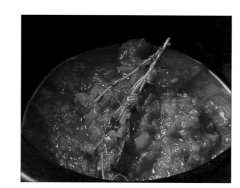

2 Put the mixture in the ceramic pot or a slow cooker and switch on to high. Cover with the lid and cook for 1½ hours.

Energy 144kcal/607kJ; Protein 23.6g; Carbohydrate 4.3g, of which sugars 4g; Fat 3.7g, of which saturates 0.5g, of which polyunsaturates 0.8g; Cholesterol 0mg; Calcium 78mg; Fibre 1.5g; Sodium 443mg.

CLAMS WITH NEAPOLITAN TOMATO SAUCE ★

THIS RECIPE TAKES ITS NAME FROM THE CITY OF NAPLES, WHERE BOTH FRESH TOMATO SAUCE AND SHELLFISH ARE TRADITIONALLY SERVED WITH VERMICELLI. HERE THE TWO ARE COMBINED TO MAKE A VERY TASTY LOW-FAT DISH THAT IS PERFECT FOR A COOL EVENING.

SERVES FOUR

INGREDIENTS
1kg/2¼lb fresh clams in their shells
250ml/8fl oz/1 cup dry white wine or
   vegetable stock
2 garlic cloves, bruised
1 large handful fresh flat leaf parsley
10ml/2 tsp extra virgin olive oil or
   sunflower oil
1 small onion, finely chopped
8 ripe plum tomatoes, skinned,
   seeded and finely chopped
½–1 fresh red chilli, seeded and
   finely chopped
350g/12oz dried vermicelli
salt and ground black pepper

1 Scrub the clams thoroughly with a brush under cold running water, and discard any that are open or do not close their shells when sharply tapped against the work surface.

2 Pour the white wine or vegetable stock into a large, heavy pan and add the bruised garlic cloves. Finely chop half the parsley and add to the wine or stock, then add the clams.

3 Cover the pan tightly with the lid and bring to the boil over a high heat. Cook, shaking the pan frequently, for about 5 minutes, or until all the clams have opened.

4 Tip the clams into a large colander set over a bowl and let the liquid drain through. Leave the clams until cool enough to handle, then remove about two-thirds of them from their shells, tipping the clam liquor into the bowl of cooking liquid.

5 Discard any clams that have failed to open. Set both shelled and unshelled clams aside, keeping the unshelled clams warm in a bowl covered with a lid.

6 Heat the oil in a non-stick pan, add the onion and cook gently, stirring frequently, for about 5 minutes, or until softened and lightly coloured. Add the tomatoes, then strain in the clam cooking liquid. Add the chilli, and salt and pepper to taste.

7 Bring to the boil, then reduce the heat, partially cover the pan and simmer gently for 15–20 minutes. Meanwhile, cook the pasta according to the packet instructions. Finely chop the remaining parsley.

8 Add the shelled clams to the tomato sauce, stir well and heat through very gently for 2–3 minutes.

9 Drain the cooked pasta well and tip it into a warmed serving bowl. Taste the sauce and adjust the seasoning, then pour the sauce over the pasta; toss to mix well. Garnish with the reserved clams, sprinkle the chopped parsley over the pasta and serve immediately.

Energy 481kcal/2040kJ; Protein 31.8g; Carbohydrate 73.4g, of which sugars 8.8g; Fat 4.3g, of which saturates 0.8g, of which polyunsaturates 1.3g; Cholesterol 84mg; Calcium 134mg; Fibre 4.3g; Sodium 1519mg.

TROUT AND PROSCIUTTO RISOTTO ROLLS ★★

THIS MAKES A DELICIOUS AND ELEGANT LOW-FAT MEAL. THE RISOTTO — MADE WITH PORCINI MUSHROOMS AND PRAWNS — IS A FINE MATCH FOR THE ROBUST FLAVOUR OF THE TROUT ROLLS.

SERVES FOUR

INGREDIENTS
    4 trout fillets, skinned
    4 slices prosciutto
    caper berries, to garnish
For the risotto
    30ml/2 tbsp olive oil
    8 large raw prawns (shrimp), peeled
      and deveined
    1 onion, chopped
    225g/8oz/generous 1 cup risotto
      rice
    about 105ml/7 tbsp white wine
    about 750ml/1¼ pints/3 cups
      simmering fish or chicken stock
    15g/½oz/¼ cup dried porcini or
      chanterelle mushrooms, soaked
      for 10 minutes in warm water
      to cover
    salt and ground black pepper

2 Add the chopped onion to the oil remaining in the pan and cook gently for 3–4 minutes, or until soft. Add the rice and stir for 3–4 minutes, or until the grains are evenly coated in oil. Add 75ml/5 tbsp of the wine and then the stock, a little at a time, stirring over a gentle heat and allowing the rice to absorb the liquid before adding more.

4 Remove the pan from the heat and stir in the prawns. Preheat the oven to 190°C/375°F/Gas 5. Lightly grease an ovenproof dish and set aside.

5 Take a trout fillet, place a spoonful of risotto at one end and roll up. Wrap each fillet in a slice of prosciutto and place in the prepared dish.

1 First make the risotto. Heat the oil in a heavy, non-stick pan or deep non-stick frying pan and cook the prawns very briefly until flecked with pink. Lift out using a slotted spoon and transfer to a plate. Keep warm.

3 Drain the mushrooms, reserving the liquid, and cut the larger ones in half. Towards the end of cooking, stir the mushrooms into the risotto with 15ml/1 tbsp of the reserved mushroom liquid. If the rice is not yet *al dente*, add a little more stock or mushroom liquid and cook for a further 2–3 minutes. Season to taste with salt and pepper.

6 Spoon any remaining risotto around the fish fillets and sprinkle over the remaining wine. Cover loosely with foil and bake in the oven for 15–20 minutes, or until the fish is cooked and tender.

7 Spoon the risotto on to a warmed serving platter, top with the trout rolls and garnish with caper berries. Serve immediately.

COOK'S TIP
There are no hard and fast rules about which type of risotto to use for this dish. Almost any risotto recipe could be used, although a vegetable or seafood risotto would be particularly suitable.

Energy 397kcal/1662kJ; Protein 33g; Carbohydrate 43.6g, of which sugars 1.1g; Fat 7.6g, of which saturates 0.3g, of which polyunsaturates 0.2g; Cholesterol 29mg; Calcium 37mg; Fibre 0.2g; Sodium 202mg.

FRESH TUNA AND TOMATO STEW ★★

A DELICIOUSLY SIMPLE LIGHT ITALIAN RECIPE THAT RELIES ON GOOD BASIC INGREDIENTS: FRESH FISH, TOMATOES AND HERBS. FOR AN AUTHENTIC FLAVOUR, SERVE WITH POLENTA OR PASTA.

SERVES FOUR

INGREDIENTS

12 baby (pearl) onions, peeled
900g/2lb ripe tomatoes
675g/1½lb fresh tuna steaks
10ml/2 tsp olive oil
2 garlic cloves, crushed
45ml/3 tbsp chopped mixed fresh herbs
2 bay leaves
2.5ml/½ tsp caster (superfine) sugar
30ml/2 tbsp sun-dried tomato
  purée (paste)
150ml/¼ pint/⅔ cup dry white wine
salt and ground black pepper
steamed baby courgettes (zucchini)
  and fresh herbs, to garnish

VARIATION
Two large mackerel make a more readily available alternative to the tuna. Simply lay the whole fish over the sauce and cook, covered with a lid, until the mackerel is cooked through.

1 Leave the onions whole and cook in a pan of boiling water for 4–5 minutes, or until softened. Drain. Plunge the tomatoes into boiling water for 30 seconds, then refresh in cold water. Peel off the skins and chop roughly.

2 Cut the tuna into 2.5cm/1in chunks. Heat the oil in a large, non-stick frying pan and quickly fry the tuna until the surface has browned. Lift the chunks out of the pan using a slotted spoon; drain.

3 Add the onions, garlic, tomatoes, chopped herbs, bay leaves, sugar, tomato purée and wine to the pan, and bring to the boil, breaking up the tomatoes with a wooden spoon.

4 Reduce the heat and simmer the sauce gently for 5 minutes. Return the tuna to the pan and cook for a further 5 minutes. Season with salt and pepper, and serve hot, garnished with baby courgettes and fresh herbs.

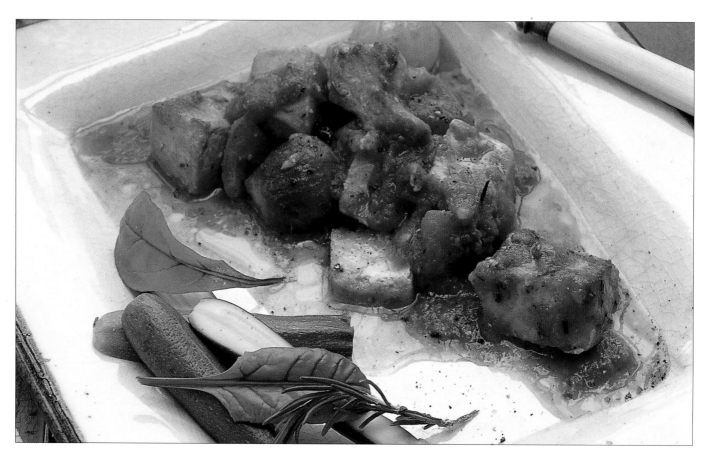

Energy 311kcal/1309kJ; Protein 42.2g; Carbohydrate 11.2g, of which sugars 10g; Fat 8.5g, of which saturates 2.3g, of which polyunsaturates 3.2g; Cholesterol 47mg; Calcium 59mg; Fibre 3g; Sodium 103mg.

MOROCCAN FISH TAGINE ★★

THIS SPICY, AROMATIC LOW-FAT DISH PROVES JUST HOW EXCITING AN INGREDIENT FISH CAN BE. SERVE IT WITH COUSCOUS FLAVOURED WITH CHOPPED FRESH MINT.

SERVES EIGHT

INGREDIENTS

1.3kg/3lb firm fish fillets, skinned
  and cut into 5cm/2in chunks
30ml/2 tbsp olive oil
4 onions, chopped
1 large aubergine (eggplant), cut into
  1cm/½in cubes
2 courgettes (zucchini), cut into
  1cm/½in cubes
400g/14oz can chopped tomatoes
400ml/14fl oz/1⅔ cups passata
  (bottled strained tomatoes)
200ml/7fl oz/scant 1 cup fish stock
1 preserved lemon, chopped
90g/3½oz/scant 1 cup pitted olives
60ml/4 tbsp chopped fresh
  coriander (cilantro)
salt and ground black pepper
fresh coriander (cilantro) sprigs,
  to garnish

For the harissa
3 large fresh red chillies, seeded
  and chopped
3 garlic cloves, peeled
15ml/1 tbsp ground coriander
30ml/2 tbsp ground cumin
5ml/1 tsp ground cinnamon
grated rind of 1 lemon
30ml/2 tbsp sunflower oil

1 Make the harissa. Whizz everything together in a blender or food processor to form a smooth paste. Set aside.

2 Put the chunks of fish in a wide bowl and add 30ml/2 tbsp of the harissa. Toss to coat all over, then cover and chill for at least 1 hour, or overnight.

3 Heat 15ml/1 tbsp of the oil in a shallow, heavy non-stick pan. Cook the onions gently for 10 minutes, or until golden brown. Stir in the remaining harissa, and cook, stirring occasionally, for 5 minutes.

4 Heat the remaining olive oil in a separate shallow pan. Add the aubergine cubes and cook for about 10 minutes, or until they are golden brown. Add the cubed courgettes and cook for a further 2 minutes.

5 Add the aubergines and courgettes to the onions, then stir in the chopped tomatoes, passata and fish stock. Bring to the boil, then reduce the heat and simmer for about 20 minutes.

6 Stir the fish chunks and preserved lemon into the pan. Add the olives and stir gently. Cover and simmer gently for about 15–20 minutes, or until the fish is just cooked through. Stir in the chopped coriander. Season to taste. Serve with couscous, if you like, and garnish with coriander sprigs.

COOK'S TIP

To make the fish go further, you could add 225g/8oz/1¼ cups cooked chickpeas to the tagine.

Energy 221kcal/925kJ; Protein 31.6g; Carbohydrate 5g, of which sugars 4.3g; Fat 8.4g, of which saturates 1.2g, of which polyunsaturates 2.9g; Cholesterol 75mg; Calcium 46mg; Fibre 2.1g; Sodium 357mg.

POULTRY AND GAME

Poultry and lean cuts of game are great for
creating nourishing and tasty low-fat dishes.
Traditional Mediterranean cooking methods such
as braising, slow-roasting and grilling are ideal
for creating a wide range of nutritious, light
meals including roasts, casseroles and tagines.
Choose from low-fat delights such as Chicken
and Apricot Filo Pie, and Chicken and Braised
Quail with Winter Vegetables.

MOROCCAN HARISSA-SPICED ROAST CHICKEN ★

THE SPICES AND FRUIT IN THIS STUFFING GIVE THE CHICKEN AN UNUSUAL FLAVOUR AND HELP TO KEEP IT MOIST. SERVE WITH BAKED POTATOES AND STEAMED GREEN BEANS FOR A DELICIOUS LOW-FAT MEAL.

3 Preheat the oven to 200°C/400°F/ Gas 6. Stuff the neck of the chicken with the fruit mixture, reserving any excess. Brush the garlic and spice oil all over the chicken. Place the chicken in a flameproof roasting pan, tuck in the bay leaves, then roast in the oven, basting occasionally with the juices, for 1–1¼ hours, or until cooked.

4 Transfer the chicken to a carving board and leave to rest while you make the sauce. Pour off and discard any excess fat from the roasting pan. Stir the honey, tomato purée, lemon juice, stock and harissa into the juices in the roasting pan. Add salt to taste. Bring to the boil, then reduce the heat and simmer, stirring frequently for 2 minutes.

5 Meanwhile, reheat any excess stuffing. Remove and discard the skin from the chicken, then carve the chicken, pour the sauce into a small bowl and serve immediately with the stuffing and chicken.

SERVES FOUR

INGREDIENTS
  1.3–1.6kg/3–3½lb chicken
  15ml/1 tbsp garlic and spice
    aromatic oil
  a few bay leaves
  10ml/2 tsp clear honey
  10ml/2 tsp tomato purée (paste)
  60ml/4 tbsp lemon juice
  150ml/¼ pint/⅔ cup chicken stock
  2.5–5ml/½–1 tsp harissa
For the stuffing
  15g/½oz/1 tbsp butter
  1 onion, chopped
  1 garlic clove, crushed
  7.5ml/1½ tsp ground cinnamon
  2.5ml/½ tsp ground cumin
  225g/8oz/1⅓ cups mixed dried fruit,
    soaked for several hours or
    overnight in water to cover
  25g/1oz/¼ cup blanched almonds,
    finely chopped (optional)
  salt and ground black pepper

1 Make the stuffing. Melt the butter in a non-stick pan. Add the onion and garlic and cook gently for 5 minutes, or until soft. Add the ground cinnamon and cumin and cook, stirring, for 2 minutes.

2 Drain the soaked dried fruit, chop it roughly and add to the stuffing mixture with the almonds; mix well. Season with salt and pepper and cook for a further 2 minutes. Transfer the mixture to a bowl and leave to cool.

COOK'S TIP
If you do not like mixed dried fruit, use a single variety such as dried apricots instead.

Energy 345kcal/1463kJ; Protein 37.4g; Carbohydrate 40.2g, of which sugars 39.9g; Fat 5g, of which saturates 2.4g, of which polyunsaturates 0.4g; Cholesterol 113mg; Calcium 38mg; Fibre 1.3g; Sodium 147mg.

ROAST CHICKEN WITH POTATOES AND LEMON ★

THIS EASY LOW-FAT DISH IDEAL FOR A FAMILY MEAL. AS WITH OTHER GREEK ROASTS, EVERYTHING IS BAKED TOGETHER SO THAT THE POTATOES ABSORB ALL THE DIFFERENT FLAVOURS.

SERVES FOUR

INGREDIENTS

  1 organic or free-range chicken,
    about 1.6kg/3½lb
  2 garlic cloves, peeled, but left whole
  15ml/1 tbsp chopped fresh thyme or
    oregano, or 5ml/1 tsp dried, plus
    2–3 sprigs fresh thyme or oregano
  800g/1¾lb potatoes
  juice of 1 lemon
  15ml/1 tbsp extra virgin olive oil
  300ml/½ pint/1¼ cups hot water
  salt and ground black pepper

4 Roast the chicken and potatoes in the oven for 30 minutes, then remove the roasting pan from the oven and carefully turn the chicken over. Season the bird with a little more salt and pepper, sprinkle over the remaining chopped fresh or dried herbs, and add more hot water, if needed. Reduce the oven temperature to 190°C/375°F/Gas 5.

5 Return the chicken and potatoes to the oven and roast them for a further 1 hour, or slightly longer, by which time both the chicken and the potatoes will be cooked and a golden colour.

6 Remove and discard the skin from the chicken, then carve the chicken and serve with a crisp leafy salad.

1 Preheat the oven to 200°C/400°F/ Gas 6. Place the chicken, breast side down, in a large roasting pan, then tuck the garlic cloves and the thyme or oregano sprigs inside the bird.

2 Peel the potatoes and quarter them lengthways. If they are very large, slice them lengthways into thinner pieces. Arrange the potatoes around the bird, then pour the lemon juice over the chicken and potatoes.

3 Season with salt and pepper, drizzle the olive oil over the top, then sprinkle over about three-quarters of the chopped fresh or dried thyme or oregano. Pour the hot water into the roasting pan.

Energy 297kcal/1259kJ; Protein 33.4g; Carbohydrate 32.2g, of which sugars 2.6g; Fat 4.7, of which saturates 1g, of which polyunsaturates 0.7g; Cholesterol 88mg; Calcium 18mg; Fibre 2g; Sodium 97mg.

CHICKEN <u>IN A</u> SALT CRUST ★★★

COOKING FOOD IN A CASING OF SALT GIVES A DELICIOUSLY MOIST, TENDER FLAVOUR THAT IS, SURPRISINGLY, NOT TOO SALTY. THE TECHNIQUE IS USED IN ITALY AND FRANCE FOR WHOLE FISH TOO.

SERVES SIX

INGREDIENTS
 1 chicken, about 1.8–2kg/4–4½lb
 about 2.25kg/5lb coarse sea salt

1 Preheat the oven to 220°C/425°F/ Gas 7. Choose a deep ovenproof dish into which the whole chicken will fit snugly. Line the dish with a double thickness of heavy foil, allowing plenty of excess foil to overhang the top edge of the ovenproof dish.

2 Truss the chicken tightly so that the salt cannot fall into the cavity. Sprinkle a thin layer of salt in the foil-lined dish then place the chicken on top.

COOK'S TIP
This recipe makes a really stunning main course when you want to serve something a little different. Take the salt-crusted chicken to the table garnished with plenty of mixed fresh herbs. Once you've scraped away the salt, transfer the chicken to a clean plate to carve it.

3 Pour the remaining salt all around and over the top of the chicken until it is completely encased. Sprinkle the top with a little water.

4 Cover tightly with the foil, then bake the chicken on the lower oven shelf for 1¾ hours, or until the chicken is cooked and tender.

5 To serve the chicken, open out the foil and ease it out of the dish. Place on a large serving platter. Crack open the salt crust on the chicken and brush away the salt before carving. Remove and discard the skin from the chicken and carve the meat into slices.

6 Serve with a selection of cooked fresh seasonal vegetables.

Energy 133kcal/561kJ; Protein 30g; Carbohydrate 0g, of which sugars 0g; Fat 1.4g, of which saturates 0.4g, of which polyunsaturates 0.3g; Cholesterol 88mg; Calcium 46mg; Fibre 0g; Sodium 75mg.

CHICKEN <u>WITH</u> LEMONS <u>AND</u> OLIVES ★

PRESERVED LEMONS AND LIMES ARE FREQUENTLY USED IN MEDITERRANEAN COOKING, PARTICULARLY IN NORTH AFRICA WHERE THEIR GENTLE FLAVOUR ENHANCES ALL KINDS OF DISHES.

SERVES FOUR

INGREDIENTS

2.5ml/½ tsp ground cinnamon
2.5ml/½ tsp ground turmeric
1 chicken, about 1.5kg/3¼lb
15ml/1 tbsp olive oil
1 large onion, thinly sliced
5cm/2in piece fresh root ginger,
  peeled and grated
600ml/1 pint/2½ cups chicken stock
2 preserved or fresh lemons or limes,
  cut into wedges
75g/3oz/¾ cup pitted brown olives
15ml/1 tbsp clear honey
60ml/4 tbsp chopped fresh
  coriander (cilantro)
salt and ground black pepper
fresh coriander (cilantro) sprigs,
  to garnish

1 Preheat the oven to 190°C/375°F/ Gas 5. Mix the ground cinnamon and turmeric in a bowl with a little salt and black pepper and rub all over the chicken skin.

2 Heat the oil in a shallow, non-stick frying pan and fry the chicken on all sides until it turns golden. Transfer the chicken to an ovenproof dish.

3 Add the onion to the pan and sauté for 3 minutes. Add the ginger and stock to the pan and bring just to the boil. Pour the stock mixture over the chicken, then cover and bake in the oven for 30 minutes. Remove the chicken from the oven.

4 Add the lemons or limes and the brown olives. Drizzle over the honey, then bake, uncovered, for a further 45 minutes, or until the chicken is cooked. Sprinkle the coriander over the chicken and season. Garnish with coriander. Remove and discard the skin from the chicken, and serve immediately.

Energy 146kcal/614kJ; Protein 24.8g; Carbohydrate 4.4g, of which sugars 4g; Fat 3.4g, of which saturates 0.6g, of which polyunsaturates 0.5g; Cholesterol 70mg; Calcium 46mg; Fibre 1.4g; Sodium 487mg.

CHICKEN LIVERS <u>WITH</u> SHERRY ★

*THE RICH FLAVOURS OF THIS LOW-FAT SPANISH DISH WORK TOGETHER VERY WELL AND THE LIGHTLY
PAN-FRIED LIVERS HAVE A WONDERFUL TEXTURE THAT LITERALLY MELTS IN THE MOUTH. SERVE WITH
PLENTY OF CRUSTY BREAD TO MOP UP THE JUICES.*

2 Finely chop the onion and garlic
using a sharp knife. Heat the olive oil
in a non-stick frying pan, add the onion,
garlic, chicken livers and thyme leaves
and cook, stirring occasionally, for about
3 minutes.

3 Stir in the sherry and cook gently,
stirring, for 1 minute. Add the sour
cream and cook, stirring, over a low
heat for a further 1–2 minutes. Add
salt and pepper to taste and serve
immediately, garnished with thyme.

SERVES FOUR

INGREDIENTS
   225g/8oz chicken livers, thawed
     if frozen
   1 small onion
   2 small garlic cloves
   15ml/1 tbsp olive oil
   5ml/1 tsp fresh thyme leaves
   30ml/2 tbsp sweet sherry
   30ml/2 tbsp sour cream
   salt and ground black pepper
   fresh thyme sprigs, to garnish

COOK'S TIP
This dish is very quick and easy to
prepare, and even quicker if you buy the
chicken livers ready-trimmed. You may
find it easier to use a pair of kitchen
scissors when trimming away the sinews.

1 Carefully trim any spots and sinews
from the chicken livers.

Energy 106kcal/441kJ; Protein 10.4g; Carbohydrate 1.9g, of which sugars 1.6g; Fat 5.6g, of which saturates 1.7g, of which polyunsaturates 0.5g; Cholesterol 218mg; Calcium 16mg; Fibre 0.2g; Sodium 48mg.

CHICKEN <u>WITH</u> GARLIC ★

USE FRESH NEW SEASON'S GARLIC IF YOU CAN FIND IT — THERE'S NO NEED TO PEEL THE CLOVES IF THE SKIN IS NOT PAPERY. IN FRANCE, SOMETIMES THE COOKED GARLIC CLOVES ARE SPREAD ON TOASTED COUNTRY BREAD.

SERVES EIGHT

INGREDIENTS

    2kg/4½lb chicken pieces
    1 large onion, halved and sliced
    3 large garlic bulbs (about
      200g/7oz), separated into cloves
      and peeled
    150ml/¼ pint/⅔ cup dry white wine
    175ml/6fl oz/¾ cup chicken stock
    4–5 fresh thyme sprigs, or
      2.5ml/½ tsp dried thyme
    1 small fresh rosemary sprig, or a
      pinch of dried rosemary
    1 bay leaf
    salt and freshly ground black pepper

1 Preheat the oven to 190°C/375°F/ Gas 5. Pat the chicken pieces dry and season with salt and pepper.

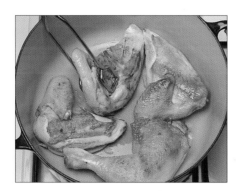

2 Put the chicken, skin side down, in a large flameproof casserole and set over a medium-high heat. Cook, turning frequently, until browned, then transfer the chicken to a plate. Cook the chicken pieces in batches, if necessary, then pour off and discard the fat after browning.

3 Add the onion and garlic to the casserole, cover and cook over a medium-low heat, stirring frequently, until lightly browned.

4 Add the wine, bring to the boil, then return the chicken to the casserole. Add the stock and herbs and bring back to the boil. Cover and transfer to the oven. Cook for 25 minutes, or until the chicken is tender and the juices run clear when the thickest part of the thigh is pierced with a knife.

5 Remove the chicken pieces from the casserole and strain the cooking liquid. Discard the herbs, transfer the solids to a blender or food processor and process until smooth. Remove and discard any fat from the cooking liquid and return to the casserole. Stir in the garlic and onion purée. Remove and discard the skin from the chicken pieces, then return the chicken to the casserole and reheat gently for 3–4 minutes before serving.

Energy 172kcal/727kJ; Protein 32.1g; Carbohydrate 4.8g, of which sugars 0.9g; Fat 1.5g, of which saturates 0.4g, of which polyunsaturates 0.3g; Cholesterol 88mg; Calcium 15mg; Fibre 1.1g; Sodium 77mg.

APRICOT AND ALMOND STUFFED CHICKEN ★★

COUSCOUS MAKES A DELICIOUS AND SIMPLE BASE FOR THIS LOW-FAT, SWEET-AND-SOUR STUFFING.
ORANGE JELLY MARMALADE ADDS TANGINESS TO THE SAUCE, AS WELL AS THICKENING IT SLIGHTLY.

SERVES FOUR

INGREDIENTS

50g/2oz/¼ cup dried apricots
150ml/¼ pint/⅔ cup orange juice
4 skinless, boneless chicken
  breast portions
50g/2oz/⅓ cup instant couscous
150ml/¼ pint/⅔ cup boiling
  chicken stock
25g/1oz/¼ cup toasted almonds,
  chopped
1.5ml/¼ tsp dried tarragon
1 egg yolk
30ml/2 tbsp orange jelly marmalade
salt and ground black pepper
boiled or steamed basmati and wild
  rice, to serve

1 Chop the dried apricots, then put them in a small bowl and pour over the orange juice. Leave to soak at room temperature while you prepare the remaining ingredients.

2 Using a sharp knife, cut a deep pocket horizontally in each chicken breast portion, taking care not to cut all the way through. Put the chicken portions between two sheets of oiled baking parchment or clear film (plastic wrap), then gently beat with a rolling pin or mallet until slightly thinner. Set aside.

VARIATION
Use dried peaches or pears in place of apricots.

3 Put the couscous in a bowl and spoon over 50ml/2fl oz/¼ cup of the stock. Leave to stand for 2–3 minutes, or until all the stock has been absorbed.

4 Drain the apricots, reserving the juice, then stir the apricots into the couscous together with the almonds and tarragon. Season with salt and pepper, then stir in just enough egg yolk to bind the mixture together.

5 Divide the stuffing equally between the chicken portions, packing it firmly into the pockets, then secure with wooden cocktail sticks (toothpicks). Place the stuffed chicken portions in the base of the ceramic cooking pot of a slow cooker.

6 Stir the orange marmalade into the remaining hot stock until dissolved, then stir in the reserved orange juice. Season with salt and pepper and pour over the chicken. Cover the pot and cook on high for 3–5 hours, or until the chicken is cooked through and tender.

7 Remove the chicken from the sauce and keep warm. Tip the sauce into a wide pan and boil rapidly on the hob, until reduced by half. Carve the chicken into slices on the diagonal and arrange on serving plates. Spoon over the sauce and serve immediately with basmati and wild rice.

COOK'S TIP
Flavoured rice, sautéed spinach or steamed green vegetables go well with this dish.

Energy 278kcal/1172kJ; Protein 39.1g; Carbohydrate 16.2g, of which sugars 9.6g; Fat 6.7g, of which saturates 1.1g, of which polyunsaturates 1.1g; Cholesterol 155mg; Calcium 37mg; Fibre 0.7g; Sodium 99mg.

POUSSINS AND NEW POTATO POT-ROAST ★

POT ROASTS ARE TRADITIONALLY ASSOCIATED WITH THE COLDER MONTHS, BUT THIS DELICIOUS LOW-FAT VERSION IS A SIMPLE SUMMER DISH THAT MAKES THE MOST OF NEW SEASON POTATOES.

SERVES FOUR

INGREDIENTS

2 poussins, about 500g/1¼lb each
15g/½oz/1 tbsp butter
15ml/1 tbsp clear honey
500g/1¼lb small new potatoes
1 red onion, halved lengthways and
  cut into thin wedges
4–5 small fresh rosemary sprigs
2 bay leaves
1 lemon, cut into wedges
450ml/¾ pint/scant 2 cups hot
  chicken stock
salt and ground black pepper

1 Soak a clay chicken brick in cold water for 20 minutes, then drain. Cut the poussins in half, along the breast bone. Set aside.

2 Melt the butter, mix it with the honey and brush the mixture over the poussins. Season with salt and pepper.

3 Place the small new potatoes and onion wedges in the base of the chicken brick. Tuck the rosemary sprigs, bay leaves and lemon wedges in among the vegetables. Pour over the hot chicken stock (see Cook's Tip).

4 Place the halved poussins on top of the vegetables. Cover the chicken brick and place it in a cold (unheated) oven. Set the oven temperature to 200°C/400°F/Gas 6 and cook for 55–60 minutes, or until the poussin juices run clear and the vegetables are tender. Uncover the chicken brick for the last 10 minutes of cooking to add more colour to the poussins, if necessary. Serve.

COOK'S TIPS
• Make sure the stock is hot, but not boiling, when it is added to the chicken brick, otherwise the brick may crack.
• A poussin is a baby chicken – usually around 4–6 weeks old. Poussins can be cooked by grilling (broiling), roasting or pot-roasting, but are especially tender and moist cooked in a chicken brick.

Energy 225kcal/10791kJ; Protein 32.3g; Carbohydrate 24.2g, of which sugars 5.4g; Fat 3.8g, of which saturates 1.8g, of which polyunsaturates 0.5g; Cholesterol 93mg; Calcium 18mg; Fibre 1.5g; Sodium 105mg.

SPICY CHICKEN CASSEROLE <u>WITH</u> RED WINE ★

THIS IS A TRADITIONAL CHICKEN DISH FROM THE GREEK ISLAND OF ALONNISOS. IT TENDS TO BE RESERVED FOR SUNDAYS. IN GREECE, IT IS USUALLY SERVED WITH PLAIN RICE OR ORZO.

SERVES FOUR

INGREDIENTS

30ml/2 tbsp extra virgin olive oil
1.6kg/3½lb organic or free-range
  chicken, jointed
1 large onion, roughly chopped
about 250ml/8fl oz/1 cup red wine
30ml/2 tbsp tomato purée (paste)
  diluted in 450ml/¾ pint/scant
  2 cups hot water
1 cinnamon stick
3–4 whole allspice
2 bay leaves
salt and ground black pepper
boiled rice or orzo, to serve

1 Heat the oil in a large non-stick frying pan or sauté pan, add the chicken pieces and cook until browned on both sides. Lift them out with tongs and set them aside.

2 Add the onion to the hot oil and cook, stirring, over a medium heat until it looks translucent.

3 Return the chicken pieces to the pan, pour the wine over and cook for 2–3 minutes, or until the wine has reduced. Add the tomato purée mixture, cinnamon, allspice and bay leaves. Season well with salt and pepper. Cover the pan, reduce the heat and cook gently for 1 hour, or until the chicken is cooked and tender. Serve with boiled rice or orzo.

VARIATION
Use 1 large red onion or 4–6 shallots in place of standard onion.

Energy 250kcal/1051kJ; Protein 37.1g; Carbohydrate 5.2g, of which sugars 4g; Fat 4.5g, of which saturates 0.9g, of which polyunsaturates 0.6g; Cholesterol 105mg; Calcium 27mg; Fibre 0.9g; Sodium 114mg.

CHICKEN AND APRICOT FILO PIE ★★★

THE FILLING FOR THIS TASTY, LOW-FAT PIE HAS A MIDDLE EASTERN FLAVOUR — MINCED CHICKEN COMBINED WITH APRICOTS, BULGUR WHEAT, NUTS AND SPICES.

SERVES SIX

INGREDIENTS
  75g/3oz/½ cup bulgur wheat
  50g/2oz/¼ cup butter
  1 onion, chopped
  450g/1lb minced (ground) chicken
    breast fillets
  50g/2oz/¼ cup ready-to-eat dried
    apricots, finely chopped
  25g/1oz/¼ cup blanched almonds,
    chopped
  5ml/1 tsp ground cinnamon
  2.5ml/½ tsp ground allspice
  50ml/2fl oz/¼ cup Greek
    (US strained plain) yogurt
  15ml/1 tbsp chopped fresh chives
  30ml/2 tbsp chopped fresh parsley
  6 large sheets filo pastry
  salt and ground black pepper
  fresh chives, to garnish

1 Preheat the oven to 200°C/400°F/ Gas 6. Put the bulgur wheat in a bowl with 120ml/4fl oz/½ cup boiling water. Leave to soak for 5–10 minutes, or until the water is absorbed.

2 Heat 15g/½ oz/1 tbsp of the butter in a non-stick pan, add the onion and minced chicken and cook gently, stirring occasionally, until pale golden.

3 Stir in the apricots, almonds and bulgur wheat and cook for a further 2 minutes. Remove from the heat and stir in the ground cinnamon and allspice, the Greek yogurt, chopped chives and chopped parsley. Season to taste with salt and pepper.

4 Melt the remaining butter. Unroll the filo pastry and cut into 25cm/10in rounds. Keep the pastry rounds covered with a clean, damp dish towel to prevent them from drying out.

5 Line a 23cm/9in loose-based flan tin (quiche pan) with three of the pastry rounds, lightly brushing each one with melted butter as you layer them. Spoon in the chicken mixture and cover with three more pastry rounds, lightly brushed with melted butter, as before.

6 Crumple the remaining pastry rounds and place them on top of the pie, then brush over any remaining melted butter. Bake the pie in the oven for about 30 minutes, or until the pastry is golden brown and crisp. Serve hot or cold, cut into wedges and garnished with chives.

VARIATIONS
• Use minced (ground) turkey breast fillets in place of the chicken.
• Use hazelnuts or pistachio nuts in place of almonds.

Energy 263kcal/1104kJ; Protein 21.9g; Carbohydrate 19.9g, of which sugars 3.8g; Fat 11.3g, of which saturates 5.2g, of which polyunsaturates 0.9g; Cholesterol 70mg; Calcium 69mg; Fibre 1.6g; Sodium 106mg.

CHICKEN AND VEGETABLE TAGINE ★★★

MOROCCAN TAGINES ARE USUALLY SERVED WITH COUSCOUS, BUT RICE MAKES AN EQUALLY DELICIOUS ACCOMPANIMENT. HERE, COUSCOUS IS STIRRED INTO THE RICE TO CREATE AN UNUSUAL DISH.

SERVES FOUR

INGREDIENTS
  25ml/1½ tbsp groundnut (peanut) oil
  4 skinless, boneless chicken breast
    portions, cut into large pieces
  1 large onion, chopped
  2 garlic cloves, crushed
  1 small parsnip, cut into
    2.5cm/1in pieces
  1 small turnip, cut into 2cm/¾in
    pieces
  3 carrots, cut into 4cm/1½in pieces
  4 tomatoes, chopped
  1 cinnamon stick
  4 whole cloves
  5ml/1 tsp ground ginger
  1 bay leaf
  1.5–2.5ml/¼–½ tsp cayenne pepper
  350ml/12fl oz/1½ cups chicken
    stock
  400g/14oz can chickpeas, drained
    and skinned
  1 red (bell) pepper, seeded
    and sliced
  150g/5oz green beans, halved
  1 piece preserved lemon peel,
    thinly sliced
  20–30 pitted brown or green olives
    (optional)
  salt, to taste
For the rice and couscous
  750ml/1¼ pints/3 cups chicken stock
  225g/8oz/generous 1 cup long grain
    white rice
  115g/4oz/⅔ cup couscous
  45ml/3 tbsp chopped fresh
    coriander (cilantro)

1 Heat 15ml/1 tbsp of the oil in a large, flameproof casserole and fry the chicken pieces for a few minutes, until evenly browned. Transfer to a plate. Heat the remaining oil in the casserole and sauté the onion, garlic, parsnip, turnip and carrots together over a medium heat, stirring frequently, for 4–5 minutes, or until the vegetables are lightly flecked with brown. Reduce the heat, cover and sweat the vegetables, stirring occasionally, for a further 5 minutes.

2 Add the tomatoes, cook for a few minutes, then add the cinnamon stick, cloves, ginger, bay leaf and cayenne pepper. Cook for 1–2 minutes.

3 Pour in the chicken stock, add the chickpeas and browned chicken pieces, and season with salt. Cover and simmer for 25 minutes.

4 Meanwhile, cook the rice and couscous mixture. Bring the chicken stock to the boil in a pan. Add the rice and simmer for about 15 minutes, or until almost tender. Remove the pan from the heat, stir in the couscous, cover tightly and leave for about 5 minutes.

5 When the vegetables in the tagine are almost tender, stir in the pepper slices and green beans and simmer for 10 minutes. Add the preserved lemon and olives, stir well and cook for a further 5 minutes, or until the vegetables are perfectly tender.

6 Stir the chopped coriander into the rice and couscous mixture and pile it on to a warmed serving plate. Serve the chicken tagine in the traditional dish, if you have one, or in a casserole.

Energy 660kcal/2774kJ; Protein 52g; Carbohydrate 92.3g, of which sugars 14.1g; Fat 10.1g, of which saturates 1.5g, of which polyunsaturates 3.3g; Cholesterol 105mg; Calcium 129mg; Fibre 9.8g; Sodium 340mg.

CHICKEN AND RED BEAN RISOTTO ★

THIS QUICK AND EASY RISOTTO, COMBINING BROWN RICE, CHICKEN, VEGETABLES AND RED KIDNEY BEANS, CREATES A TASTY LOW-FAT FAMILY SUPPER DISH.

SERVES FOUR TO SIX

INGREDIENTS

1 onion, chopped
2 garlic cloves, crushed
1 fresh red chilli, seeded and
  finely chopped
175g/6oz mushrooms, sliced
2 celery sticks, chopped
225g/8oz/generous 1 cup long grain
  brown rice
450ml/¾ pint/scant 2 cups chicken
  or vegetable stock
150ml/¼ pint/⅔ cup white wine
400g/14oz can red kidney beans
225g/8oz skinless, boneless chicken
  breast portions, diced
200g/7oz can corn
115g/4oz/¾ cup sultanas
  (golden raisins)
175g/6oz small broccoli florets
30–45ml/2–3 tbsp chopped mixed
  fresh herbs
salt and ground black pepper

1 Put the onion, garlic, chilli, mushrooms, celery, rice, stock and wine in a large, non-stick pan. Cover, bring to the boil, then reduce the heat and simmer for 15 minutes.

2 Rinse and drain the kidney beans. Stir the chicken, kidney beans, corn kernels and sultanas into the pan. Cook, stirring occasionally, for a further 20 minutes, or until almost all the liquid has been absorbed and the rice is tender.

3 Meanwhile, cook the broccoli in a separate pan of boiling water for 5 minutes, then drain.

4 Stir the broccoli and chopped herbs into the risotto, season to taste with salt and pepper and serve immediately.

Energy 368kcal/1553kJ; Protein 19.8g; Carbohydrate 65.6g, of which sugars 20.2g; Fat 1.9g, of which saturates 0.3g, of which polyunsaturates 0.7g; Cholesterol 26mg; Calcium 94mg; Fibre 6.3g; Sodium 395mg.

ITALIAN CHICKEN ★

*THIS SIMPLE ITALIAN PEASANT CASSEROLE HAS ALL THE FLAVOURS OF TRADITIONAL ITALIAN
INGREDIENTS AND IS A DELICIOUS, LOW-FAT SUPPER DISH.*

2 Return the chicken to the pan, then add the passata, wine and chopped fresh or dried oregano and stir to mix. Season well and bring to the boil, stirring, then cover the pan tightly.

3 Reduce the heat and simmer gently, stirring occasionally, for 30–35 minutes, or until the chicken is tender and the juices run clear, not pink, when it is pierced with the point of a sharp knife.

4 Stir in the cannellini beans and simmer for a further 5 minutes, or until heated through. Meanwhile, preheat the grill (broiler) to high. Sprinkle the breadcrumbs over the casserole and cook under the grill until golden brown. Serve immediately, garnished with oregano sprigs.

SERVES SIX

INGREDIENTS
  5ml/1 tsp olive oil
  8 chicken thighs, skinned
  1 onion, thinly sliced
  2 red (bell) peppers, seeded
    and sliced
  1 garlic clove, crushed
  300ml/½ pint/1¼ cups passata
    (bottled strained tomatoes)
  150ml/¼ pint/⅔ cup dry white wine
  1 large fresh oregano sprig, chopped,
    or 5ml/1 tsp dried oregano
  400g/14oz can cannellini beans,
    rinsed and drained
  45ml/3 tbsp fresh breadcrumbs
  salt and ground black pepper
  fresh oregano sprigs, to garnish

1 Heat the oil in a non-stick frying pan, add the chicken and cook until golden brown all over. Remove the chicken to a plate and keep hot. Add the onion and peppers to the pan and sauté gently until softened, but not brown. Add the garlic.

VARIATIONS
• Use 1 red onion in place of a standard onion.
• Use black-eyed beans (peas) in place of cannellini beans.

Energy 218kcal/919kJ; Protein 20.5g; Carbohydrate 23.9g, of which sugars 8.4g; Fat 3.3g, of which saturates 0.8g, of which polyunsaturates 0.9g; Cholesterol 70mg; Calcium 75mg; Fibre 5.9g; Sodium 385mg.

TURKEY AND PASTA BAKE ★

SERVE THIS FLAVOURFUL TURKEY, VEGETABLE AND PASTA BAKE WITH A MIXED GREEN SALAD OR
A SELECTION OF STEAMED FRESH VEGETABLES, FOR A TEMPTING MID-WEEK MEAL.

SERVES FOUR

INGREDIENTS
   275g/10oz minced (ground)
     turkey breast
   150g/5oz smoked turkey
     rashers (strips), chopped
   1–2 garlic cloves, crushed
   1 onion, finely chopped
   2 carrots, diced
   30ml/2 tbsp tomato purée (paste)
   300ml/½ pint/1¼ cups
     chicken stock
   225g/8oz/2 cups dried rigatoni
   30ml/2 tbsp freshly grated
     Parmesan cheese
   salt and ground black pepper

3 Preheat the oven to 180ºC/350ºF/ Gas 4. Cook the pasta in a large pan of salted, boiling water until *al dente*. Drain thoroughly, then mix the pasta with the turkey sauce.

4 Transfer the mixture to a shallow ovenproof dish and sprinkle with grated Parmesan cheese. Bake in the oven for 20–30 minutes, or until lightly browned. Serve immediately.

1 Place the minced turkey in a non-stick pan and cook, breaking up any large pieces with a wooden spoon, until well browned all over.

2 Add the chopped turkey rashers, garlic, onion, carrots, tomato purée, stock and seasoning. Bring to the boil, then reduce the heat, cover and simmer, stirring occasionally, for 1 hour.

Energy 358kcal/1515kJ; Protein 36.3g; Carbohydrate 45.9g, of which sugars 5.6g; Fat 4.5g, of which saturates 2g, of which polyunsaturates 0.8g; Cholesterol 68mg; Calcium 121mg; Fibre 2.7g; Sodium 161mg.

SPAGHETTI ALLA CARBONARA ★★

THIS TASTY LOW-FAT VERSION OF THE CLASSIC DISH CREATES A LIGHT AND TEMPTING MID-WEEK LUNCH OR SUPPER, IDEAL SERVED WITH A MIXED LEAF SALAD.

SERVES FOUR

INGREDIENTS

150g/5oz smoked turkey
   rashers (strips)
1 onion, chopped
1–2 garlic cloves, crushed
150ml/¼ pint/⅔ cup chicken stock
150ml/¼ pint/⅔ cup dry white wine
200g/7oz reduced-fat soft cheese
450g/1lb fresh chilli and garlic-
   flavoured spaghetti
30ml/2 tbsp chopped fresh parsley
salt and ground black pepper
shavings of fresh Parmesan cheese,
   to serve (optional)

1 Cut the turkey rashers into 1cm/½in lengths, then fry them quickly in a non-stick pan for 2–3 minutes. Add the onion, garlic and stock to the pan. Bring to the boil, cover and simmer for 5 minutes, or until the onion is tender.

2 Add the wine and boil rapidly until reduced by half, then whisk in the soft cheese until smooth.

3 Meanwhile, cook the spaghetti in a large pan of salted, boiling water for 10–12 minutes or until *al dente*. Drain thoroughly.

4 Return the pasta to the rinsed-out pan. Add the sauce and chopped parsley, toss well to mix and serve immediately sprinkled with shavings of Parmesan cheese, if you like.

Energy 481kcal/2039kJ; Protein 29.2g; Carbohydrate 77.6g, of which sugars 6.4g; Fat 6.3g, of which saturates 2.9g, of which polyunsaturates 1.1g; Cholesterol 33mg; Calcium 114mg; Fibre 3.7g; Sodium 247mg.

ROLLED STUFFED CANNELLONI ★★

SERVE THIS FLAVOURFUL ITALIAN PASTA DISH WITH A MIXED GREEN SALAD AND FRESH CRUSTY BREAD,
FOR A SATISFYING LOW-FAT SUPPER ALL THE FAMILY WILL ENJOY.

SERVES FOUR

INGREDIENTS
  12 sheets lasagne
  fresh basil leaves, to garnish
For the filling
  2–3 garlic cloves, crushed
  1 small onion, finely chopped
  150ml/¼ pint/⅔ cup white wine
  450g/1lb minced (ground)
    turkey breast fillets
  15ml/1 tbsp dried basil
  15ml/1 tbsp dried thyme
  40g/1½oz fresh white breadcrumbs
  salt and ground black pepper
For the sauce
  25g/1oz/2 tbsp reduced-fat spread
  25g/1oz/¼ cup plain (all-purpose)
    flour
  300ml/½ pint/1¼ cups semi-skimmed
    (low-fat) milk
  4 sun-dried tomatoes, chopped
  15ml/1 tbsp chopped mixed fresh
    herbs (basil, parsley and marjoram)
  30ml/2 tbsp freshly grated
    Parmesan cheese

1 Make the filling. Put the garlic, onion and half the wine into a pan. Cover and cook for about 5 minutes, or until tender. Increase the heat, add the minced turkey and break up with a wooden spoon. Cook quickly until all the liquid has evaporated and the turkey begins to brown slightly.

2 Reduce the heat, add the remaining wine, the dried herbs and seasoning. Cover and cook for 20 minutes. Remove from the heat and stir in the breadcrumbs, then leave to cool.

3 Cook the lasagne in a pan of salted, boiling water until *al dente*. Cook in batches to prevent the lasagne sheets from sticking together. Drain thoroughly, then rinse in cold water. Pat dry.

4 Place the lasagne sheets on a chopping board. Spoon some turkey mixture along one long edge of each sheet and roll it up to encase the filling. Cut the tubes in half.

5 Preheat the oven to 200°C/400°F/ Gas 6. Make the sauce. Put the half-fat spread, flour and milk into a pan, heat gently, whisking constantly, until thickened and smooth. Add the chopped tomatoes, chopped herbs and seasoning.

6 Spoon a thin layer of the sauce into a shallow ovenproof dish and arrange a layer of stuffed cannelloni on top. Spoon over a layer of sauce, and cover with the remaining cannelloni and sauce. Sprinkle with Parmesan, then bake in the oven for 10–15 minutes, or until lightly browned. Serve, garnished with basil leaves.

Energy 645kcal/2731kJ; Protein 47g; Carbohydrate 92g, of which sugars 8.6g; Fat 9.8g, of which saturates 3.5g, of which polyunsaturates 2.7g; Cholesterol 76mg; Calcium 239mg; Fibre 3.6g; Sodium 282mg.

BRAISED QUAIL <u>WITH</u> WINTER VEGETABLES ★★★

QUAIL ARE BOTH PLENTIFUL AND VERY POPULAR IN SPAIN. ROASTING AND BRAISING ARE THE TWO CLASSIC TECHNIQUES FOR COOKING QUAIL. HERE, IN THIS DELICIOUS LOW-FAT DISH, THEY ARE COOKED AND SERVED IN A RED WINE SAUCE, THEN ELEGANTLY DISPLAYED ON CRISP CROÛTES.

4 Add the remaining olive oil to the casserole with the carrots, turnips and shallots and cook until just colouring. Return the quail to the casserole, breast sides down, and pour in the red wine. Cover the casserole and bake in the oven for about 30 minutes, or until the quail are tender.

5 Meanwhile, make the croûtes. Using a 10cm/4in plain cutter, stamp out rounds from the bread. Heat the oil in a non-stick frying pan and cook the bread over a high heat until golden on both sides. Drain on kitchen paper and keep warm.

6 Remove and discard the skin from the quail. Place the croûtes on warmed serving plates and set a quail on top of each one. Arrange the vegetables around the quail, cover and keep hot.

7 Boil the cooking juices rapidly until reduced to a syrupy consistency. Add the brandy and warm through, then season to taste. Drizzle the sauce over the quail, garnish with parsley and serve immediately.

SERVES FOUR

INGREDIENTS
4 quail, cleaned
175g/6oz small carrots, scrubbed
175g/6oz baby turnips
20ml/4 tsp olive oil
4 shallots, halved
450ml/¾ pint/scant 2 cups red wine
30ml/2 tbsp Spanish brandy
salt and ground black pepper
fresh flat leaf parsley, to garnish
For the croûtes
4 slices stale bread, crusts removed
15ml/1 tbsp olive oil

1 Preheat the oven to 220°C/425°F/ Gas 7. Season the quail with salt and black pepper.

2 Using a sharp knife, cut the carrots and baby turnips into chunks. (If the carrots are very small, you can leave them whole, if you prefer.)

3 Heat half the olive oil in a flameproof casserole and add the quail. Cook until browned all over, using two wooden spoons or a pair of tongs to turn the birds. Remove from the casserole and set aside.

Energy 437kcal/1827kJ; Protein 50.5g; Carbohydrate 6.9g, of which sugars 6.3g; Fat 13g, of which saturates 3g, of which polyunsaturates 2.7g; Cholesterol 0mg; Calcium 107mg; Fibre 2.3g; Sodium 161mg.

MARINATED PIGEON IN RED WINE ★★★

GREAT CLOUDS OF MIGRATING PIGEONS FLY OVER THE MOUNTAINS OF SPAIN, AND SHOOTING THEM IS A BIG SPORT. HERE THEY ARE MARINATED IN SPICED VINEGAR AND RED WINE, THEN COOKED IN THE MARINADE. CABBAGE IS A FAMILIAR PARTNER TO PIGEON, BUT PURÉED CELERIAC ALSO GOES VERY WELL.

SERVES FOUR

INGREDIENTS

  4 pigeons (US squabs), weighing about
    225g/8oz each, cleaned and skinned
  10ml/2 tsp olive oil
  1 onion, roughly chopped
  225g/8oz/3 cups brown cap (cremini)
    mushrooms, sliced
  plain (all-purpose) flour, for dusting
  300ml/½ pint/1¼ cups beef or
    game stock
  30ml/2 tbsp chopped fresh parsley
  salt and ground black pepper
  fresh flat leaf parsley, to garnish
For the marinade
  10ml/2 tsp olive oil
  1 onion, chopped
  1 carrot, chopped
  1 celery stick, chopped
  3 garlic cloves, sliced
  6 allspice berries, bruised
  2 bay leaves
  8 black peppercorns, bruised
  120ml/4fl oz/½ cup red wine vinegar
  150ml/¼ pint/⅔ cup red wine

2 Preheat the oven to 150°C/300°F/ Gas 2. Heat the oil in a large flameproof casserole, add the onion and mushrooms and cook for about 5 minutes, or until the onion has softened.

3 Meanwhile, remove the pigeons to a plate with a slotted spoon and strain the marinade into a bowl, then set both aside separately.

4 Sprinkle the flour over the pigeons, then add them to the casserole, breast sides down. Pour in the marinade and stock, and add the chopped parsley and seasoning. Cover and cook for 1½ hours or until cooked and tender.

5 Adjust the seasoning to taste, then serve the pigeons on warmed plates with the sauce. Garnish with parsley.

1 Starting a day ahead, combine all the ingredients for the marinade in a large, non-metallic dish. Add the pigeons and turn them in the marinade, then cover and chill in the refrigerator, turning occasionally, for 12 hours.

VARIATION
If you are unable to buy pigeon, this recipe works equally well with rabbit or hare. Buy portions and make deep slashes in the flesh so that the marinade soaks in and flavours right to the centre.

Energy 232kcal/965kJ; Protein 22.9g; Carbohydrate 1.7g, of which sugars 1.2g; Fat 14.9g, of which saturates 0.7g, of which polyunsaturates 0.5g; Cholesterol 0mg; Calcium 42mg; Fibre 1.4g; Sodium 88mg.

LAMB, PORK, BEEF AND VEAL

*Lean cuts of meat such as lamb, pork, beef and
veal are ideal for creating a wide range
of nutritious, low-fat dishes. In the
Mediterranean, popular cooking methods such as
braising and grilling, as well as marinating
meat before cooking, are good for creating classic,
tasty, low-fat dishes such as Spiced Lamb and
Vegetable Couscous, Kleftico, Beef Stew with
Red Wine and Peas, and Osso Bucco.*

SPICED LAMB ᴬᴺᴰ VEGETABLE COUSCOUS ★★

A DELICIOUS MEDITERRANEAN-STYLE STEW OF TENDER LAMB AND VEGETABLES, SERVED WITH PLENTY OF COUSCOUS, CREATES THIS FLAVOURFUL LOW-FAT MEAL.

SERVES SIX

INGREDIENTS

350g/12oz lean lamb fillet, cut into
  2cm/¾in cubes
30ml/2 tbsp plain (all-purpose)
  flour, seasoned
10ml/2 tsp sunflower oil
1 onion, chopped
2 garlic cloves, crushed
1 red (bell) pepper, seeded and diced
5ml/1 tsp ground coriander
5ml/1 tsp ground cumin
5ml/1 tsp ground allspice
2.5ml/½ tsp hot chilli powder
300ml/½ pint/1¼ cups lamb or
  vegetable stock
400g/14oz can chopped tomatoes
225g/8oz carrots, sliced
175g/6oz parsnips, sliced
175g/6oz courgettes (zucchini), sliced
175g/6oz/2⅓ cups closed cup
  mushrooms, quartered
225g/8oz frozen broad (fava) beans
115g/4oz/¾ cup sultanas
  (golden raisins)
450g/1lb/2¾ cups quick-cook
  couscous
salt and ground black pepper
fresh parsley sprigs, to garnish

2 Add any remaining flour and the ground spices and cook, stirring continuously, for 1 minute.

3 Gradually add the stock, continuing to stir, then add the tomatoes, carrots and parsnips, and mix well.

5 Add the courgettes, mushrooms, broad beans and sultanas. Cover, return to the boil and simmer, stirring occasionally, for a further 20–30 minutes, or until the lamb and vegetables are tender. Season to taste with salt and pepper.

6 Meanwhile, soak the couscous according to the packet instructions. Drain. Pile the cooked couscous on to a warmed serving platter and top with the lamb and vegetable stew. Garnish with parsley. Serve immediately.

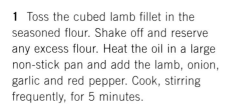

1 Toss the cubed lamb fillet in the seasoned flour. Shake off and reserve any excess flour. Heat the oil in a large non-stick pan and add the lamb, onion, garlic and red pepper. Cook, stirring frequently, for 5 minutes.

4 Bring to the boil, stirring, then reduce the heat, cover and simmer, stirring occasionally, for 30 minutes.

VARIATIONS
• Use lean beef or pork in place of lamb.
• Use raisins or chopped dried apricots in place of sultanas (golden raisins).

Energy 445kcal/1869kJ; Protein 22.2g; Carbohydrate 71.2g, of which sugars 22g; Fat 9.7g, of which saturates 3.4g, of which polyunsaturates 1.5g; Cholesterol 44mg; Calcium 100mg; Fibre 7g; Sodium 78mg.

ROAST LAMB <u>WITH</u> FIGS ★★★

LAMB FILLET IS AN EXPENSIVE CUT OF MEAT, BUT BECAUSE IT IS VERY LEAN AND THEREFORE LOWER IN FAT, THERE IS VERY LITTLE WASTE. SERVE WITH BAKED POTATOES AND STEAMED GREEN BEANS.

SERVES SIX

INGREDIENTS
    15ml/1 tbsp olive oil
    1kg/2¼lb lamb fillet
    9 fresh figs
    150ml/¼ pint/⅔ cup ruby port
    salt and ground black pepper

1 Preheat the oven to 190°C/375°F/ Gas 5. Heat the oil in a flameproof roasting pan over a medium heat. Add the lamb fillet and sear on all sides until evenly browned.

2 Cut the figs in half and arrange them around the lamb. Season the lamb with salt and black pepper and roast for 30 minutes. Pour the port over the figs.

3 Return the lamb to the oven and roast for a further 30–45 minutes. The meat should still be slightly pink in the middle so be careful not to overcook it.

4 Transfer the lamb to a chopping board and leave to rest for about 5 minutes, then carve into slices and serve.

COOK'S TIP
Fresh figs are grown mainly in Greece and Turkey and they are at their best from June until the end of September. Ripe figs have plump, soft flesh with a powdery, white bloom on the surface. They are perishable and will only keep fresh for a day or two.

Energy 422kcal/1768kJ; Protein 33.8g; Carbohydrate 18.9g, of which sugars 18.9g; Fat 15g, of which saturates 8.9g, of which polyunsaturates 1g; Cholesterol 127mg; Calcium 89mg; Fibre 2.3g; Sodium 163mg.

LAMB <u>WITH</u> RED PEPPERS <u>AND</u> RIOJA ★★★

WORLD-FAMOUS FOR ITS RED WINE, RIOJA, SPAIN, ALSO PRODUCES EXCELLENT RED PEPPERS. TOGETHER THEY GIVE THIS LOW-FAT STEW A RICH FLAVOUR. BOILED POTATOES ARE A GOOD ACCOMPANIMENT.

<u>SERVES FOUR</u>

INGREDIENTS
   15ml/1 tbsp plain (all-purpose) flour
   450g/1lb lean lamb, cubed
   10ml/2 tsp olive oil
   2 red onions, sliced
   4 garlic cloves, sliced
   10ml/2 tsp paprika
   1.5ml/¼ tsp ground cloves
   400ml/14fl oz/1⅔ cups red Rioja
   150ml/¼ pint/⅔ cup lamb stock
   2 bay leaves
   2 fresh thyme sprigs
   3 red (bell) peppers, halved
    and seeded
  salt and ground black pepper
  bay leaves and fresh thyme sprigs,
   to garnish (optional)

1 Preheat the oven to 160ºC/325ºF/ Gas 3. Season the flour, add the lamb and toss lightly to coat all over. Shake off and discard any excess flour.

2 Heat the oil in a non-stick frying pan and cook the lamb until browned all over. Transfer to an ovenproof dish. Add the onions and garlic to the pan and cook, stirring occasionally, until soft. Add to the meat in the dish.

3 Add the paprika, ground cloves, Rioja, stock, bay leaves and thyme sprigs to the pan and bring the mixture to a gentle simmer. Add the red peppers. Pour the mixture over the meat, onions and garlic in the ovenproof dish and mix well. Cover the dish with a lid or foil and bake in the oven for about 30 minutes, or until the meat is cooked and tender. Garnish with more bay leaves and thyme sprigs, if you like. Serve.

Energy 342kcal/1427kJ; Protein 24g; Carbohydrate 12.3g, of which sugars 9g; Fat 14.7g, of which saturates 6.2g, of which polyunsaturates 1g; Cholesterol 86mg; Calcium 33mg; Fibre 2.4g; Sodium 110mg.

MEDITERRANEAN LAMB <u>WITH</u> VEGETABLES ★★★

A GOOD SELECTION OF VEGETABLES COMBINE WITH LEAN LAMB CHOPS AND HERBS TO CREATE THIS DELICIOUS, WARMING LOW-FAT FAMILY MEAL, IDEAL SERVED WITH BAKED POTATOES.

SERVES SIX

INGREDIENTS

juice of 1 lemon
15ml/1 tbsp soy sauce
15ml/1 tbsp dry sherry
1 garlic clove, crushed
10ml/2 tsp chopped fresh rosemary
6 lean chump or loin lamb chops, fat removed
1 red onion, cut into 8 pieces
1 onion, cut into 8 pieces
1 each red, yellow and green (bell) peppers, seeded and cut into chunks
4 courgettes (zucchini), thickly sliced
350g/12oz/4½ cups button (white) mushrooms
15ml/1 tbsp olive oil
4 plum tomatoes, skinned
400g/14oz can baby corn
60ml/4 tbsp chopped fresh basil
15–30ml/1–2 tbsp balsamic vinegar
salt and ground black pepper
fresh basil sprigs, to garnish

1 In a shallow non-metallic dish, mix together the lemon juice, soy sauce, sherry, garlic and chopped rosemary. Add the lamb chops to the marinade and turn them to coat all over. Cover and refrigerate for 2 hours.

2 Preheat the oven to 200°C/400°F/ Gas 6. Put the onions, peppers, courgettes and mushrooms in a non-stick roasting pan, drizzle over the oil and toss the vegetables together to mix. Bake in the oven for 25 minutes.

3 Quarter the tomatoes and stir into the roast vegetables with the baby corn. Bake for a further 10 minutes, or until all the vegetables are just tender and slightly browned at the edges. Add the chopped basil, sprinkle over the balsamic vinegar and season to taste with salt and pepper, stirring to mix well.

4 Meanwhile, preheat the grill (broiler) to medium. Place the lamb chops on a grill (broiling) pan and grill (broil), turning once, for about 6 minutes on each side, or until cooked. Brush the chops with any remaining marinade while they are cooking, to prevent them drying out. Place the chops on warmed serving plates with the vegetables and garnish with basil sprigs. Serve.

Energy 197kcal/819kJ; Protein 16.1g; Carbohydrate 8.7g, of which sugars 7.8g; Fat 10.7g, of which saturates 3.4g, of which polyunsaturates 1.2g; Cholesterol 38mg; Calcium 56mg; Fibre 4.1g; Sodium 815mg.

KLEFTIKO ★★★

FOR THIS LIGHT CLASSIC GREEK RECIPE, MARINATED LAMB IS SLOW-COOKED TO DEVELOP A MELTINGLY TENDER TASTE. THE DISH IS SEALED, WITH FLOUR DOUGH TO TRAP SUCCULENCE AND FLAVOUR.

SERVES FOUR

INGREDIENTS
    juice of 1 lemon
    15ml/1 tbsp chopped fresh oregano
    4 lean lamb leg steaks or chump
      chops with bones, fat removed
    10ml/2 tsp olive oil
    2 large onions, thinly sliced
    2 bay leaves
    150ml/¼ pint/⅔ cup dry white wine
    225g/8oz/2 cups plain
      (all-purpose) flour
    salt and ground black pepper

1 Mix together the lemon juice, chopped oregano and salt and pepper, and brush this mixture over both sides of the lamb steaks or chops. Leave to marinate in a cool place for at least 4 hours or overnight.

2 Preheat the oven to 160°C/325°F/ Gas 3. Drain the lamb, reserving the marinade, and dry the meat with kitchen paper. Heat the oil in a large non-stick frying pan and cook the lamb over a high heat until browned on both sides.

3 Transfer the lamb to a shallow, ovenproof pie dish. Sprinkle the sliced onions and bay leaves around the lamb, then pour over the white wine and the reserved marinade. Set aside.

COOK'S TIPS
• They are not essential for this dish, but lean lamb steaks or chops with bones will provide lots of additional flavour.
• Boiled potatoes will make a delicious accompaniment.

4 In a bowl, mix the flour with sufficient water to make a firm dough. Moisten the rim of the pie dish. Roll out the dough on a lightly floured surface and use to cover the dish so that it is tightly sealed.

5 Bake in the oven for 2 hours, then break away and discard the dough crust and serve the lamb hot, with boiled potatoes, if you like.

Energy 267kcal/1113kJ; Protein 23g; Carbohydrate 6.2g, of which sugars 4.4g; Fat 14.3g, of which saturates 6.1g, of which polyunsaturates 0.8g; Cholesterol 86mg; Calcium 31mg; Fibre 1.1g; Sodium 101mg.

LAMB AND SEVEN–VEGETABLE COUSCOUS ★★★

SEVEN IS A MAGICAL NUMBER IN MOROCCO AND THERE ARE MANY RECIPES FOR THIS GLORIOUS CELEBRATION COUSCOUS. THE VEGETABLES ARE CARROTS, PARSNIPS, TURNIPS, ONIONS, COURGETTES, TOMATOES AND FRENCH BEANS. YOU COULD SUBSTITUTE DIFFERENT VEGETABLES, IF YOU WISH.

SERVES SIX

INGREDIENTS
    20ml/4 tsp sunflower or olive oil
    450g/1lb lean lamb, cut into
      bite-size pieces
    2 chicken breast quarters, skinned
      and halved
    2 onions, chopped
    350g/12oz carrots, cut into chunks
    225g/8oz parsnips, cut into chunks
    115g/4oz turnips, cut into cubes
    6 tomatoes, skinned and chopped
    900ml/1½ pints/3¾ cups
      chicken stock
    good pinch of ground ginger
    1 cinnamon stick
    400g/14oz can chickpeas, rinsed
      and drained
    400g/14oz/2⅓ cups couscous
    2 small courgettes (zucchini), cut
      into julienne strips
    115g/4oz French (green) beans,
      trimmed and halved if necessary
    50g/2oz/⅓ cup raisins
    a little harissa or Tabasco sauce
    salt and ground black pepper

1 Heat half the oil in a large non-stick pan or flameproof casserole and cook the lamb, in batches if necessary, stirring frequently, until evenly browned. Transfer to a plate with a slotted spoon. Add the chicken pieces to the pan and cook until evenly browned. Transfer to the plate with the lamb.

2 Heat the remaining oil in the pan and add the onions. Cook over a gentle heat, stirring occasionally, for 2–3 minutes, then add the carrots, parsnips and turnips. Stir well, cover with a lid and "sweat" over a gentle heat, stirring once or twice, for 5–6 minutes.

3 Add the tomatoes, lamb, chicken and stock to the pan. Season, add the ginger and cinnamon. Bring to the boil, reduce the heat, simmer for 45 minutes, until tender.

4 Meanwhile, skin the chickpeas by placing them in a bowl of cold water and rubbing them between your fingers. Prepare the couscous according to the instructions on the packet.

5 Add the chickpeas, courgettes, beans and raisins to the meat mixture, stir gently and cook for 10–15 minutes, or until tender. Pile the couscous on to a serving plate. Make a well in the centre.

6 Transfer the meat to a plate, remove the bones. Spoon 4 spoonfuls of stock from the pan into a small pan. Stir the chicken into the stew and heat gently. Add the harissa or Tabasco sauce to the stock juices and heat gently until hot. Spoon the lamb and vegetable stew over the couscous. Serve the harissa sauce in a separate bowl.

VARIATIONS
Use lean beef or pork in place of lamb.
Use swede (rutabaga) in place of turnips or parsnips.

Energy 546kcal/2292kJ; Protein 38.9g; Carbohydrate 68g, of which sugars 19.5g; Fat 14.9g, of which saturates 4.8g, of which polyunsaturates 2.1g; Cholesterol 92mg; Calcium 126mg; Fibre 8.8g; Sodium 278mg.

BULGUR WHEAT, BACON AND LENTIL PILAFF ★★★

BULGUR WHEAT IS A REALLY USEFUL LOW-FAT STORE CUPBOARD INGREDIENT. IT HAS A NUTTY TASTE AND TEXTURE AND ONLY NEEDS SOAKING BEFORE SERVING IN A SALAD, OR WARMING THROUGH FOR A HOT DISH.

SERVES FOUR

INGREDIENTS
  115g/4oz/½ cup green lentils
  115g/4oz/⅔ cup bulgur wheat
  5ml/1 tsp ground coriander
  5ml/1 tsp ground cinnamon
  10ml/2 tsp olive oil
  225g/8oz rindless lean back bacon
    rashers (strips), chopped
  1 red onion, chopped
  1 garlic clove, crushed
  5ml/1 tsp cumin seeds
  30ml/2 tbsp roughly chopped
    fresh parsley
  salt and ground black pepper

1 Soak the lentils and bulgur wheat separately in cold water for 1 hour, then drain. Tip the lentils into a pan. Stir in the coriander, cinnamon and 475ml/16fl oz/2 cups water. Bring to the boil, then simmer until the lentils are tender and the liquid has been absorbed.

2 Meanwhile, heat the oil in a non-stick pan and cook the bacon until crisp. Remove and drain on kitchen paper. Add the onion and garlic to the oil remaining in the pan and cook for 10 minutes, or until soft and golden brown. Stir in the cumin seeds and cook for a further 1 minute. Return the bacon to the pan.

3 Stir the drained bulgur wheat into the cooked lentils, then add the mixture to the frying pan. Season with salt and pepper and heat through. Stir in the chopped parsley and serve.

COOK'S TIP
If possible, use Puy lentils, which have a superior flavour, aroma and texture.

Energy 300kcal/1257kJ; Protein 18.3g; Carbohydrate 32.4g, of which sugars 1.8g; Fat 11.6g, of which saturates 3.8g, of which polyunsaturates 1.5g; Cholesterol 30mg; Calcium 49mg; Fibre 2.2g; Sodium 881mg.

PANCETTA AND BROAD BEAN RISOTTO ★★

THIS DELICIOUS RISOTTO MAKES A HEALTHY AND FILLING LOW-FAT MEAL, WHEN SERVED WITH A MIXED GREEN SALAD. USE LEAN SMOKED BACK BACON INSTEAD OF PANCETTA, IF YOU LIKE.

2 Heat the olive oil in the casserole. Add the onion, garlic and pancetta or bacon and cook gently, stirring occasionally, for about 5 minutes.

3 Add the rice to the pan and cook, stirring, for 1 minute. Add 300ml/ ½ pint/1¼ cups of the hot stock and simmer, stirring frequently, until it has been absorbed.

SERVES FOUR

INGREDIENTS
225g/8oz frozen baby broad (fava) beans
10ml/2 tsp olive oil
1 onion, chopped
2 garlic cloves, finely chopped
115g/4oz smoked pancetta or lean smoked back bacon, diced
350g/12oz/1¾ cups risotto rice
about 1.2 litres/2 pints/5 cups simmering chicken stock
30ml/2 tbsp chopped mixed fresh herbs, such as parsley, thyme and oregano
salt and ground black pepper
coarsely chopped fresh parsley, to garnish
shavings of fresh Parmesan cheese, to serve (optional) (see Cook's Tip)

1 Cook the broad beans in a large flameproof casserole of lightly salted, boiling water for about 3 minutes, or until tender. Drain and set aside.

COOK'S TIP
To make thin Parmesan cheese shavings, take a rectangular block or long wedge of fresh Parmesan cheese and firmly scrape a vegetable peeler down the side of the cheese to make shavings. The swivel-bladed type of peeler is best for this job.

4 Continue adding the stock, a ladleful at a time, stirring frequently, until the rice is just tender and creamy, and almost all of the liquid has been absorbed. This will take 30–35 minutes. It may not be necessary to add all the stock.

5 Stir the broad beans, chopped herbs and seasoning into the risotto. Heat gently until hot, then serve garnished with the chopped parsley and sprinkled with shavings of Parmesan cheese, if you like.

Energy 444kcal/1858kJ; Protein 16.2g; Carbohydrate 77.9g, of which sugars 1.8g; Fat 7.2g, of which saturates 2.1g, of which polyunsaturates 1g; Cholesterol 15mg; Calcium 76mg; Fibre 4.4g; Sodium 452mg.

CANNELLONI ★★

THIS TASTY, LOW-FAT VERSION OF THIS POPULAR AND CLASSIC ITALIAN PASTA DISH IS IDEAL SERVED WITH A MIXED BABY LEAF SALAD AND FRESH CRUSTY BREAD FOR A TEMPTING MID-WEEK LUNCH OR SUPPER.

SERVES FOUR

INGREDIENTS
  2 garlic cloves, crushed
  2 x 400g/14oz cans chopped tomatoes
  10ml/2 tsp soft light brown sugar
  15ml/1 tbsp chopped fresh basil
  15ml/1 tbsp chopped fresh marjoram
  450g/1lb frozen chopped spinach
  large pinch freshly grated nutmeg
  115g/4oz cooked lean ham,
    minced (ground)
  200g/7oz cottage cheese
  12–14 dried cannelloni tubes
  50g/2oz reduced-fat mozzarella
    cheese, diced
  25g/1oz mature (sharp) Cheddar
    cheese, grated
  25g/1oz fresh white breadcrumbs
  salt and ground black pepper
  fresh flat leaf parsley sprigs, to garnish

4 Pipe the filling into each tube of uncooked cannelloni. It is easiest to hold them upright with one end flat on a chopping board, while piping from the other end.

5 Preheat the oven to 180°C/350°F/ Gas 4. Spoon half the tomato sauce into the bottom of a 20cm/8in square ovenproof dish. Lay two rows of filled cannelloni on top of the sauce.

6 Sprinkle over the diced mozzarella and cover with the remaining tomato sauce.

7 Combine the Cheddar cheese and breadcrumbs and sprinkle over the top. Bake in the oven for 30–40 minutes. Garnish with flat leaf parsley sprigs and serve immediately.

1 To make the sauce, put the garlic, chopped tomatoes, sugar and chopped herbs into a non-stick pan, bring to the boil and cook uncovered over a medium heat, stirring occasionally, for 30 minutes, or until fairly thick.

2 Meanwhile, make the filling. Put the spinach into a separate pan, cover and cook slowly until thawed. Break up with a fork, then increase the heat to cook off any water. Season with salt, pepper and nutmeg.

3 Turn the spinach into a bowl, cool slightly, then add the minced ham and cottage cheese. Stir to mix well. Spoon the ham mixture into a piping (pastry) bag fitted with a plain nozzle.

Energy 421kcal/1782kJ; Protein 25.5g; Carbohydrate 61.6g, of which sugars 12.6g; Fat 9.5g, of which saturates 4.9g, of which polyunsaturates 1.3g; Cholesterol 38mg; Calcium 218mg; Fibre 4.5g; Sodium 661mg.

PORK IN SWEET-AND-SOUR SAUCE ★★

THE COMBINATION OF SWEET AND SOUR FLAVOURS IS POPULAR WITH MEAT AND LIVER. THIS RECIPE IS GIVEN EXTRA BITE WITH THE ADDITION OF CRUSHED MIXED PEPPERCORNS.

SERVES FOUR

INGREDIENTS
    1 whole pork fillet, about 350g/12oz
        total weight
    25ml/1½ tbsp plain (all-purpose) flour
    15ml/1 tbsp olive oil
    250ml/8fl oz/1 cup dry white wine
    30ml/2 tbsp white wine vinegar
    10ml/2 tsp granulated sugar
    15ml/1 tbsp mixed peppercorns,
        coarsely ground
    salt and ground black pepper
    broad beans tossed with grilled
        (broiled) lean bacon, to serve

1 Cut the pork fillet diagonally into thin slices. Place between two sheets of clear film (plastic wrap) and pound lightly with a rolling pin to flatten them evenly.

2 Sprinkle the flour into a shallow bowl. Season well, then coat the meat all over with the flour, shaking off and discarding any excess flour.

3 Heat the oil in a wide heavy pan or non-stick frying pan and add as many slices of pork as the pan will hold. Cook over a medium to high heat for 2–3 minutes on each side, or until crispy and tender. Remove with a fish slice or metal spatula and set aside. Repeat with the remaining pork.

4 Mix the wine, wine vinegar and sugar in a bowl. Pour the mixture into the pan and stir vigorously over a high heat until reduced, scraping the pan to incorporate the sediment. Stir in the ground peppercorns, then return the pork to the pan. Spoon the sauce over the pork until it is evenly coated and heated through. Serve immediately.

COOK'S TIP
Serve fresh crusty bread with this dish and use to mop up the juices.

Energy 194kcal/812kJ; Protein 19.4g; Carbohydrate 5.2g, of which sugars 0.5g; Fat 6.3g, of which saturates 1.6g, of which polyunsaturates 0.9g; Cholesterol 55mg; Calcium 21mg; Fibre 0.2g; Sodium 64mg.

AFELIA ★★

THIS LIGHTLY SPICED PORK STEW MAKES A REALLY DELICIOUS LOW-FAT SUPPER DISH SERVED SIMPLY, AS IT WOULD BE IN CYPRUS, WITH WARMED BREAD, A LEAFY SALAD AND A FEW OLIVES.

SERVES FOUR

INGREDIENTS
  675g/1½lb lean pork fillet
  20ml/4 tsp coriander seeds
  2.5ml/½ tsp caster (superfine) sugar
  20ml/4 tsp olive oil
  2 large onions, sliced
  300ml/½ pint/1¼ cups red wine
  salt and ground black pepper
  fresh coriander (cilantro),
    to garnish

1 Cut the pork into small chunks, removing and discarding any visible fat. Crush the coriander seeds with a mortar and pestle until fairly finely ground.

2 Mix the coriander seeds with the sugar and salt and pepper and rub all over the meat. Leave to marinate in a cool place for up to 4 hours.

COOK'S TIP
A coffee grinder can also be used to grind the coriander seeds. Alternatively, use 15ml/1 tbsp ground coriander.

3 Preheat the oven to 160°C/325°F/ Gas 3. Heat half of the oil in a non-stick frying pan over a high heat. Add the pork to the pan and brown quickly all over, then transfer to an ovenproof dish.

4 Add the remaining oil and the onions to the pan and cook until the onions are beginning to colour. Stir in the wine and a little seasoning, and bring to the boil.

5 Pour the onion and wine mixture over the meat; cover with a lid. Bake for 1 hour, or until the meat is very tender. Serve garnished with fresh coriander.

Energy 320kcal/1337kJ; Protein 37.4g; Carbohydrate 8.1g, of which sugars 5.8g; Fat 10g, of which saturates 2.8g, of which polyunsaturates 1.5g; Cholesterol 106mg; Calcium 42mg; Fibre 1.4g; Sodium 127mg.

HONEY ROAST PORK WITH HERBS ★

HERBS AND HONEY ADD FLAVOUR AND SWEETNESS TO TENDERLOIN — THE LEANEST CUT OF PORK — TO CREATE THIS FLAVOURFUL, LOW-FAT DISH.

SERVES FOUR

INGREDIENTS
  450g/1lb lean pork tenderloin
    or fillet
  30ml/2 tbsp set (crystallized) honey
  30ml/2 tbsp Dijon mustard
  5ml/1 tsp chopped fresh rosemary
  2.5ml/½ tsp chopped fresh thyme
  1.5ml/¼ tsp whole tropical
    peppercorns
  fresh rosemary and thyme sprigs,
    to garnish
For the red onion confit
  4 red onions
  350ml/12fl oz/1½ cups
    vegetable stock
  15ml/1 tbsp red wine vinegar
  15ml/1 tbsp caster (superfine) sugar
  1 garlic clove, crushed
  30ml/2 tbsp ruby port
  pinch of salt

1 Preheat the oven to 180°C/350°F/ Gas 4. Trim off and discard any visible fat from the pork. Put the honey, mustard, chopped rosemary and thyme in a small bowl and mix them together well.

2 Crush the peppercorns using a mortar and pestle. Spread the honey mixture evenly over the pork and sprinkle with the crushed peppercorns. Place in a non-stick roasting pan and bake in the oven for 35–45 minutes.

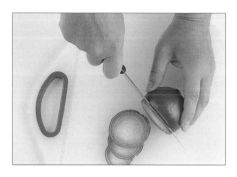

3 Meanwhile, make the red onion confit. Slice the onions into rings and put them into a heavy pan.

4 Add the stock, vinegar, sugar and garlic to the pan. Bring to the boil, then reduce the heat, cover and simmer for 15 minutes.

5 Uncover the pan and add the port, then continue to simmer, stirring occasionally, until the onions are soft and the juices are thick and syrupy. Season to taste with salt.

6 Cut the pork into slices and arrange on warmed plates, to serve.

Energy 231kcal/968kJ; Protein 25.6g; Carbohydrate 20.4g, of which sugars 17.6g; Fat 4.8g, of which saturates 1.6g, of which polyunsaturates 0.9g; Cholesterol 71mg; Calcium 42mg; Fibre 1.8g; Sodium 84mg.

PORK WITH MARSALA AND JUNIPER ★★

SICILIAN MARSALA GIVES SAVOURY DISHES A RICH, FRUITY AND ALCOHOLIC TANG. USE GOOD QUALITY
PORK TO ENHANCE THE FLAVOUR OF THE SAUCE. SERVE WITH COOKED NOODLES AND GREEN VEGETABLES.

SERVES FOUR

INGREDIENTS
    25g/1oz dried ceps
    4 lean pork escalopes
    10ml/2 tsp balsamic vinegar
    8 garlic cloves
    15g/½oz/1 tbsp butter
    45ml/3 tbsp Marsala
    several fresh rosemary sprigs
    10 juniper berries, crushed
    salt and ground black pepper

1 Put the dried mushrooms in a bowl and just cover with hot water. Leave to soak for 15–20 minutes, then strain, reserving the mushrooms and soaking water separately. Set aside.

2 Brush the pork with 5ml/1 tsp of the vinegar and season with salt and pepper. Set aside. Put the garlic cloves in a small pan, cover with boiling water and cook for 10 minutes, or until soft. Drain and set aside.

3 Melt the butter in a large non-stick frying pan. Add the pork and fry quickly until browned on the underside. Turn the meat over and cook for a further 1 minute.

4 Add the Marsala, rosemary sprigs, soaked mushrooms, 60ml/4 tbsp of the mushroom soaking water, the garlic, juniper berries and remaining vinegar.

5 Simmer gently for about 3 minutes, or until the pork is cooked through. Season lightly with salt and pepper and serve immediately.

VARIATION
Use dried porcini mushrooms in place of dried ceps.

Energy 229kcal/957kJ; Protein 32.1g; Carbohydrate 1.4g, of which sugars 1.4g; Fat 9.1g, of which saturates 4.1g, of which polyunsaturates 1.2g; Cholesterol 103mg; Calcium 12mg; Fibre 0g; Sodium 128mg.

LASAGNE ★★

THIS IS A DELICIOUS LOW-FAT VERSION OF THE CLASSIC ITALIAN LASAGNE, IDEAL SERVED WITH A MIXED SALAD AND CRUSTY BREAD FOR A TEMPTING SUPPER WITH FRIENDS.

SERVES EIGHT

INGREDIENTS

  1 large onion, chopped
  2 garlic cloves, crushed
  500g/1¼lb extra-lean minced
    (ground) beef or turkey
  450ml/¾ pint/scant 2 cups passata
    (bottled strained tomatoes)
  5ml/1 tsp mixed dried herbs
  225g/8oz frozen spinach, thawed
  200g/7oz lasagne verdi
  200g/7oz cottage cheese
  mixed salad, to serve
For the sauce
  25g/1oz/2 tbsp half-fat spread
  25g/1oz/¼ cup plain (all-purpose)
    flour
  300ml/½ pint/1¼ cups skimmed milk
  1.5ml/¼ tsp freshly grated nutmeg
  25g/1oz/⅓ cup freshly grated
    Parmesan cheese
  salt and ground black pepper

1 Put the onion, garlic and beef or turkey in a non-stick pan. Cook quickly, stirring with a wooden spoon to separate the pieces, for 5 minutes, or until the meat is lightly browned all over.

VARIATIONS
• Use extra-lean minced (ground) lamb, pork or chicken in place of beef or turkey.
• Use grated mature (sharp) Cheddar cheese in place of Parmesan.

2 Add the passata, dried herbs and seasoning and stir to mix. Bring to the boil, then reduce the heat, cover and simmer, stirring occasionally, for about 30 minutes.

3 Meanwhile, make the sauce. Put all the sauce ingredients, except the Parmesan cheese, into a pan. Cook gently, whisking continuously, until the sauce thickens and is bubbling and smooth. Remove from the heat. Adjust the seasoning to taste, add the Parmesan cheese to the sauce and stir to mix.

4 Preheat the oven to 190°C/375°F/ Gas 5. Arrange the spinach leaves on sheets of kitchen paper and pat them until they are dry.

5 Layer the meat mixture, lasagne, cottage cheese and spinach in a 2 litre/3½ pint/8 cup ovenproof dish, starting and ending with a layer of meat mixture.

6 Spoon the cheese sauce evenly over the top to cover the meat completely, then bake in the oven for 40–50 minutes, or until bubbling. Serve with a mixed salad and fresh crusty bread.

Energy 279kcal/1173kJ; Protein 21.9g; Carbohydrate 27.4g, of which sugars 6.7g; Fat 9.8g, of which saturates 4g, of which polyunsaturates 1.6g; Cholesterol 38mg; Calcium 180mg; Fibre 2.3g; Sodium 183mg.

TAGINE OF BEEF WITH PEAS AND SAFFRON ★★★

THIS NUTRITIOUS TAGINE CAN BE MADE WITH BEEF OR LAMB. SAFFRON IMPARTS A PUNGENT TASTE. THE
PEAS, TOMATOES AND LEMON ADDED AT THE END OF COOKING ENLIVEN THE GINGERY BEEF MIXTURE.

SERVES SIX

INGREDIENTS

   600g/1¼lb lean chuck steak or
    braising steak, trimmed of any fat
    and cubed
   10ml/2 tsp olive oil
   1 onion, chopped
   25g/1oz fresh root ginger, peeled
    and finely chopped
   5ml/1 tsp ground ginger
   pinch of cayenne pepper
   pinch of saffron threads
   1.2kg/2½lb shelled fresh peas
   2 tomatoes, skinned and chopped
   1 preserved lemon, chopped
   a handful of brown kalamata olives
   salt and ground black pepper
   bread or couscous, to serve (optional)

1 Put the cubed steak in a tagine, flameproof casserole or heavy, non-stick pan with the olive oil, onion, fresh and ground ginger, cayenne and saffron threads, and season with salt and pepper. Pour in enough water to cover the meat completely, and bring to the boil, then reduce the heat, cover and simmer for about 1½ hours, or until the meat is very tender. Cook for a little longer, if necessary.

2 Add the peas, tomatoes, preserved lemon and olives. Stir well, then cook, uncovered, for about 10 minutes, or until the peas are tender and the sauce has reduced. Adjust the seasoning to taste and serve with bread or plain couscous, if you like.

Energy 359kcal/1494kJ; Protein 36.9g; Carbohydrate 24.4g, of which sugars 6.2g; Fat 13.4g, of which saturates 4.6g, of which polyunsaturates 2g; Cholesterol 58mg; Calcium 52mg; Fibre 9.9g; Sodium 69mg.

BEEF STEW WITH RED WINE AND PEAS ★★★

THIS RICH, BUT LOW-FAT, MEATY STEW IS PERFECT FOR A WINTER LUNCH OR SUPPER. SERVE IT WITH BOILED OR MASHED POTATOES TO SOAK UP THE DELICIOUSLY TASTY WINE AND TOMATO SAUCE.

SERVES FOUR

INGREDIENTS

30ml/2 tbsp plain (all-purpose) flour
10ml/2 tsp chopped fresh or dried thyme
500g/1lb lean braising or stewing steak, cut into large cubes
15ml/1 tbsp olive oil
1 medium onion, roughly chopped
450ml/¾ pint/scant 2 cups passata (bottled strained tomatoes)
250ml/8fl oz/1 cup beef stock
250ml/8fl oz/1 cup red wine
2 garlic cloves, crushed
30ml/2 tbsp tomato purée (paste)
275g/10oz/2 cups shelled fresh peas
5ml/1 tsp granulated sugar
salt and ground black pepper
fresh thyme sprigs, to garnish

1 Preheat the oven to 160°C/325°F/ Gas 3. Put the flour in a shallow dish and add the chopped fresh or dried thyme. Season with plenty of salt and pepper. Add the beef cubes and turn them in the seasoned flour until each cube is evenly coated on all sides.

2 Heat the oil in a large flameproof casserole over a medium to high heat, add the beef and brown on all sides. Remove the beef with a slotted spoon and drain on kitchen paper.

3 Add the onion to the pan, scraping the base of the pan to mix in any residue. Cook gently, stirring frequently, for about 3 minutes, or until the onions have softened, then stir in the passata, stock, wine, garlic and tomato purée. Bring to the boil, stirring.

4 Return the beef to the pan and stir well to coat with the sauce. Cover and cook in the oven for 1½ hours.

5 Stir in the peas and sugar. Return the casserole to the oven and cook for a further 30 minutes, or until the beef is tender. Season to taste with salt and pepper and garnish with fresh thyme sprigs before serving.

VARIATION

Use frozen peas instead of fresh. Add them 10 minutes before the end of cooking.

Energy 401kcal/1671kJ; Protein 36.9g; Carbohydrate 18.8g, of which sugars 5.7g; Fat 15g, of which saturates 5.4g, of which polyunsaturates 1.3g; Cholesterol 73mg; Calcium 52mg; Fibre 4.4g; Sodium 106mg.

S T E A K WITH W A R M T O M A T O S A L S A ★★★

A REFRESHING, TANGY, MEDITERRANEAN-STYLE SALSA OF TOMATOES, SPRING ONIONS AND BALSAMIC VINEGAR MAKES A COLOURFUL TOPPING FOR CHUNKY, PAN-FRIED STEAKS.

SERVES TWO

INGREDIENTS

    2 lean steaks, about 2cm/¾in thick
    3 large plum tomatoes
    2 spring onions (scallions)
    30ml/2 tbsp balsamic vinegar
    salt and ground black pepper

1 Trim and discard any excess fat from the steaks, then season on both sides with salt and pepper. Heat a non-stick frying pan and cook the steaks for about 3 minutes on each side for medium rare. Cook for a little longer, if you like your steak well done.

2 Meanwhile, put the tomatoes in a heatproof bowl, cover with boiling water and leave for 1–2 minutes, or until the skins start to split. Drain, allow to cool and skin the tomatoes, then halve them and scoop out and discard the seeds. Dice the tomato flesh. Thinly slice the spring onions.

3 Transfer the steaks to plates and keep warm. Add the tomatoes, spring onions, balsamic vinegar, 30ml/2 tbsp water and a little seasoning to the cooking juices in the pan and stir briefly until the mixture is warm, scraping up any meat residue.

4 Spoon the warm salsa over the steaks and serve immediately.

Energy 291kcal/1215kJ; Protein 35.3g; Carbohydrate 5g, of which sugars 5g; Fat 14.5g, of which saturates 5.9g, of which polyunsaturates 0.9g; Cholesterol 87mg; Calcium 22mg; Fibre 1.7g; Sodium 110mg.

ITALIAN-STYLE MEATBALLS ★★★

*THESE TASTY, LOW-FAT AND SUCCULENT MEATBALLS IN A COLOURFUL PEPPER SAUCE ARE DELICIOUS
SERVED WITH RICE OR PASTA, AND THEY ARE ALWAYS A HIT WITH CHILDREN AS WELL AS ADULTS.*

SERVES FOUR

INGREDIENTS
    10ml/2 tsp sunflower oil
    1 shallot, chopped
    2 garlic cloves, finely chopped
    15ml/1 tbsp fresh thyme leaves
    500g/1lb/2½ cups extra-lean minced
        (ground) beef
    1 slice white bread, crusts removed,
        made into crumbs
    1 egg
    salt and ground black pepper
    fresh thyme leaves, to garnish
For the sauce
    3 red (bell) peppers, halved and seeded
    1 onion, quartered
    400g/14oz can chopped tomatoes

1 Heat the oil in a non-stick frying pan,
add the shallot and garlic and cook for
5 minutes, or until softened. Remove the
pan from the heat and add the thyme
leaves, then turn the mixture into a bowl.

2 Add the minced beef, breadcrumbs,
egg and seasoning to the shallot
mixture. Mix until all the ingredients
are thoroughly combined. Shape the
mixture into 20 small meatballs, then
chill them until the sauce is ready.

3 To make the sauce, preheat the grill
(broiler) to high. Arrange the peppers
on a grill (broiling) rack with the pieces
of onion. Grill (broil), turning frequently,
for 12–15 minutes, or until the pepper
skins are blackened. Remove from the
heat, cover the peppers with a clean
dish towel and leave to cool. Skin the
peppers, then place them in a blender or
food processor with the onion and the
tomatoes. Process until smooth, then
add seasoning to taste. Set aside.

COOK'S TIP
Both the meatballs and sauce freeze
well. Freeze the meatballs after shaping.
Thaw thoroughly before cooking.

4 Cook the meatballs in a large, non-
stick frying pan, gently rolling them
around to brown them evenly all over,
for about 10–15 minutes.

5 Add the puréed pepper and tomato
mixture and bring to the boil, then
reduce the heat and simmer for
10 minutes. Transfer to a warmed
serving dish and sprinkle with thyme
leaves to garnish. Serve immediately.

Energy 341kcal/1427kJ; Protein 33g; Carbohydrate 18.3g, of which sugars 12.9g; Fat 15g, of which saturates 5.6g, of which polyunsaturates 2.1g; Cholesterol 120mg; Calcium 44mg; Fibre 3.7g; Sodium 160mg.

VEAL CASSEROLE WITH BROAD BEANS ★★

THIS DELICATE SPANISH STEW, FLAVOURED WITH SHERRY AND PLENTY OF GARLIC, IS A LOW-FAT SPRING DISH MADE WITH NEW VEGETABLES. LEAN LAMB IS EQUALLY GOOD COOKED IN THIS WAY.

SERVES SIX

INGREDIENTS
25ml/1½ tbsp olive oil
1.3–1.6kg/3–3½lb lean veal, cut into
   5cm/2in cubes
1 large onion, chopped
6 large garlic cloves, unpeeled
1 bay leaf
5ml/1 tsp paprika
250ml/8fl oz/1 cup fino sherry
115g/4oz/scant 1 cup shelled,
   skinned broad (fava) beans
60ml/4 tbsp chopped fresh flat
   leaf parsley
salt and ground black pepper

1 Heat 15ml/1 tbsp oil in a large flameproof casserole. Add half the meat and brown well on all sides. Transfer to a plate. Brown the rest of the meat and remove from the pan.

2 Add the remaining oil to the pan, add the onion and cook until soft. Return the meat to the casserole and stir well to mix with the onion.

3 Add the garlic cloves, bay leaf, paprika and sherry. Season with salt and black pepper. Bring to simmering point, then cover and cook very gently for 30–40 minutes.

4 Add the broad beans to the casserole about 10 minutes before the end of the cooking time. Adjust the seasoning to taste and stir in the chopped parsley just before serving.

Energy 330kcal/1385kJ; Protein 47.7g; Carbohydrate 3.8g, of which sugars 1.6g; Fat 8.8g, of which saturates 2.4g, of which polyunsaturates 1.2g; Cholesterol 182mg; Calcium 49mg; Fibre 1.8g; Sodium 247mg.

SPAGHETTI WITH TASTY MEATBALLS ★★

MEATBALLS SIMMERED IN A TASTY, LOW-FAT, SWEET AND SPICY TOMATO SAUCE ARE TRULY DELICIOUS SERVED WITH SPAGHETTI. CHILDREN LOVE THEM AND YOU CAN EASILY LEAVE OUT THE CHILLIES, IF YOU PREFER.

SERVES SIX

INGREDIENTS

350g/12oz/1½ cups extra-lean
   minced (ground) beef
1 egg
60ml/4 tbsp roughly chopped fresh
   flat leaf parsley
2.5ml/½ tsp crushed dried red chillies
1 thick slice white bread,
   crusts removed
30ml/2 tbsp semi-skimmed
   (low-fat) milk
10ml/2 tsp olive oil
300ml/½ pint/1¼ cups passata
   (bottled strained tomatoes)
400ml/14fl oz/1⅔ cups
   vegetable stock
5ml/1 tsp granulated sugar
350–450g/12oz–1lb fresh or
   dried spaghetti
salt and ground black pepper
a little freshly grated Parmesan
   cheese, to serve (optional)

1 Put the minced beef in a large bowl. Add the egg, half the chopped parsley and half the crushed chillies. Season with plenty of salt and pepper. Set aside.

2 Tear the bread into small pieces and place in a small bowl. Moisten with the milk. Leave to soak for a few minutes, then squeeze out the excess milk and crumble the bread over the meat mixture. Mix everything together with a wooden spoon, then use your hands to squeeze and knead the mixture so that it becomes smooth and quite sticky.

3 Wash your hands, rinse them under the cold tap, then pick up small pieces of the mixture and roll them between your palms to make about 40–60 small balls. Place the meatballs on a tray and chill in the refrigerator for about 30 minutes.

4 Heat the oil in a large, non-stick frying pan. Cook the meatballs in batches until browned on all sides. Pour the passata and stock into a large pan. Heat gently, then add the remaining chillies and the sugar, with salt and pepper to taste. Add the meatballs to the passata mixture. Bring to the boil, then reduce the heat, cover and simmer for 20 minutes.

5 Cook the pasta according to the packet instructions. When it is *al dente*, drain, then tip it into a warmed serving bowl. Pour the sauce over the pasta and toss gently to mix. Sprinkle with the remaining chopped parsley, and serve with grated Parmesan, if you like.

Energy 333kcal/1409kJ; Protein 21.1g; Carbohydrate 48.4g, of which sugars 4g; Fat 7.5g, of which saturates 2.3g, of which polyunsaturates 1.1g; Cholesterol 68mg; Calcium 55mg; Fibre 2.7g; Sodium 103mg.

SPAGHETTI BOLOGNESE ★

A VERY POPULAR AND CLASSIC ITALIAN DISH, THIS TASTY BOLOGNESE SAUCE IS FULL OF FLAVOUR AND IS LOW IN FAT TOO.

SERVES SIX

INGREDIENTS
  1 onion, chopped
  2–3 garlic cloves, crushed
  300ml/½ pint/1¼ cups beef or
    chicken stock
  450g/1lb/2 cups extra-lean minced
    (ground) turkey or beef
  2 x 400g/14oz cans chopped
    tomatoes
  5ml/1 tsp dried basil
  5ml/1 tsp dried oregano
  60ml/4 tbsp tomato purée (paste)
  450g/1lb/6 cups button (white)
    mushrooms, quartered and sliced
  150ml/¼ pint/⅔ cup red wine
  450g/1lb dried spaghetti
  salt and ground black pepper

1 Put the onion and garlic into a non-stick pan with half of the stock. Bring to the boil and cook, stirring occasionally, for 5 minutes, or until the onion is tender and the stock has reduced completely.

2 Add the minced turkey or beef and cook, breaking up the meat with a fork, for 5 minutes. Add the tomatoes, dried herbs and tomato purée and mix well. Bring to the boil, then reduce the heat, cover and simmer, stirring occasionally, for 1 hour.

3 In a separate non-stick pan, cook the mushrooms with the wine, stirring occasionally, for 5 minutes, or until the wine has evaporated. Add the mushrooms to the meat mixture with salt and pepper to taste, and stir to mix.

4 Meanwhile cook the pasta in a large pan of salted boiling water according to the instructions on the packet until *al dente*. Drain thoroughly. Serve the cooked spaghetti on warmed plates, topped with the meat sauce.

COOK'S TIP
Sautéeing the vegetables in stock rather than oil is an easy way of cutting down on calories and fat. Choose fat-free stock to reduce them even more.

Energy 396kcal/1682kJ; Protein 30.2g; Carbohydrate 62.3g, of which sugars 8.8g; Fat 2.8g, of which saturates 0.6g, of which polyunsaturates 1.3g; Cholesterol 43mg; Calcium 43mg; Fibre 4.8g; Sodium 82mg.

RAVIOLI WITH BOLOGNESE SAUCE ★★★

SERVE THIS TASTY ITALIAN-STYLE PASTA DISH WITH A MIXED LEAF SALAD AND FRESH CRUSTY BREAD FOR A FLAVOURFUL LOW-FAT FAMILY MEAL.

SERVES SIX

INGREDIENTS
  200g/7oz/1¾ cups plain (all-purpose)
    flour), plus extra for dusting
  pinch of salt
  2 eggs
  10ml/2 tsp cold water
For the filling
  225g/8oz cottage cheese
  30ml/2 tbsp freshly grated
    Parmesan cheese
  1 egg white, beaten, plus extra
    for brushing
  1.5ml/¼ tsp freshly grated nutmeg
For the sauce
  1 onion, finely chopped
  1 garlic clove, crushed
  150ml/¼ pint/⅔ cup beef stock
  350g/12oz extra-lean minced
    (ground) beef
  30ml/2 tbsp tomato purée (paste)
  120ml/4fl oz/½ cup red wine
  400g/14oz can chopped tomatoes
  2.5ml/½ tsp chopped fresh rosemary
  1.5ml/¼ tsp ground allspice
  salt and ground black pepper

1 To make the basic pasta dough, sift the flour and salt on to a clean work surface and make a well in the centre.

2 Put the eggs and water into the well. Using a fork, beat the eggs gently together, then gradually draw in the flour from the sides, to make a thick paste.

3 When the mixture becomes too stiff to use a fork, use your hands to mix to a firm dough. Knead the dough for about 5 minutes, or until smooth. (This can be done in an electric food mixer fitted with a dough hook, if you like.) Wrap in clear film (plastic wrap) to prevent it from drying out and leave to rest for 20–30 minutes before use.

4 To make the filling, place the cottage cheese, grated Parmesan, egg white, nutmeg and seasoning in a bowl and mix together thoroughly.

5 Roll the pasta into thin sheets, then place a small teaspoon of filling along the pasta in rows 5cm/2in apart.

6 Moisten between the mounds of filling with beaten egg white. Lay a second sheet of pasta lightly over the top, and press between each pocket to remove any air and seal firmly.

7 Cut into rounds with a serrated ravioli or pastry cutter. Transfer to a floured dish towel and rest for at least 30 minutes before cooking.

8 To make the Bolognese sauce, place the onion, garlic and stock in a pan and cook for 5 minutes, or until the stock has reduced. Add the beef and cook quickly, breaking up the meat, until it is browned. Add the tomato purée, wine, tomatoes, rosemary and allspice. Bring to the boil, reduce the heat and simmer for 1 hour. Season to taste.

9 Cook the ravioli in a large pan of salted, boiling water for 4–5 minutes. Drain thoroughly. Serve the ravioli on warmed plates, topped with the Bolognese sauce.

Energy 359kcal/1503kJ; Protein 24g; Carbohydrate 30g, of which sugars 4.3g; Fat 15g, of which saturates 6.6g, of which polyunsaturates 0.9g; Cholesterol 109mg; Calcium 178mg; Fibre 1.8g; Sodium 246mg.

VEAL SHANKS WITH TOMATOES AND WHITE WINE ★★

THIS LOW-FAT VERSION OF THE FAMOUS DISH OSSO BUCCO IS RICH AND HEARTY. IT IS TRADITIONALLY SERVED WITH RISOTTO ALLA MILANESE, BUT PLAIN BOILED RICE GOES EQUALLY WELL. THE LEMONY GREMOLATA GARNISH HELPS TO CUT THE RICHNESS OF THE DISH, AS DOES A CRISP GREEN SALAD — SERVE IT AFTER THE OSSO BUCCO AND BEFORE A LIGHT DESSERT, TO REFRESH THE PALATE.

SERVES SIX

INGREDIENTS

30ml/2 tbsp plain (all-purpose) flour
4 pieces of lean osso bucco
2 small onions
15ml/1 tbsp olive oil
1 large celery stick, finely chopped
1 carrot, finely chopped
2 garlic cloves, finely chopped
400g/14oz can chopped tomatoes
300ml/½ pint/1¼ cups dry
   white wine
300ml/½ pint/1¼ cups chicken or
   veal stock
1 strip of thinly pared lemon rind
2 bay leaves, plus extra for
   garnishing (optional)
salt and ground black pepper
For the gremolata
30ml/2 tbsp finely chopped fresh
   flat leaf parsley
finely grated rind of 1 lemon
1 garlic clove, finely chopped

VARIATIONS
Use chopped fresh coriander (cilantro) in place of parsley.

1 Preheat the oven to 160°C/325°F/Gas 3. Season the flour with salt and pepper and spread it out in a shallow dish. Add the pieces of veal and turn them in the flour until evenly coated all over. Shake off and discard any excess flour.

2 Slice one of the onions and separate it into rings. Heat the oil in a large flameproof casserole over a medium heat, then add the veal, with the onion rings, and brown the veal on both sides. Remove the veal with tongs and set aside on kitchen paper to drain.

3 Chop the remaining onion and add it to the pan with the celery, carrot and garlic. Stir the bottom of the pan to incorporate the pan juices and sediment. Cook gently, stirring frequently, for about 5 minutes, or until the vegetables soften slightly.

COOK'S TIP
Osso bucco is available from large supermarkets and good butchers. Choose pieces about 2cm/¾in thick.

4 Add the tomatoes, wine, stock, lemon rind and bay leaves, then season to taste with salt and pepper. Bring to the boil, stirring. Return the veal to the pan and coat with the sauce. Cover and cook in the oven for 2 hours, or until the veal is tender when pierced with a fork.

5 Meanwhile, make the gremolata. In a small bowl, mix together the chopped parsley, lemon rind and garlic. Remove the casserole from the oven and lift out and discard the strip of lemon rind and the bay leaves. Taste the sauce for seasoning and adjust if necessary. Serve the osso bucco hot, sprinkled with the gremolata and garnished with extra bay leaves, if you like.

Energy 319kcal/1340kJ; Protein 34.5g; Carbohydrate 17.6g, of which sugars 10g; Fat 7.6g, of which saturates 1.9g, of which polyunsaturates 1.2g; Cholesterol 126mg; Calcium 80mg; Fibre 3.4g; Sodium 191mg.

DESSERTS

In many Mediterranean countries, dessert often comprises a simple serving of fresh fruit, but for special occasions or a sweet treat, a number of low-fat or fat-free desserts can be enjoyed. Choose from frozen delights such as Iced Clementines or Lemon Sorbet, fruity favourites such as Fresh Fig Compote, or oven-baked treats including Fresh Fig Filo Tart and Yogurt Cake with Pistachio Nuts.

FRESH FIGS <u>WITH</u> HONEY <u>AND</u> WINE ★

ANY VARIETY OF FRESH FIGS CAN BE USED IN THIS TEMPTING LOW-FAT RECIPE, THEIR RIPENESS DETERMINING THE COOKING TIME.

SERVES SIX

INGREDIENTS

450ml/¾ pint/scant 2 cups dry
  white wine
75g/3oz/⅓ cup clear honey
50g/2oz/¼ cup caster
  (superfine) sugar
1 small orange
8 whole cloves
450g/1lb fresh figs
1 cinnamon stick
fresh mint sprigs or bay leaves,
  to decorate
low-fat Greek (US strained plain)
  yogurt, to serve

VARIATION
Use fresh apricots or halved (and stoned)
fresh peaches or nectarines in place
of figs.

1 Put the wine, honey and sugar in
a heavy pan and heat gently, stirring
constantly, until the sugar dissolves.

2 Stud the orange with the cloves
and add to the syrup with the figs and
cinnamon stick. Cover and simmer very
gently for 5–10 minutes, or until the figs
are softened. Transfer to a serving dish
and leave to cool.

3 Decorate the figs with mint sprigs
or bay leaves, then serve with low-fat
Greek yogurt, if you like.

COOK'S TIP
Choose fresh figs that are plump and
firm for this recipe, and use them
quickly as they don't store well.

Energy 194kcal/822kJ; Protein 1.4g; Carbohydrate 36.4g, of which sugars 36.4g; Fat 0.5g, of which saturates 0g, of which polyunsaturates 0g; Cholesterol 0mg; Calcium 95mg; Fibre 2.5g; Sodium 26mg.

MOROCCAN DRIED FRUIT SALAD ★

THIS IS A WONDERFUL COMBINATION OF FRESH AND DRIED FRUIT AND MAKES AN EXCELLENT LIGHT DESSERT THROUGHOUT THE YEAR. USE FROZEN RASPBERRIES OR BLACKBERRIES IN WINTER.

SERVES FOUR

INGREDIENTS
115g/4oz/½ cup dried apricots
115g/4oz/½ cup dried peaches
1 fresh pear
1 fresh apple
1 fresh orange
115g/4oz/⅔ cup mixed raspberries
  and blackberries
1 cinnamon stick
50g/2oz/¼ cup caster
  (superfine) sugar
15ml/1 tbsp clear honey
30ml/2 tbsp lemon juice

1 Soak the apricots and peaches in a bowl of water for 1–2 hours or until plump, then drain and halve or quarter them. Set aside.

2 Peel and core the pear and apple and cut the flesh into cubes. Peel the orange with a sharp knife, removing all the white pith, and cut the flesh into wedges. Place all the fruit in a large pan with the raspberries and blackberries.

3 Add 600ml/1 pint/2½ cups water, the cinnamon stick, sugar and honey and bring to the boil, stirring constantly. Reduce the heat, cover and simmer very gently for 10–12 minutes, then remove the pan from the heat. Stir in the lemon juice. Allow to cool, then pour the mixture into a bowl and chill in the refrigerator for 1–2 hours before serving.

Energy 160kcal/682kJ; Protein 2.6g; Carbohydrate 38.9g, of which sugars 38.9g; Fat 0.4g, of which saturates 0g, of which polyunsaturates 0.1g; Cholesterol 0mg; Calcium 57mg; Fibre 4.8g; Sodium 10mg.

MELON <u>WITH</u> GRILLED STRAWBERRIES ★

SPRINKLING THE STRAWBERRIES WITH A LITTLE SUGAR, THEN GRILLING THEM, HELPS BRING OUT THEIR FLAVOUR. SERVE THIS DELICIOUS FAT-FREE DESSERT ON ITS OWN OR WITH A SCOOP OF LEMON SORBET.

SERVES FOUR

INGREDIENTS
   115g/4oz/1 cup strawberries
   15ml/1 tbsp icing
      (confectioners') sugar
   ½ cantaloupe melon

1 Preheat the grill (broiler) to high. Hull the strawberries and cut them in half. Arrange the fruit in a single layer, cut side up, on a baking sheet or in an ovenproof dish and dust with the icing sugar.

VARIATION
Use half an Ogen melon or charentais melon in place of cantaloupe melon.

2 Grill (broil) the strawberries for 4–5 minutes, or until the sugar starts to bubble and turn golden.

3 Meanwhile, scoop out and discard the seeds from the half melon using a spoon. Using a sharp knife, remove and discard the skin, then cut the flesh into wedges and arrange on a serving plate with the grilled strawberries. Serve immediately.

Energy 46kcal/197kJ; Protein 1g; Carbohydrate 10.9g, of which sugars 10.9g; Fat 0.2g, of which saturates 0g, of which polyunsaturates 0g; Cholesterol 0mg; Calcium 32mg; Fibre 1.6g; Sodium 12mg.

FRESH FIG COMPOTE ★

LIGHTLY POACHING FIGS IN A VANILLA AND COFFEE SYRUP BRINGS OUT THEIR WONDERFUL FLAVOUR, TO CREATE THIS TEMPTING LIGHT MEDITERRANEAN-STYLE DESSERT.

SERVES SIX

INGREDIENTS
    400ml/14fl oz/1⅔ cups
      brewed coffee
    115g/4oz/½ cup clear honey
    1 vanilla pod (bean)
    12 slightly under-ripe
      fresh figs
    low-fat Greek (US strained plain)
      yogurt, to serve (optional)

COOK'S TIPS
• Rinse and dry the vanilla pod (bean); it can be used several times.
• Figs come in three main varieties – red, white and black – and all three are suitable for cooking. Naturally high in sugar, they are sweet and succulent and complement well the stronger flavours of coffee and vanilla.

1 Choose a frying pan with a lid, large enough to hold the figs in a single layer. Pour in the coffee and add the honey.

2 Split the vanilla pod lengthways and scrape the seeds into the pan. Add the vanilla pod, then bring the mixture to a rapid boil and cook until reduced to about 175ml/6fl oz/¾ cup.

3 Wash the figs and pierce the skins several times with a sharp skewer. Cut in half and add to the syrup. Reduce the heat, cover and simmer for 5 minutes. Remove the figs from the syrup with a slotted spoon and set aside to cool.

4 Strain the syrup over the figs. Allow to stand at room temperature for 1 hour before serving with yogurt, if you like.

Energy 131kcal/558kJ; Protein 1.3g; Carbohydrate 32.3g, of which sugars 32.3g; Fat 0.5g, of which saturates 0g, of which polyunsaturates 0g; Cholesterol 0mg; Calcium 84mg; Fibre 2.5g; Sodium 23mg.

ICED CLEMENTINES ★

THESE PRETTY, SORBET-FILLED FRUITS FREEZE WELL, AND WILL PROVE PERFECT FOR AN IMPROMPTU SUMMER PARTY, A PICNIC OR SIMPLY A REFRESHING FAT-FREE TREAT ON A HOT SUMMER'S AFTERNOON.

MAKES TWELVE

INGREDIENTS
    16 large clementines
    175g/6oz/scant 1 cup caster
      (superfine) sugar
    105ml/7 tbsp water
    juice of 2 lemons
    a little fresh orange juice
      (if necessary)
    fresh mint or lemon balm leaves,
      to decorate

VARIATION
Use satsumas or mandarin oranges in place of clementines.

1 Slice the tops off 12 of the clementines to make lids. Set aside on a baking sheet. Loosen the clementine flesh with a sharp knife then carefully scoop it out into a bowl, keeping the shells intact. Scrape out and discard as much of the membrane from the shells as possible. Add the shells to the lids and put them in the freezer.

2 Put the sugar and water in a heavy pan and heat gently, stirring, until the sugar dissolves. Bring to the boil, then boil for 3 minutes without stirring. Remove the pan from the heat and leave the syrup to cool, then stir in the lemon juice.

3 Finely grate the rind from the remaining 4 clementines. Squeeze the fruits and add the juice and rind to the syrup.

4 Process the clementine flesh in a blender or food processor, then press it through a sieve placed over a bowl to extract as much juice as possible. Add this juice to the syrup. You need about 900ml/1½ pints/3¾ cups of liquid. Make up with fresh orange juice, if necessary.

5 To make the sorbet (sherbet) by hand: Pour the mixture into a shallow freezerproof container and freeze for 3–4 hours, beating twice as the sorbet thickens. **Using an ice cream maker:** Churn the mixture until it holds its shape.

6 Pack the sorbet into the clementine shells, mounding them up slightly in the centre. Position the lids and return to the freezer for several hours or overnight.

7 Transfer the frozen clementines to the refrigerator about 30 minutes before serving, to soften. Serve decorated with mint or lemon balm leaves.

Energy 77kcal/329kJ; Protein 0.6g; Carbohydrate 19.9g, of which sugars 19.9g; Fat 0.1g, of which saturates 0g, of which polyunsaturates 0g; Cholesterol 0mg; Calcium 24mg; Fibre 0.6g; Sodium 3mg.

LEMON SORBET ★

This smooth, tangy sorbet originates from the Andalucia region of Spain, and creates a refreshing light dessert that all the family will enjoy.

SERVES SIX

INGREDIENTS
200g/7oz/1 cup caster
  (superfine) sugar
300ml/½ pint/1¼ cups water
4 lemons, washed
1 large (US extra large) egg white
a little granulated sugar,
  for sprinkling

1 Put the caster sugar and water into a heavy pan and bring slowly to the boil, stirring occasionally, until the sugar has just dissolved.

2 Using a vegetable peeler, pare the rind thinly from two of the lemons directly into the pan. Simmer for about 2 minutes without stirring, then remove the pan from the heat. Leave the syrup to cool, then chill.

3 Squeeze the juice from all the lemons and carefully strain it into the syrup, making sure all the pips (seeds) are removed. Take the lemon rind out of the syrup and set it aside until you make the decoration.

4 If you have an ice cream maker, strain the syrup into the machine tub and churn for 10 minutes, or until thickening.

5 In a bowl, lightly whisk the egg white with a fork, then pour it into the machine. Continue to churn for 10–15 minutes, or until firm enough to scoop.

6 If working by hand, strain the syrup into a plastic tub or a similar shallow freezerproof container and freeze for 4 hours, or until the mixture is mushy.

7 Scoop the mushy mixture into a blender or food processor and process until smooth. Whisk the egg white with a fork until it is just frothy. Spoon the sorbet back into its container; beat in the egg white. Freeze for 1 hour.

8 To make the sugared rind decoration, use the blanched rind from step 2. Cut into very thin strips and sprinkle with granulated sugar on a plate. Scoop the sorbet into bowls or glasses; decorate with the sugared lemon rind.

VARIATION
Sorbet (sherbet) can be made from any citrus fruit. As a guide, you will need 300ml/½ pint/1¼ cups of fresh fruit juice and the pared rind of half the squeezed fruits. For example, use four oranges or two oranges and two lemons, or, to make a grapefruit sorbet, use the rind of one ruby grapefruit and the juice of two.

Energy 133kcal/569kJ; Protein 0.7g; Carbohydrate 34.8g, of which sugars 34.8g; Fat 0g, of which saturates 0g, of which polyunsaturates 0g; Cholesterol 0mg; Calcium 18mg; Fibre 0g; Sodium 12mg.

WATERMELON ICE ★

THIS SIMPLE, REFRESHING FAT-FREE DESSERT IS PERFECT AFTER A HOT AND SPICY LOW-FAT MEAL. THE AROMATIC FLAVOUR OF KAFFIR LIME LEAVES GOES PERFECTLY WELL WITH WATERMELON.

SERVES SIX

INGREDIENTS
  90ml/6 tbsp caster (superfine) sugar
  4 kaffir lime leaves, torn into
    small pieces
  500g/1¼lb watermelon

1 Put the sugar and lime leaves in a pan with 105ml/7 tbsp water. Heat gently until the sugar has dissolved, then pour into a large bowl and set aside to cool.

2 Cut the watermelon into wedges with a large knife. Cut the flesh from the rind, remove and discard the seeds and chop the flesh. Place the flesh in a blender or food processor and process to a slush, then mix in the sugar syrup. Chill for 3–4 hours.

3 Strain the chilled mixture into a shallow freezerproof container and freeze for 2 hours, then beat with a fork to break up the ice crystals. Freeze for a further 3 hours, beating at half-hourly intervals, then freeze until firm. Transfer the ice to the refrigerator about 30 minutes before serving.

Energy 85kcal/363kJ; Protein 0.5g; Carbohydrate 21.6g, of which sugars 21.6g; Fat 0.3g, of which saturates 0.1g, of which polyunsaturates 0.1g; Cholesterol 0mg; Calcium 14mg; Fibre 0.1g; Sodium 3mg.

PEACH AND ALMOND GRANITA ★★★

INFUSED ALMONDS MAKE A RICHLY FLAVOURED "MILK" THAT FORMS THE BASIS OF THIS LIGHT, TANGY DESSERT, WHICH WOULD BE THE IDEAL CHOICE TO FOLLOW A FILLING MAIN COURSE.

SERVES SIX

INGREDIENTS
115g/4oz/1 cup ground almonds
900ml/1½ pints/3¾ cups water
150g/5oz/¾ cup caster
 (superfine) sugar
5ml/1 tsp almond extract
juice of 2 lemons
6 fresh peaches
Amaretto liqueur, to serve (optional)

1 Put the ground almonds in a pan and pour in 600ml/1 pint/2½ cups of the water. Bring just to the boil, then reduce the heat and simmer gently for 2 minutes. Remove from the heat and leave to stand for 30 minutes.

2 Strain the mixture through a fine sieve (strainer) placed over a bowl, and press lightly with the back of a spoon to extract as much liquid as possible. Pour the liquid into a clean, heavy pan. Discard the infused almonds.

3 Add the sugar and almond extract to the pan, with half the lemon juice and the remaining water. Heat gently until the sugar dissolves, then bring to the boil. Reduce the heat and simmer gently for 3 minutes without stirring, taking care that the almond syrup does not boil over. Leave to cool.

COOK'S TIP
If you want to make the granita ahead, serve the granita in tall glasses, instead of peach shells.

4 Cut the peaches in half and remove the stones. Using a small knife, scoop out about half the flesh to enlarge the cavities. Put the flesh in a blender or food processor. Brush the exposed flesh with the remaining lemon juice; chill the peaches.

5 Add the almond syrup to the peach flesh in the blender or food processor, and process until smooth. Pour into a shallow freezerproof container and freeze until ice crystals have formed around the edges. Stir with a fork, then freeze again until more crystals have formed around the edges. Repeat until the mixture has the consistency of crushed ice.

6 Lightly break up the granita with a fork to loosen the mixture. Spoon into the peach halves and place two on each serving plate. Drizzle a little amaretto liqueur over the top, if you like.

Energy 239kcal/1005kJ; Protein 4.9g; Carbohydrate 32.8g, of which sugars 32.3g; Fat 10.8g, of which saturates 0.9g, of which polyunsaturates 2g; Cholesterol 0mg; Calcium 64mg; Fibre 2.5g; Sodium 5mg.

CLEMENTINES WITH STAR ANISE AND CINNAMON ★

THIS FRESH FAT-FREE DESSERT, DELICATELY FLAVOURED WITH MULLING SPICES, IS IDEAL FOR WARMING A WINTER'S DAY AND IT MAKES THE PERFECT ENDING FOR A LOW-FAT MEDITERRANEAN-STYLE MEAL.

SERVES SIX

INGREDIENTS
350ml/12fl oz/1½ cups sweet
   dessert wine
75g/3oz/⅓ cup caster (superfine)
   sugar
6 star anise
1 cinnamon stick
1 vanilla pod (bean)
1 strip thinly pared lime rind
30ml/2 tbsp Cointreau
12 clementines

VARIATIONS
• Tangerines or small oranges can be used instead of clementines.
• Use thinly pared lemon rind in place of lime rind.

1 Put the wine, sugar, star anise and cinnamon stick in a pan. Split the vanilla pod and add it to the pan with the lime rind. Bring to the boil, then reduce the heat and simmer for 10 minutes. Remove the pan from the heat and allow to cool, then stir in the Cointreau.

COOK'S TIPS
When buying vanilla pods (beans), test them for freshness – simply bend the vanilla pods: they should be supple and resilient. To obtain a stronger flavour from a vanilla pod (bean), use the tiny, oily seeds rather than infusing the whole pod. Cut the pod in half lengthways, and using the tip of a sharp knife, scrape out the seeds from inside the opened pod, then add the seeds directly to the dish as required.

2 Peel the clementines, removing all the pith and white membranes. Cut some of the clementines in half and arrange them all in a glass dish. Pour over the spiced wine and chill overnight.

Energy 145kcal/612kJ; Protein 0.9g; Carbohydrate 23.5g, of which sugars 23.5g; Fat 0.1g, of which saturates 0g, of which polyunsaturates 0g; Cholesterol 0mg; Calcium 40mg; Fibre 1g; Sodium 12mg.

ZABAGLIONE ★★

LIGHT AS AIR AND WONDERFULLY ALCOHOLIC, THIS LOW-FAT WARM EGG CUSTARD IS A MUCH-LOVED CLASSIC ITALIAN DESSERT. ALTHOUGH IT IS TRADITIONALLY MADE WITH MARSALA, YOU CAN REPLACE THIS FORTIFIED WINE WITH MADEIRA OR SWEET SHERRY.

SERVES FOUR

INGREDIENTS
4 egg yolks
50g/2oz/¼ cup caster
  (superfine) sugar
60ml/4 tbsp Marsala, Madeira or
  sweet sherry
amaretti, to serve (optional)

VARIATION
For a special treat, make a chocolate version of this low-fat dessert. Whisk in 30ml/2 tbsp unsweetened cocoa powder with the wine or sherry and serve dusted with cocoa powder and icing sugar.

1 Place the egg yolks and sugar in a large heatproof bowl, and whisk with an electric whisk until the mixture is pale and thick.

2 Gradually add the Marsala, Madeira or sherry to the egg mixture, 15ml/ 1 tbsp at a time, whisking well after each addition.

3 Place the bowl over a pan of gently simmering water and continue to whisk for 5–7 minutes, or until the mixture becomes thick; when the beaters are lifted they should leave a thick trail on the surface of the mixture. Do not be tempted to underbeat the mixture, as the zabaglione will be too runny and will be likely to separate.

4 Pour into four warmed, stemmed glasses and serve immediately with amaretti for dipping, if you like.

COOK'S TIP
Zabaglione is also delicious served as a sauce with cooked fruit desserts. Try serving it with poached pears, grilled (broiled) peaches or baked bananas to create a really special pudding.

Energy 134kcal/561kJ; Protein 3g; Carbohydrate 14.9g, of which sugars 14.9g; Fat 5.5g, of which saturates 1.6g, of which polyunsaturates 0.6g; Cholesterol 202mg; Calcium 31mg; Fibre 0g; Sodium 10mg.

ORANGES WITH CARAMEL WIGS ★

THIS DELICIOUS DESSERT IS A PRETTY VARIATION ON AN ORANGE SALAD. THE SLIGHTLY BITTER, CARAMELIZED ORANGE RIND AND SYRUP CONTRAST WITH THE SWEET, JUICY ORANGES.

5 Put half the sugar into a small pan and add 15ml/1 tbsp cold water. Heat gently until the mixture caramelizes, shaking the pan a little if one side starts to brown too fast. As soon as the mixture colours, dip the bottom of the pan into cold water. Add 30ml/2 tbsp hot water and the orange rind to the caramel, then stir until the caramel dissolves. Turn the rind on to a plate to cool.

6 Make a caramel syrup for serving. Put the remaining sugar in a small pan with 15ml/1 tbsp cold water, and make caramel as before. When it has coloured nicely, stand well back, pour in the boiling water and stir with a wooden spoon to dissolve. Add the reserved juices and pour into a serving jug (pitcher).

7 To serve, arrange the orange strips in a criss-cross pattern on top of each orange. Remove the cocktail sticks and pour a little caramel syrup round the base of each orange.

SERVES SIX

INGREDIENTS
    6 oranges
    115g/4oz/²⁄₃ cup caster
      (superfine) sugar
    120ml/4fl oz/½ cup boiling water

1 Using a vegetable peeler, thinly pare the rind off a few of the oranges to make 12 long strips. Set aside.

2 Using a sharp knife, peel all the oranges, reserving the rind and discarding the pith. Reserve any juice and freeze the oranges separately for 30 minutes.

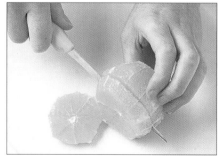

3 Slice the oranges, then re-shape and secure each with a cocktail stick (toothpick). Chill in the refrigerator.

4 To make the wigs, simmer the rind in a small pan of boiling water for about 5 minutes, then drain, rinse, and repeat this procedure. Trim and shape the rind with scissors. Set aside.

Energy 120kcal/512kJ; Protein 1.4g; Carbohydrate 30.2g, of which sugars 30.2g; Fat 0.1g, of which saturates 0g, of which polyunsaturates 0g; Cholesterol 0mg; Calcium 67mg; Fibre 2g; Sodium 7mg.

ORANGE AND DATE SALAD ★

*WITH FEW INGREDIENTS, THIS TEMPTING, LOW-FAT DESSERT IS SIMPLICITY ITSELF TO PUT TOGETHER,
YET IS WONDERFULLY FRESH-TASTING AND ESSENTIALLY MOROCCAN.*

SERVES FOUR TO SIX

INGREDIENTS
    5 oranges
    15–30ml/1–2 tbsp orange flower
      water or rose water (optional)
    lemon juice, to taste (optional)
    115g/4oz/⅔ cup stoned (pitted)
      dates
    50g/2oz/½ cup pistachio nuts
    icing (confectioners') sugar, to taste
    a few toasted almonds, to decorate
      (optional)

COOK'S TIP
Use ready-to-eat dried dates, natural
dates or fresh dates for this recipe.

VARIATION
Use blanched almonds or hazelnuts in
place of pistachio nuts.

1 Peel the oranges with a sharp knife,
removing all the pith, then cut the flesh
into segments, catching the juice in a
small bowl. Place the orange segments
in a serving dish.

2 Stir in the juice from the bowl
together with a little orange flower or
rose water, if using, and sharpen with
lemon juice, if you like.

3 Chop the dates and pistachio nuts,
then sprinkle them over the salad with a
little icing sugar. Chill in the refrigerator
for 1 hour.

4 Just before serving, sprinkle over a
few toasted almonds, if using, and a
little extra icing sugar.

Energy 111kcal/467kJ; Protein 2.9g; Carbohydrate 15.2g, of which sugars 15g; Fat 4.7g, of which saturates 0.6g, of which polyunsaturates 1.5g; Cholesterol 0mg; Calcium 61mg; Fibre 2.6g; Sodium 51mg.

FRESH FIG FILO TART ★★

FIGS COOK WONDERFULLY WELL AND TASTE SUPERB IN THIS DELICIOUS LOW-FAT TART FROM THE
MEDITERRANEAN — THE RIPER THE FIGS, THE BETTER.

2 Using scissors, cut off any excess pastry, leaving a little overhanging the edge. Arrange the figs in the filo case.

3 Sift the flour into a bowl and stir in the caster sugar. Add the eggs and a little of the milk; whisk until smooth. Gradually whisk in the remaining milk and the almond extract. Pour the mixture over the figs and bake for 1 hour, or until the batter is set and golden.

SERVES EIGHT

INGREDIENTS
25g/1oz/2 tbsp butter, melted, plus a
  little extra for greasing
five 35 × 25cm/14 × 10in sheets filo
  pastry, thawed if frozen
6 fresh figs, cut into wedges
75g/3oz/⅔ cup plain (all-purpose) flour
75g/3oz/6 tbsp caster (superfine) sugar
4 eggs
450ml/¾ pint/scant 2 cups milk
2.5ml/½ tsp almond extract
15ml/1 tbsp icing (confectioners')
  sugar, for dusting
low-fat Greek (US strained plain)
  yogurt, to serve

1 Preheat the oven to 190°C/375°F/
Gas 5. Grease a 25 × 16cm/10 × 6¼in
baking tin (pan) with butter. Brush each
filo sheet in turn with melted butter and
use to line the prepared tin.

4 Remove the tart from the oven and allow it to cool in the tin on a wire rack for 10 minutes. Dust with the icing sugar and serve with Greek yogurt, if you like.

Energy 189kcal/797kJ; Protein 6.5g; Carbohydrate 27.7g, of which sugars 20.5g; Fat 6.7g, of which saturates 3g, of which polyunsaturates 0.5g; Cholesterol 105mg; Calcium 138mg; Fibre 1.4g; Sodium 88mg.

MANGO STACKS WITH RASPBERRY COULIS ★★

THIS MAKES A VERY HEALTHY YET STUNNING DESSERT — IT IS LOW IN FAT AND CONTAINS NO ADDED SUGAR. HOWEVER, IF THE RASPBERRIES ARE A LITTLE SHARP, YOU MAY PREFER TO ADD A PINCH OF SUGAR TO THE PURÉE. THE INCLUSION OF SEASONAL FRUIT MAKES THIS DESSERT A LITTLE BIT SPECIAL.

SERVES FOUR

INGREDIENTS
3 large filo pastry sheets, thawed
  if frozen
40g/1½oz/3 tbsp butter, melted
2 small ripe mangoes
115g/4oz/⅔ cup raspberries, thawed
  if frozen

1 Preheat the oven to 200°C/400°F/ Gas 6. Arrange the filo sheets on a clean work surface and cut out four 10cm/4in rounds from each.

2 Brush each pastry round with the melted butter and place the rounds on two non-stick baking sheets. Bake in the oven for 5 minutes, or until crisp and golden.

3 Transfer to wire racks and cool.

4 Peel the mangoes, remove and discard the stones and cut the flesh into thin slices. Put the raspberries in a blender or food processor with 45ml/ 3 tbsp water and process to a purée. Place a pastry round on each of four serving plates. Top with a quarter of the mango and drizzle with a little of the raspberry purée. Repeat until all the ingredients have been used, finishing with a layer of mango and a drizzle of raspberry purée. Serve.

Energy 167kcal/702kJ; Protein 2.2g; Carbohydrate 21.7g, of which sugars 11.9g; Fat 8.6g, of which saturates 5.4g, of which polyunsaturates 0.4g; Cholesterol 21mg; Calcium 36mg; Fibre 3.1g; Sodium 63mg.

MOIST ORANGE AND ALMOND CAKE ★★★

THE KEY TO GETTING THE BEST RESULTS FROM THIS DELICIOUS LOW-FAT RECIPE IS TO COOK THE ORANGE SLOWLY FIRST, SO IT IS FULLY TENDER BEFORE BEING BLENDED. DON'T USE A MICROWAVE TO SPEED THINGS UP — THIS MAKES ORANGE SKIN TOUGH.

SERVES FOURTEEN

INGREDIENTS
    1 large orange
    3 eggs
    225g/8oz/1¼ cups caster
      (superfine) sugar
    5ml/1 tsp baking powder
    225g/8oz/2 cups ground almonds
    25g/1oz/¼ cup plain
      (all-purpose) flour
    icing (confectioners') sugar,
      for dusting
    low-fat Greek (US strained plain)
      yogurt and orange slices, to serve
      (optional)

1 Wash the orange and pierce it with a skewer. Put it in a deep pan and pour over water to cover completely. Bring to the boil then reduce the heat, cover and simmer for 1 hour, or until the skin is very soft. Drain, then cool.

2 Preheat the oven to 180°C/350°F/ Gas 4. Grease a 20cm/8in round cake tin (pan) and line it with baking parchment. Cut the orange in half and discard the pips (seeds). Place the orange and skin in a blender or food processor and process until smooth.

3 In a bowl, whisk the eggs and caster sugar together until thick. Fold in the baking powder, almonds and flour. Fold in the orange purée.

4 Pour into the prepared tin and level the surface, then bake in the oven for 1 hour, or until a skewer inserted into the centre comes out clean. Cool the cake in the tin for 10 minutes, then turn out on to a wire rack, peel off the lining paper and cool completely. Dust the top liberally with icing sugar and serve as a dessert with Greek yogurt, if you like. For added colour, tuck thick orange slices under the cake just before serving.

Energy 187kcal/782kJ; Protein 5.1g; Carbohydrate 20g, of which sugars 18.2g; Fat 10.2g, of which saturates 1.1g, of which polyunsaturates 1.8g; Cholesterol 41mg; Calcium 60mg; Fibre 1.4g; Sodium 19mg.

YOGURT CAKE WITH PISTACHIO NUTS ★★★

SOME YOGURT CAKES ARE DRY AND SERVED WITH TEA, OTHERS ARE BATHED IN LEMON SYRUP AND SERVED AT ROOM TEMPERATURE, AND THEN THERE IS THIS TYPE, WHICH IS DELICIOUS WARM OR CHILLED WITH HALF-FAT CRÈME FRAÎCHE OR LOW-FAT YOGURT AND FRESH PASSION FRUIT.

SERVES SIX

INGREDIENTS

3 eggs, separated
75g/3oz/⅔ cup caster
  (superfine) sugar
seeds from 2 vanilla pods (beans)
300ml/½ pint/1¼ cups Greek
  (US strained plain) yogurt
grated rind and juice of 1 lemon
scant 15ml/1 tbsp plain
  (all-purpose) flour
small handful of pistachio nuts,
  roughly chopped
90ml/6 tbsp half-fat crème fraîche
  and 6 fresh passion fruit or
  50g/2oz/½ cup mixed fresh summer
  berries, to serve

5 Place the dish in a roasting pan and pour in enough cold water to come about halfway up the outside of the dish. Bake in the oven for about 20 minutes, or until the mixture is risen and just set.

6 Sprinkle the pistachio nuts evenly over the cake and bake for a further 20 minutes, or until it is browned on top.

7 Serve the cake warm or chilled with crème fraîche and a spoonful of passion fruit drizzled over the top. Alternatively, sprinkle with a few mixed summer berries such as redcurrants, blackcurrants and blueberries.

COOK'S TIP
If possible, when buying nuts such as pistachio nuts, buy unshelled nuts. They will keep for twice as long as shelled nuts, as long as they are fresh when you buy them.

1 Preheat the oven to 180°C/350°F/ Gas 4. Line a 25cm/10in square ovenproof dish with baking parchment and grease well.

2 In a bowl, beat the egg yolks with two-thirds of the sugar, until pale and fluffy. Beat in the vanilla seeds, then stir in the yogurt, lemon rind and juice, and the flour.

3 In a separate bowl, whisk the egg whites until stiff, then gradually whisk in the remaining sugar to form soft peaks.

4 Fold the whisked egg whites into the yogurt mixture. Turn the mixture into the lined dish and spread evenly.

Energy 229kcal/955kJ; Protein 8.6g; Carbohydrate 17.7g, of which sugars 15.4g; Fat 14.8g, of which saturates 5.5g, of which polyunsaturates 2.1g; Cholesterol 95mg; Calcium 125mg; Fibre 0.8g; Sodium 121mg.

BREADS

*It's hard to beat the delicious aroma of freshly
baked bread wafting from your kitchen, and
yeasted and unyeasted breads form an important
part of meals throughout the Mediterranean.
Choose from a tempting selection of low-fat
traditional breads such as Focaccia, Ciabatta,
French Baguettes and Olive Bread.*

FOCACCIA ★

THIS IS A DELICIOUS FLATTISH BREAD, ORIGINATING FROM GENOA IN ITALY, MADE WITH FLOUR, OLIVE OIL AND SALT. THERE ARE MANY VARIATIONS, FROM MANY REGIONS, INCLUDING STUFFED VARIETIES AND VERSIONS TOPPED WITH ONIONS, OLIVES OR HERBS.

MAKES ONE LOAF
SERVES EIGHT

INGREDIENTS
    25g/1oz fresh yeast
    400g/14oz/3½ cups strong white
      bread flour
    10ml/2 tsp salt
    45ml/3 tbsp olive oil
    10ml/2 tsp coarse sea salt

1 Lightly grease a 25cm/10in tart tin (pan) and set aside. In a small bowl, dissolve the yeast in 120ml/4fl oz/½ cup warm water. Allow to stand for 10 minutes. Sift the flour into a large bowl, make a well in the centre, and add the yeast mixture, salt and 25ml/1½ tbsp oil. Mix in the flour and add more water, if necessary, mixing to make a dough.

2 Turn out on to a floured surface and knead the dough for about 10 minutes, or until smooth and elastic. Return to the bowl, cover with a cloth, and leave to rise in a warm place for 2–2½ hours, or until the dough has doubled in bulk.

3 Knock back (punch down) the dough and knead again for a few minutes. Press into the prepared tin, and cover with a damp cloth. Leave to rise in a warm place for 30 minutes.

4 Preheat the oven to 200°C/400°F/ Gas 6. Poke the dough all over with your fingers, to make little dimples in the surface. Brush the remaining oil over the dough using a pastry brush. Sprinkle with the coarse sea salt.

5 Bake in the oven for 20–25 minutes, or until the bread is a pale golden colour. Carefully remove from the tin and leave to cool on a wire rack. The bread is best eaten on the day of making, but it also freezes very well.

Energy 208kcal/878kJ; Protein 4.7g; Carbohydrate 38.9g, of which sugars 0.8g; Fat 4.8g, of which saturates 0.7g, of which polyunsaturates 0.6g; Cholesterol 0mg; Calcium 70mg; Fibre 1.6g; Sodium 493mg.

CIABATTA ★

THIS IRREGULAR-SHAPED ITALIAN BREAD IS SO CALLED BECAUSE IT LOOKS LIKE AN OLD SHOE OR SLIPPER. IT IS MADE WITH A VERY WET DOUGH FLAVOURED WITH OLIVE OIL; COOKING PRODUCES A BREAD WITH HOLES AND A WONDERFULLY CHEWY CRUST.

MAKES THREE LOAVES
EACH LOAF SERVES FOUR

INGREDIENTS
For the biga starter
  7g/¼oz fresh yeast
  175–200ml/6–7fl oz/¾–scant 1 cup
    lukewarm water
  350g/12oz/3 cups unbleached plain
    (all-purpose) flour, plus extra for
    dusting
For the dough
  15g/½oz fresh yeast
  400ml/14fl oz/1⅔ cups lukewarm
    water
  60ml/4 tbsp lukewarm milk
  500g/1¼lb/5 cups unbleached strong
    white bread flour
  10ml/2 tsp salt
  45ml/3 tbsp extra virgin olive oil

1 In a small bowl, cream the yeast for the biga starter with a little of the water. Sift the flour into a large bowl. Gradually mix in the yeast mixture and enough of the remaining water to form a firm dough.

2 Turn out the biga starter dough on to a lightly floured surface and knead for about 5 minutes, or until smooth and elastic. Return the dough to the bowl, cover with lightly oiled clear film (plastic wrap) and leave in a warm place for 12–15 hours, or until the dough has risen and is starting to collapse.

3 Sprinkle three baking sheets with flour. In a small bowl, mix the yeast for the dough with a little of the water until creamy, then mix in the remainder. Add the yeast mixture to the biga and gradually mix in.

4 Mix in the milk, beating thoroughly with a wooden spoon. Using your hand, gradually beat in the flour, lifting the dough as you mix. Mixing the dough will take 15 minutes or more and form a very wet mix, impossible to knead on a work surface.

5 With a spoon, carefully tip one-third of the dough at a time on to the baking sheets without knocking back (punching down) the dough in the process.

VARIATION
To make tomato-flavoured ciabatta, add 115g/4oz/1 cup chopped, drained sun-dried tomatoes in olive oil. Add with the olive oil in step 5. Remember this will increase the fat and calorie content of the loaves.

6 Using floured hands, shape into rough oblong loaves, about 2.5cm/1in thick. Flatten slightly with splayed fingers. Sprinkle with flour; leave to rise in a warm place for 30 minutes.

7 Meanwhile, preheat the oven to 220°C/425°F/Gas 7. Bake the loaves in the oven for 25–30 minutes, or until golden brown and sounding hollow when tapped on the base. Transfer to a wire rack to cool.

Energy 269kcal/1139kJ; Protein 6.8g; Carbohydrate 55.3g, of which sugars 1.3g; Fat 3.8g, of which saturates 0.6g, of which polyunsaturates 0.7g; Cholesterol 0mg; Calcium 105mg; Fibre 2.2g; Sodium 332mg.

FRENCH BAGUETTES ★

BAGUETTES HAVE MANY USES: SPLIT HORIZONTALLY AND FILL WITH LEAN MEATS, LOW-FAT CHEESES AND SALADS; SLICE DIAGONALLY AND TOAST THE SLICES TO SERVE WITH SOUP; OR SIMPLY CUT INTO CHUNKS AND SERVE ON ITS OWN. FRENCH BAGUETTES ARE BEST EATEN ON THE DAY OF BAKING.

MAKES THREE LOAVES
EACH LOAF SERVES THREE

INGREDIENTS
  500g/1¼lb/5 cups unbleached strong
    white bread flour
  115g/4oz/1 cup fine French plain
    (all-purpose) flour
  10ml/2 tsp salt
  15g/½oz fresh yeast

COOK'S TIP
Baguettes are difficult to reproduce at home as they require a very hot oven and steam. However, by using less yeast and a triple fermentation you can produce a bread with a superior taste and far better texture than mass-produced baguettes.

1 Sift the flours and salt into a large bowl. Add the yeast to 550ml/18fl oz/2½ cups lukewarm water in a separate bowl and stir until combined. Gradually beat in half the flour mixture to form a batter. Cover with clear film (plastic wrap) and leave for about 3 hours, or until nearly trebled in size.

2 Add the remaining flour a little at a time, beating with your hand. Turn out on to a lightly floured surface and knead for 8–10 minutes to form a moist dough. Place the dough in a lightly oiled bowl, cover with lightly oiled clear film and leave to rise, in a warm place, for about 1 hour.

3 Knock back (punch down) the dough, turn out on to a floured surface and divide into three equal pieces. Shape each into a ball and then into a 15 x 7.5cm/6 x 3in rectangle. Fold the bottom third up lengthways and the top third down and press down. Seal the edges. Repeat two or three more times until each loaf is an oblong. Leave to rest for a few minutes between foldings.

4 Stretch each piece of dough into a 35cm/14in long loaf. Pleat a floured dish towel on a baking sheet to make three moulds for the loaves. Place the loaves between the pleats, cover with lightly oiled clear film and leave to rise in a warm place for 45–60 minutes.

5 Preheat the oven to maximum. Roll the loaves on to a baking sheet, spaced apart. Slash the top of each diagonally several times. Place at the top of the oven, spray the inside of the oven with water and bake for 20–25 minutes. Spray the oven twice during the first 5 minutes of baking. Allow to cool.

Energy 233kcal/991kJ; Protein 6.4g; Carbohydrate 53.1g, of which sugars 1g; Fat 0.9g, of which saturates 0.1g, of which polyunsaturates 0.4g; Cholesterol 0mg; Calcium 96mg; Fibre 2.1g; Sodium 439mg.

PANINI ALL'OLIO ★

ITALIAN-STYLE DOUGH ENRICHED AND FLAVOURED WITH EXTRA VIRGIN OLIVE OIL IS VERSATILE FOR MAKING DECORATIVE LOW-FAT ROLLS. CHILDREN WILL LOVE HELPING TO MAKE AND SHAPE THESE ROLLS. THE ROLLS ARE SURE TO DISAPPEAR AS SOON AS THEY ARE COOL ENOUGH TO EAT.

MAKES SIXTEEN ROLLS

INGREDIENTS
  450g/1lb/4 cups unbleached strong
    white bread flour
  10ml/2 tsp salt
  15g/½oz fresh yeast
  60ml/4 tbsp extra virgin olive oil,
    plus a little extra for brushing

1 Lightly oil three baking sheets. Sift the flour and salt together in a large bowl and make a well in the centre. Measure 250ml/8fl oz/1 cup lukewarm water. Cream the yeast with half the water, then stir in the remainder. Add to the well with the oil and mix to a dough.

2 Turn the dough out on to a lightly floured surface and knead for 8–10 minutes, or until smooth and elastic. Place the dough in a lightly oiled bowl, cover with lightly oiled clear film (plastic wrap) and leave to rise in a warm place for about 1 hour, or until nearly doubled in bulk.

3 Turn the dough on to a lightly floured surface and knock back (punch down). Divide into 12 equal pieces and shape into rolls. To make twists, roll each piece of dough into a strip 30cm/12in long and 4cm/1½in wide. Twist each strip into a loose spiral and join the ends together to make a circle. Place on the baking sheets, spaced well apart. Lightly brush with olive oil, cover with lightly oiled clear film and leave to rise in a warm place for 20–30 minutes.

4 To make fingers, flatten each piece of dough into an oval and roll to about 23cm/9in long. Roll up from the wider end. Gently stretch the dough roll to 20–23cm/8–9in long. Cut in half. Place on the baking sheets, spaced well apart. Lightly brush the dough with olive oil, cover with lightly oiled clear film and leave to rise in a warm place for 20–30 minutes.

5 To make artichoke shapes, shape each piece of dough into a ball and space well apart on the baking sheets. Lightly brush with oil, cover with lightly oiled clear film and leave to rise in a warm place for 20–30 minutes. Using scissors, snip 5mm/¼in deep cuts in a circle on the top of each ball, then make five larger horizontal cuts around the sides.

6 Preheat the oven to 200°C/400°F/ Gas 6. Bake the rolls in the oven for 15 minutes. Transfer to a wire rack to cool.

Energy 121kcal/509kJ; Protein 2.6g; Carbohydrate 21.9g, of which sugars 0.4g; Fat 3.1g, of which saturates 0.5g, of which polyunsaturates 0.4g; Cholesterol 0mg; Calcium 39mg; Fibre 0.9g; Sodium 247mg.

PITTA BREAD ★

SOFT, SLIGHTLY BUBBLY PITTA BREAD IS A PLEASURE TO MAKE. IT CAN BE FILLED WITH SALAD OR LITTLE CHUNKS OF LEAN MEAT COOKED ON THE BARBECUE, OR IT CAN BE TORN INTO PIECES AND DIPPED IN SAVOURY DIPS SUCH AS LOW-FAT HUMMUS OR TZATZIKI.

MAKES TWELVE

INGREDIENTS
500g/1¼lb/5 cups strong white bread flour, or half white and half wholemeal (whole-wheat)
12.5ml/2½ tsp easy-blend (rapid-rise) dried yeast
15ml/1 tbsp salt
15ml/1 tbsp olive oil

1 Combine the flour, yeast and salt. Combine the oil and 250ml/8fl oz/1 cup water in a bowl, then add half of the flour mixture, stirring in the same direction, until the dough is stiff. Knead in the remaining flour until smooth. Place the dough in a clean bowl, cover with a clean dish towel and leave in a warm place for 30 minutes to 2 hours.

2 Turn the dough on to a lightly floured surface and knead for 10 minutes, or until smooth. Lightly oil the bowl, place the dough in it, cover again and leave to rise in a warm place for about 1 hour, or until doubled in size.

3 Divide the dough into 12 equal pieces. With lightly floured hands, flatten each piece, then roll out into a round measuring about 20cm/8in and about 5mm–1cm/¼–½in thick. Keep the rolled breads covered while you make the remaining pittas.

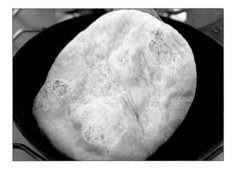

4 Heat a frying pan over a medium-high heat. When hot, place one piece of flattened dough in the pan and cook for 15–20 seconds. Turn it over and cook the second side for about 1 minute.

5 When large bubbles start to form on the bread, turn it over again. It should puff up. Using a clean dish towel, gently press on the bread where the bubbles have formed. Cook for a total of 3 minutes, then remove the pitta from the pan. Repeat with the remaining dough rounds. Wrap the pitta breads in a clean dish towel, stacking them as each one is cooked. Serve the pittas hot, while they are soft and moist.

VARIATION
To bake the breads, preheat the oven to 220°C/425°F/Gas 7. Fill an unglazed or partially glazed dish with hot water and place in the bottom of the hot oven. Use either a non-stick baking sheet or a lightly oiled baking sheet and heat in the oven for a few minutes. Place two or three pieces of flattened dough on to the hot baking sheet and place in the hottest part of the oven. Bake for 2–3 minutes until puffed up. Repeat with the remaining dough.

Energy 150kcal/638kJ; Protein 3.9g; Carbohydrate 32.4g, of which sugars 0.6g; Fat 1.5g, of which saturates 0.2g, of which polyunsaturates 0.3g; Cholesterol 0mg; Calcium 58mg; Fibre 1.3g; Sodium 165mg.

RED ONION AND ROSEMARY FOCACCIA ★

FOCACCIA IS AN APPETIZING ITALIAN FLAT BREAD MADE WITH OLIVE OIL, IDEAL SERVED AS A LOW-FAT ACCOMPANIMENT TO MEAT DISHES, SOUPS OR STEWS. HERE IT IS GIVEN ADDED FLAVOUR WITH RED ONION, FRESH ROSEMARY AND A SPRINKLING OF COARSE SEA SALT.

MAKES ONE LOAF
SERVES EIGHT

INGREDIENTS
  350g/12oz/3 cups strong white
    bread flour
  2.5ml/½ tsp salt
  10ml/2 tsp easy-blend (rapid-rise)
    dried yeast
  about 250ml/8fl oz/1 cup
    lukewarm water
  45ml/3 tbsp olive oil
  1 small red onion
  leaves from 1 large fresh
    rosemary sprig
  5ml/1 tsp coarse sea salt

1 Lightly grease or flour a baking sheet and set it aside. Sift the flour and salt into a large bowl. Stir in the yeast, then make a well in the centre of the dry ingredients.

2 Pour in the water and 30ml/2 tbsp of the oil. Mix well to make a dough, adding a little more water if the mixture seems too dry.

3 Turn the dough out on to a lightly floured surface and knead it for about 10 minutes, or until smooth and elastic.

4 Place the dough in a lightly oiled bowl, cover and leave to rise in a warm place for about 1 hour, or until doubled in bulk. Knock back (punch down) and knead the dough on a lightly floured surface for 2–3 minutes.

5 Preheat the oven to 220°C/425°F/ Gas 7. Roll the dough to a circle 1cm/½in thick, transfer to the baking sheet and brush with the remaining oil.

6 Halve the onion, then slice it thinly. Press the slices lightly over the dough, then sprinkle with the rosemary leaves and sea salt.

7 Using your fingertips, make deep indentations all over the surface of the dough. Cover the surface with oiled clear film (plastic wrap), then leave to rise in a warm place for 30 minutes. Remove the clear film and bake the loaf for 25–30 minutes, or until golden. Transfer to a wire rack to cool. Serve in slices or wedges.

COOK'S TIPS
• Use flavoured olive oil, such as chilli or herb oil, for extra flavour.
• Strong wholemeal (whole-wheat) bread flour or a mixture of wholemeal and white flour works well in this recipe.

Energy 189kcal/798kJ; Protein 4.2g; Carbohydrate 34.6g, of which sugars 1.1g; Fat 4.7g, of which saturates 0.7g, of which polyunsaturates 0.6g; Cholesterol 0mg; Calcium 63mg; Fibre 1.5g; Sodium 124mg.

MEDITERRANEAN OLIVE AND OREGANO BREAD ★

THIS DELICIOUS BREAD IS AN EXCELLENT LOW-FAT ACCOMPANIMENT TO ALL SALADS AND PASTA DISHES, AND IS PARTICULARLY GOOD SERVED WARM.

MAKES ONE LOAF
SERVES EIGHT

INGREDIENTS
  300ml/¼ pint/1¼ cups warm water
  5ml/1 tsp dried yeast
  pinch of granulated sugar
  15ml/1 tbsp olive oil
  1 onion, chopped
  450g/1lb/4 cups strong white
    bread flour
  5ml/1 tsp salt
  1.5ml/¼ tsp ground black pepper
  50g/2oz/½ cup pitted black olives,
    roughly chopped
  15ml/1 tbsp black olive paste
  15ml/1 tbsp chopped fresh oregano
  15ml/1 tbsp chopped fresh parsley

1 Lightly grease a baking sheet and set aside. Put half the warm water in a jug (cup). Sprinkle the yeast on top. Add the sugar, mix well and leave for 10 minutes.

2 Heat the olive oil in a non-stick frying pan and fry the onion until golden brown.

3 Sift the flour into a large bowl with the salt and pepper. Make a well in the centre. Add the yeast mixture, the fried onion (with the oil), the olives, olive paste, chopped herbs and remaining water. Gradually incorporate the flour and mix to form a soft dough, adding a little extra water if necessary.

4 Turn the dough on to a floured surface and knead for 5 minutes, or until smooth and elastic. Place the dough in a lightly oiled bowl, cover with a damp dish towel and leave to rise in a warm place for about 2 hours, or until doubled in bulk.

5 Turn the dough on to a floured surface and knead again for a few minutes. Shape into a 20cm/8in round and place on the prepared baking sheet. Using a sharp knife, make criss-cross cuts over the top, cover and leave in a warm place for 30 minutes, or until well risen. Meanwhile, preheat the oven to 220°C/425°F/Gas 7.

6 Dust the loaf with a little flour. Bake for 10 minutes, then reduce the oven temperature to 200°C/400°F/Gas 6. Bake for a further 20 minutes, or until the loaf sounds hollow when it is tapped underneath. Transfer to a wire rack to cool slightly before serving. Serve in slices or wedges.

Energy 215kcal/910kJ; Protein 5.6g; Carbohydrate 44.4g, of which sugars 1.4g; Fat 2.9g, of which saturates 0.4g, of which polyunsaturates 0.5g; Cholesterol 0mg; Calcium 93mg; Fibre 2.2g; Sodium 144mg.

MOROCCAN HOLIDAY BREAD ★★

THE ADDITION OF CORNMEAL AND SEEDS GIVES THIS SUPERB LOAF AN INTERESTING FLAVOUR AND TEXTURE. SERVE IT WITH COOKED LEAN SLICED MEATS, OR SIMPLY AS AN ACCOMPANIMENT.

MAKES ONE LOAF
SERVES SIX

INGREDIENTS
275g/10oz/2½ cups unbleached
   strong white bread flour
50g/2oz/½ cup cornmeal
5ml/1 tsp salt
20g/¾oz fresh yeast
120ml/4fl oz/½ cup lukewarm water
120ml/4fl oz/½ cup lukewarm
   semi-skimmed (low-fat) milk
15ml/1 tbsp pumpkin seeds
15ml/1 tbsp sesame seeds
30ml/2 tbsp sunflower seeds

VARIATIONS
• Incorporate all the seeds into the dough in step 5 and leave the top of the loaf plain.
• Use sesame seeds instead of sunflower seeds for the topping.

1 Lightly grease a baking sheet and set aside. Mix the flour, cornmeal and salt in a large bowl.

2 Cream the yeast with a little of the water in a jug (cup). Stir in the remaining water and the milk. Pour into the centre of the flour and mix to form a fairly soft dough.

3 Turn out the dough on to a lightly floured surface and knead for about 5 minutes, or until smooth and elastic. Place the dough in a lightly oiled bowl, cover with lightly oiled clear film (plastic wrap) and leave in a warm place for about 1 hour, or until doubled in bulk.

4 Turn out the dough on to a lightly floured surface and knock back (punch down). Gently knead the pumpkin and sesame seeds into the dough. Shape into a round ball and flatten slightly.

5 Place on the prepared baking sheet, cover with lightly oiled clear film or slide into a large, lightly oiled plastic food bag and leave to rise in a warm place for 45 minutes, or until doubled in bulk.

6 Meanwhile, preheat the oven to 200°C/400°F/Gas 6. Brush the top of the loaf with water and sprinkle evenly with the sunflower seeds. Bake the loaf in the oven for 30–35 minutes, or until it is golden and sounds hollow when tapped on the base. Transfer the loaf to a wire rack to cool. Serve in slices.

Energy 241kcal/1017kJ; Protein 7.1g; Carbohydrate 42.7g, of which sugars 1.7g; Fat 5.6g, of which saturates 0.9g, of which polyunsaturates 2.2g; Cholesterol 1mg; Calcium 139mg; Fibre 2.2g; Sodium 339mg.

PROSCIUTTO AND PARMESAN BREAD ★

SERVE THIS DELICIOUS BREAD ON ITS OWN OR WITH A SELECTION OF LOW-FAT CHEESES, COOKED LEAN SLICED MEATS AND SALADS FOR A TASTY LIGHT LUNCH OR SUPPER.

SERVES EIGHT

INGREDIENTS

225g/8oz/2 cups self-raising (self-rising) wholemeal (whole-wheat) flour
225g/8oz/2 cups self-raising (self-rising) white flour
5ml/1 tsp baking powder
5ml/1 tsp salt
5ml/1 tsp ground black pepper
75g/3oz prosciutto, chopped
25g/1oz/⅓ cup freshly grated Parmesan cheese
30ml/2 tbsp chopped fresh parsley
45ml/3 tbsp Meaux or wholegrain mustard
350ml/12fl oz/1½ cups buttermilk
skimmed milk, to glaze

1 Preheat the oven to 200°C/400°F/ Gas 6. Flour a baking sheet and set aside. Place the wholemeal flour in a bowl and sift in the white flour, baking powder and salt. Add the pepper and prosciutto. Set aside about 15ml/1 tbsp of the grated Parmesan and stir the rest into the flour mixture. Stir in the chopped parsley. Make a well in the centre.

2 Mix the mustard and buttermilk in a jug (cup), pour into the flour mixture and quickly mix to form a soft dough.

3 Turn the dough on to a floured surface and knead briefly. Shape into an oval loaf, brush with milk and sprinkle with the remaining Parmesan cheese. Place on the prepared baking sheet.

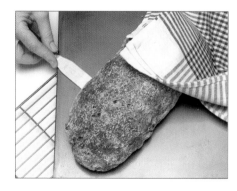

4 Bake the loaf in the oven for 25–30 minutes, or until golden brown. Transfer to a wire rack to cool. Serve in slices.

Energy 226kcal/960kJ; Protein 9.6g; Carbohydrate 44.7g, of which sugars 2.9g; Fat 2.2g, of which saturates 0.9g, of which polyunsaturates 0.4g; Cholesterol 10mg; Calcium 300mg; Fibre 2g; Sodium 616mg.

CHEESE AND ONION HERBSTICKS ★

AN EXTREMELY TASTY MEDITERRANEAN-STYLE BREAD WHICH IS VERY GOOD SERVED WITH LOW-FAT SOUP OR SALADS FOR A HEALTHY LUNCH OR SUPPER. USE AN EXTRA-STRONG CHEESE.

MAKES TWO LOAVES
EACH LOAF SERVES FOUR

INGREDIENTS
  300ml/½ pint/1¼ cups warm water
  5ml/1 tsp dried yeast
  pinch of granulated sugar
  15ml/1 tbsp sunflower oil
  1 red onion, chopped
  450g/1lb/4 cups strong white
    bread flour
  5ml/1 tsp salt
  5ml/1 tsp dry mustard powder
  45ml/3 tbsp chopped mixed fresh
    herbs, such as thyme, parsley,
    marjoram or sage
  75g/3oz/¾ cup half-fat mature
    (sharp) Cheddar cheese, grated

1 Lightly grease 2 baking sheets and set aside. Put the water in a jug (cup). Sprinkle the yeast on top. Add the sugar, mix well and leave for 10 minutes.

2 Heat the oil in a non-stick frying pan and fry the onion until well coloured.

3 Sift the flour, salt and mustard into a large bowl. Add the chopped herbs. Set aside 30ml/2 tbsp of the cheese. Stir the remaining cheese into the flour mixture and make a well in the centre. Add the yeast mixture with the fried onions and oil, then gradually incorporate the flour and mix to form a soft dough, adding extra water, if necessary.

4 Turn the dough on to a floured surface and knead for 5 minutes, or until smooth and elastic. Place the dough in a lightly oiled bowl, cover with a damp dish towel and leave to rise in a warm place for about 2 hours, or until doubled in bulk.

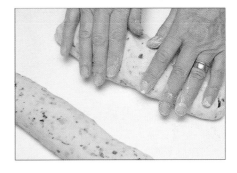

5 Turn the dough on to a floured surface, knead briefly, then divide the mixture in half and roll each piece into a 30cm/12in-long stick. Place each stick on a baking sheet and make diagonal cuts along the top.

6 Sprinkle the sticks with the reserved cheese. Cover and leave in a warm place for 30 minutes, or until well risen. Meanwhile, preheat the oven to 220°C/425°F/Gas 7. Bake the sticks in the oven for 25 minutes, or until they sound hollow when they are tapped underneath. Transfer to a wire rack to cool. Serve in slices or chunks.

Energy 226kcal/961kJ; Protein 8.2g; Carbohydrate 43.1g, of which sugars 1.2g; Fat 3.6g, of which saturates 1.2g, of which polyunsaturates 1.2g; Cholesterol 4mg; Calcium 278mg; Fibre 1.9g; Sodium 511mg.

POLENTA BREAD ★★

POLENTA IS WIDELY USED IN ITALIAN COOKING. HERE IT IS COMBINED WITH PINE NUTS TO MAKE A TRULY ITALIAN BREAD WITH A FANTASTIC FLAVOUR.

MAKES ONE LOAF
SERVES EIGHT

INGREDIENTS
  50g/2oz/½ cup polenta
  300ml/½ pint/1¼ cups lukewarm
    water
  15g/½oz fresh yeast
  2.5ml/½ tsp clear honey
  225g/8oz/2 cups unbleached strong
    white bread flour
  25g/1oz/2 tbsp butter
  25g/1oz/¼ cup pine nuts
  7.5ml/1½ tsp salt
For the topping
  1 egg white
  15ml/1 tbsp water
  additional pine nuts, for sprinkling
    (optional)

1 Lightly grease a baking sheet and set aside. Mix the polenta and 250ml/8fl oz/ 1 cup of the water together in a pan and slowly bring to the boil, stirring continuously with a wooden spoon.

2 Reduce the heat and simmer, stirring occasionally, for 2–3 minutes. Remove the pan from the heat and set aside to cool for 10 minutes, or until just warm.

3 In a small bowl, mix the yeast with the remaining water and the honey until creamy. Sift 115g/4oz/1 cup of the flour into a large bowl. Gradually beat in the yeast mixture, then gradually stir in the polenta mixture to combine. Turn out on to a lightly floured surface and knead for 5 minutes, or until smooth and elastic.

4 Place the dough in a lightly oiled bowl. Cover the bowl with lightly oiled clear film (plastic wrap). Leave the dough to rise in a warm place for about 2 hours, or until it has doubled in bulk.

5 Meanwhile, melt the butter in a small pan, add the pine nuts and cook over a medium heat, stirring, until pale golden. Remove the pan from the heat and set aside to cool.

6 Add the remaining flour and the salt to the polenta dough and mix to form a soft dough. Knead in the pine nuts and melted butter. Turn out on to a lightly floured surface and knead for 5 minutes, or until the dough is smooth and elastic.

7 Place the dough in a lightly oiled bowl, cover with lightly oiled clear film and leave to rise in a warm place for 1 hour, or until doubled in bulk.

8 Knock back (punch down) the dough and turn it out on to a lightly floured surface. Cut the dough into 2 equal pieces and roll each piece into a fat sausage about 38cm/15in long. Plait (braid) together and place on the prepared baking sheet. Cover with lightly oiled clear film and leave to rise in a warm place for 45 minutes. Meanwhile, preheat the oven to 200°C/400°F/Gas 6.

9 Lightly beat the egg white with the water and brush over the loaf. Sprinkle with pine nuts, if using, and bake in the oven for 30 minutes, or until golden and sounding hollow when tapped on the base. Transfer to a wire rack to cool. Cut into slices to serve.

Energy 162kcal/682kJ; Protein 3.9g; Carbohydrate 26g, of which sugars 0.5g; Fat 5.3g, of which saturates 1.8g, of which polyunsaturates 1.5g; Cholesterol 7mg; Calcium 100mg; Fibre 1.1g; Sodium 128mg.

OLIVE BREAD ★

BLACK AND GREEN OLIVES AND GOOD QUALITY FRUITY OLIVE OIL COMBINE TO MAKE THIS STRONGLY FLAVOURED AND IRRESISTIBLE LIGHT ITALIAN BREAD.

MAKES ONE LOAF
SERVES EIGHT

INGREDIENTS
275g/10oz/2½ cups unbleached strong white bread flour
50g/2oz/½ cup strong wholemeal (whole-wheat) bread flour
7g/¼oz sachet easy-blend (rapid-rise) dried yeast
2.5ml/½ tsp salt
210ml/7½fl oz/scant 1 cup lukewarm water
15ml/1 tbsp extra virgin olive oil, plus a little extra for brushing
115g/4oz/1 cup pitted mixed black and green olives, coarsely chopped

1 Lightly grease a baking sheet and set aside. Mix the flours, yeast and salt together in a large bowl and make a well in the centre.

2 Add the water and oil to the centre of the flour and mix to form a soft dough. Knead the dough on a lightly floured surface for 8–10 minutes, or until smooth and elastic. Place the dough in a lightly oiled bowl, cover with lightly oiled clear film (plastic wrap) and leave to rise in a warm place for 1 hour, or until doubled in bulk.

3 Turn out on to a lightly floured surface and knock back (punch down) the dough. Flatten out and sprinkle with the olives. Fold up and knead the dough to distribute the olives evenly. Leave to rest for 5 minutes, then shape into an oval loaf. Place on the prepared baking sheet.

4 Make 6 deep cuts in the top of the loaf using a sharp knife and gently push the sections over slightly. Cover with lightly oiled clear film and leave to rise in a warm place for 30–45 minutes, or until doubled in bulk.

5 Meanwhile, preheat the oven to 200°C/400°F/Gas 6. Brush the bread with a little olive oil, then bake in the oven for 35 minutes, or until golden and sounding hollow when tapped underneath. Transfer to a wire rack to cool. Serve in slices.

VARIATION
Increase the proportion of wholemeal (whole-wheat) flour to make the loaf more rustic.

Energy 153kcal/646kJ; Protein 3.6g; Carbohydrate 28.7g, of which sugars 0.6g; Fat 3.4g, of which saturates 0.5g, of which polyunsaturates 0.5g; Cholesterol 0mg; Calcium 60mg; Fibre 1.6g; Sodium 325mg.

PANE TOSCANO ★

THIS DELICIOUS BREAD IS MADE WITHOUT SALT AND PROBABLY ORIGINATES FROM THE DAYS WHEN
SALT WAS HEAVILY TAXED. TO COMPENSATE, IT IS USUALLY SERVED WITH SALTY FOODS SUCH AS OLIVES.

MAKES ONE LOAF
SERVES EIGHT

INGREDIENTS
  550g/1¼lb/5 cups unbleached strong
    white bread flour
  350ml/12fl oz/1½ cups boiling water
  15g/½oz fresh yeast
  60ml/4 tbsp lukewarm water

1 First make the starter. Sift 175g/6oz/
1½ cups of the flour into a large bowl.
Pour over the boiling water, leave for a
couple of minutes, then mix well. Cover
the bowl with a damp dish towel and
leave for 10 hours.

2 Lightly flour a baking sheet and
set aside. In a small bowl, cream the
yeast with the lukewarm water. Stir
into the starter.

3 Gradually add the remaining flour
and mix to form a dough. Turn out on to
a lightly floured surface and knead for
5–8 minutes, or until smooth and elastic.

4 Place the dough in a lightly oiled
bowl, cover with lightly oiled clear film
(plastic wrap) and leave to rise in a
warm place for 1–1½ hours, or until
doubled in bulk.

5 Turn out the dough on to a lightly
floured surface, knock back (punch
down) and shape into a round.

COOK'S TIP
Salt controls the action of yeast in
bread so the leavening action is more
noticeable. Don't let this unsalted bread
over-rise or it may collapse.

6 Fold the sides of the round into the
centre and seal. Place seam side up on
the prepared baking sheet. Cover with
lightly oiled clear film and leave to rise
in a warm place for 30–45 minutes or
until doubled in size.

7 Flatten the loaf to about half its risen
height and flip over. Cover with a large
upturned bowl and leave to rise in a
warm place for 30 minutes.

8 Meanwhile, preheat the oven to
220°C/425°F/Gas 7. Slash the top of
the loaf several times using a sharp
knife, if you like. Bake in the oven
for 30–35 minutes, or until golden.
Transfer to a wire rack to cool. Serve
in slices or wedges.

Energy 235kcal/997kJ; Protein 6.5g; Carbohydrate 53.4g, of which sugars 1g; Fat 0.9g, of which saturates 0.1g, of which polyunsaturates 0.4g; Cholesterol 0mg; Calcium 96mg; Fibre 2.1g; Sodium 2mg.

SESAME BREADSTICKS ★

HOME-MADE BREADSTICKS ARE IDEAL SERVED ON THEIR OWN, OR WITH A SELECTION OF LOW-FAT DIPS FOR A TASTY SNACK OR APPETIZER.

MAKES THIRTY

INGREDIENTS
225g/8oz/2 cups strong white
  bread flour
5ml/1 tsp salt
7g/¼oz sachet easy-blend (rapid-rise)
  dried yeast
30ml/2 tbsp sesame seeds
30ml/2 tbsp olive oil

1 Lightly grease or flour 2 or 3 baking sheets and set aside. Preheat the oven to 230°C/450°F/Gas 8. Sift the flour into a large bowl. Stir in the salt, yeast and sesame seeds and make a well in the centre.

2 Add the olive oil to the flour mixture and enough warm water to make a firm dough. Tip out the dough on to a lightly floured surface and knead for 5–10 minutes, or until smooth and elastic.

3 Place in a lightly oiled bowl and cover with a clean dish towel. Leave to rise in a warm place for about 40 minutes, or until it has doubled in size.

4 Knock back (punch down) the dough, then knead lightly until smooth. Pull off small balls of dough, then using your hands, roll out each ball on a lightly floured surface to form a thin sausage about 25cm/10in long.

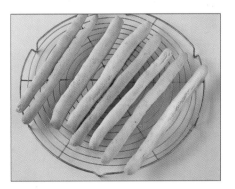

5 Place the breadsticks on the prepared baking sheets and bake in the oven for 15 minutes, or until crisp and golden. Transfer the breadsticks to a wire rack to cool, then store them in an airtight container until ready to serve.

Energy 38kcal/161kJ; Protein 0.9g; Carbohydrate 5.8g, of which sugars 0.1g; Fat 1.4g, of which saturates 0.2g, of which polyunsaturates 0.4g; Cholesterol 0mg; Calcium 17mg; Fibre 0.3g; Sodium 66mg.

INDEX

ACKNOWLEDGEMENTS

Recipes: Pepita Aris, Catherine Atkinson, Mary Banks, Alex Barker, Ghillie Basan,
Judy Bastyra, Angela Boggiano, Jacqueline Clark, Maxine Clark, Trish Davies,
Roz Denny, Joanna Farrow, Jennie Fleetwood, Brian Glover, Nicola Graimes,
Carole Handslip, Christine Ingram, Becky Johnson, Lucy Knox, Sally Mansfield,
Christine McFadden, Jane Milton, Sallie Morris, Rena Salaman,
Jenni Shapter, Marlena Spieler, Liz Trigg, Jenny White, Kate Whiteman,
Lucy Whiteman, Jeni Wright.

Home economists: Eliza Baird, Alex Barker, Caroline Barty, Joanna Farrow,
Annabel Ford, Christine France, Carole Handslip, Kate Jay, Becky Johnson,
Jill Jones, Bridget Sargeson, Jennie Shapter, Carol Tennant, Sunil Vijayakar,
Jenny White.

Photographers: Frank Adam, Tim Auty, Martin Brigdale, Louisa Dare, Nicki Dowey,
Gus Filgate, Ian Garlick, Michelle Garrett, John Heseltine, Amanda Heywood,
Janine Hosegood, Dave Jordan, Dave King, William Lingwood,
Thomas Odulate,Craig Roberson, Simon Smith, Sam Stowell.